PRAISE FOR *UNFOLLOW YOUR PASSION*

"Trespicio helps us reevaluate what society has taught us we need, like passion and plans and a bucket list. It's quite liberating to realize that there's more than one way to live a life that means something, and that you can do so without leaving your comfort zone."

—*The Washington Post*
(Named it one of the "Best feel-good books of 2021")

"It's a rare book that can effectively mix words from Viktor Frankl and Dilbert, but this one pulls it off. Trespicio dishes pragmatic advice with finesse."

—*Publishers Weekly*

"An especially meaningful and much-needed read as the workplace continues to change."

—*Booklist*

"Learn how to redefine what passion means to you under Trespicio's gentle but brutally honest guidance."

—*POPSUGAR*

"Funny, relatable, and endlessly compelling. I wish I'd had this book when I started out."

—Farnoosh Torabi, *So Money* podcast

"Engaging, no-nonsense, and challenges conventional thinking in all the best ways? Terri Trespicio's *Unfollow Your Passion* is everything I love in a self-help book and then some!"

—Sarah Knight, *New York Times* bestselling author of
*The Life-Changing Magic of Not Giving a F*ck*

"As the original multi-passionate entrepreneur, I've been saying for years that the push for a single passion is outdated. In *Unfollow Your Passion*, Terri Trespicio writes with power, style, and wit about the question we all struggle with: What is it I should, or can, do with my life?"

—Marie Forleo, *New York Times* bestselling author of
Everything Is Figureoutable

unfollow your passion

HOW TO CREATE A LIFE THAT MATTERS TO YOU

Terri Trespicio

ATRIA PAPERBACK

New York London Toronto Sydney New Delhi

An Imprint of Simon & Schuster, Inc.
1230 Avenue of the Americas
New York, NY 10020

First Atria Paperback edition January 2023

For information about special discounts for bulk purchases, please contact Simon & Schuster Special Sales at 1-866-506-1949 or business@simonandschuster.com.

The Simon & Schuster Speakers Bureau can bring authors to your live event. For more information or to book an event, contact the Simon & Schuster Speakers Bureau at 1-866-248-3049 or visit our website at www.simonspeakers.com.

Interior design by Suet Chong

Manufactured in the United States of America

1 3 5 7 9 10 8 6 4 2

Library of Congress Cataloging-in-Publication Data

Names: Trespicio, Terri, author.
Title: Unfollow your passion : how to create a life
that matters to you / Terri Trespicio.
Description: First Atria Books hardcover edition. | New York :
Atria Books 2022. | Includes bibliographical references and index.
Identifiers: LCCN 2021043101 (print) | LCCN 2021043102 (ebook) |
ISBN 9781982169244 (hardcover) | ISBN 9781982169268 (ebook)
Subjects: LCSH: Self-actualization (Psychology) |
Self-consciousness (Awareness) | Success.
Classification: LCC BF637.S4 T75 2022 (print) | LCC BF637.S4 (ebook) |
DDC 158.1–dc23/eng/20211004
LC record available at https://lccn.loc.gov/2021043101
LC ebook record available at https://lccn.loc.gov/2021043102

ISBN 978-1-9821-6924-4
ISBN 978-1-9821-6925-1 (pbk)
ISBN 978-1-9821-6926-8 (ebook)

To my uncle, Rev. Robert Barone

CONTENTS

part three

unleash

INTRODUCTION

Don't aim at success. The more you aim at it and make it a target, the more you are going to miss it.
—Viktor E. Frankl, *Man's Search for Meaning*

It didn't rain every day in 1996, but it felt like it did. I was twenty-two, temping for a socially awkward ob-gyn who smoked in his office. I worked in a windowless room, booking surgeries for women at odds with their ovaries. These were the days when you had to call "in" to your answering machine to check your messages. Every hour or so I'd call my own number and wait for the robot to come up empty. For a chain of indistinguishable days, I stepped out of the building at 5:00 p.m., unfolded the umbrella like a damp wing, and huddled beneath it, biting back tears the whole way to the T.

I lived alone in a walk-up on Strathmore Road in Brighton, Massachusetts. I ate watching reruns in front of a TV on a wheeled cart. That's what comfort was: temporarily staving off hunger under the spell of shows you knew the ending to. Around 9:00 p.m., I'd call home. My mother would pick up the phone, as she did yesterday and would tomorrow. I cried into the phone; she listened in her loving and tireless way. Then I'd go to bed.

A few months earlier, I'd been in the car with my dad after graduation, and as we exited the campus and headed onto the Mass Pike he said, in a jovial way, though I wasn't feeling jovial, "So? What are you going to do now?"

"I have no idea." And then I stopped talking because I thought I would cry.

"You'll be OK," he said.

Since then, things had flattened out. I experienced a kind of miserable synesthesia, in which life became flavorless, colorless, textureless; I woke up each day inside the sensory deprivation tank of my brain, unsure of where I ended or began. I stood in the kitchen, eating cereal over the sink.

That spring, I had been busy and brimming with potential, my world like a sky crammed with stars: good grades, great friends, a boyfriend. I graduated Phi Beta Kappa, summa cum laude, won a cash grant awarded to the senior with promise of a writing career, moved into a sunny summer sublet with friends.

When summer ended, I was on my own. I invented errands. One Saturday I drove to the Chestnut Hill mall, believing what I needed was a pair of small hoop earrings. I sat in the car, looking at two glaring bits of metal in a box, and felt a nauseating swell of self-loathing. On the way home, sitting at a red light at Cleveland Circle, I realized with numb clarity that there was nothing to look forward to anymore, except that in a few moments the light would turn.

Fear sprouted a fresh green blade: *What if this is it? What if I'm never going anywhere and nothing ever happens again?*

I'm guessing you've been there too.

Maybe you thought you had it together and now find yourself eating straight out of a box, wondering WTF your life even is. Maybe you're six months out of college, ten years into a marriage, twenty years into a career. You liked it, maybe loved it, and now resent it. You may have suffered large losses, disasters. Or perhaps nothing seemed to happen. When asked how you are, you say you "can't complain." And you mean it. You can't complain. *This is life,* you think.

I'd been temping for six months or so when I got an informational interview at a then little-known business publication called *Inc.* magazine. The editor offered me a position as an editorial assistant on the spot. I was afraid—that I wouldn't know how to do it and thus would fail, that the salary was too low, that I didn't know anything about business. Though you know how you learn about business? *Work at a fucking business magazine.* I'd like to leap back right now to 1996, march myself into *Inc.*'s lovely waterfront offices by my own earlobe, and say, "$18,500 a year? Great. We'll take it."

I had the mistaken idea that I was supposed to know what to do, and that I had to know more or be more than I was to do anything of worth. And that I should figure *that* out first.

One night over the phone, my mother said, "Honey, you don't plan your life, then live it. You create it *by* living it. Please take a job, *any* job." And so I did. I took a full-time job as an executive assistant at a management consulting firm. I needed the structure, the people, the benefits, the work. And that job, that basic office job, is what ultimately turned my life around and got it moving. Yes, I learned hard skills, soft skills, I learned to do things. But after a year or so, I also felt differently about myself and what I *could* do. It didn't matter that I had no interest in management consulting, or that I would leave that job—which I did—and go back to school, and get another job after that. The momentum began the way it always does: By moving. The direction almost didn't matter.

Nothing Is More Frustrating than Feeling Stuck

I know what it's like to feel you've done everything you were "supposed" to do and yet things aren't clicking into place. When you know you're perfectly smart and capable, but your self-confidence acts like a trick knee—sturdy and functional one moment, but can easily give out the next. You can't point to any one thing that's *wrong* either. You may not be *stuck* stuck, but more like you've shifted into neutral, where you're not secure, but also not moving, and things feel out of your control. And when you ask people in your life what they think, they tell you you're doing great! So now on top of *not* feeling great, you feel crazy or ungrateful, or both.

We look to all sorts of remedies to ease this nagging, existential ache. Whether it's self-care or exercise or volunteering or, well, drinking, which isn't so bad in moderation (says the person who subscribes to a wine club). Maybe you meditate, do yoga, go for long walks, keep a gratitude journal. All great things! You should totally keep doing them.

But there's a deeper excavation that can be foundational, and it requires questioning the beliefs we have about what we "should" be doing, and why—and which, at the heart of it all, can be flawed, unhelpful, and actually keep you from feeling like the whole and sovereign person you are. Ideas that contradict themselves, and which women in particular are told to adhere to, like: Be grateful for what you have, but get out of your comfort zone; be compliant and take risks; keep yourself busy and you'll be indispensable; try new things, but stick with what you know; and my (least) favorite, follow your passion and everything will work out—and you'll never work again. Ha! That's funny.

Why You Need This Book—Stat

Whether you're in a blind panic or nursing an existential ache, even the craving for change causes uncomfortable feelings to arise—you may feel ashamed for wanting more, or something else altogether. Fears and worries swirl around your head like a cloud of gnats and it's hard to know which to pay attention to and which to bat away. You might be sick to death of the job you have or like it enough to worry that you might never, ever leave. Maybe you want *off* this runaway train, or you're trying to get your poky old horse to giddyap. You just know things could be better, but you might not be sure how.

You should know that you're in very good company. And if you're wondering what you should do with your life next, rest assured that no one can tell you what you *can't* do. But they also can't tell you what you *must* do. Not your favorite teacher or coach, a monk or your mom.

The good news: No one knows any better than you do.

The bad news: No one knows any better than you do.

We think we're supposed to know something by now, but where on earth did we get that idea? Did we think ultimate knowledge would be bequeathed to us with a title change, a degree, a deed to a house? Because as you might have discovered, it's not.

Fact is, we'll spend a good part of our lives walking through doorways the way we sometimes walk into the kitchen, forgetting for a moment what we intended to do there and finding something else instead. Something way better. And that's why the shift you're dying to make doesn't start with what passion to chase or what position to apply for; it starts with the recalibration of what freedom really feels like, and a rewiring of the "fears" that the world has told us to have. What this means is not worrying about the "right" move, but discovering what it means to *be* a sovereign person, to exercise power over your options, decisions, and desires—without being ruled by any of them. To realize that you don't need to know exactly where you're headed to start walking, nor do you need permission to do it.

What You're About to Do

I have a plan for us, and the first order of business, in part 1, is to *unsubscribe*—from old beliefs and dumb ideas, from patriarchal notions and biases that have been handed down and forced down our throats for too long. We'll request to be removed—at once!—from this list of agendas and expectations that have been blowing up your inbox since you had dial-up internet. When you do, you free yourself from the tyranny of dopey ideas about where your comfort zone ends (and why it's totally cool to stay on this side of it); why you don't have to do things just to say you did them; and why you need not be ashamed of your baggage, which will absolutely fit in the overhead compartment.

Then, in part 2, we *uncover*—your brilliant skills, your unique perspective, and why what you practice means more than what you happen to be into right now. You'll rediscover your natural talent for improvisation and the real source of your calling and learn how to make a living without selling your soul. You'll also identify what it is that makes you indispensable—without having to rely on anyone, ever again.

Part 3 exists because even when you've done everything intentionally and well, life will take a hard left when you least expect it. You'll find out how you can have fun and fulfillment without ultimate control, and why there not only will but *should* be times when it all gets too boring for words. You'll explore your commitments to determine which are worth keeping and how to access your best, most brilliant ideas without judgment or criticism. Above all, you'll discover why you don't need to be "fixed" to lead a fulfilling life, and how true freedom comes not when things go your way, but when you let things go.

I will not let you so much as *once* double-text your purpose and then cry when it won't text back. We're not doing that. And rather than hit all the tourist sites you've visited a zillion times down the how-to highway (self-care, hot baths, mindfulness meditation), we're going to head off road to places you might not have gone, or maybe not in a long time. We'll tour holy cities but bail on church; swing by my sister's wedding, pop into an improv class, even stop by your old office. We're going to unfollow the asinine advice, the tired dictums, even our passion. Why? Because passion is a dog and it can't resist a good chase. So let's give him one.

If you feel you've lost the thread on your life or anything resembling motivation, what can help is to actually *get* lost—and by that I mean immerse yourself in the nonlinear, explore the full dimension of who you are, what you've experienced, and all the things you have right in front of you that you might have overlooked. Because a rigid, must-do approach to anything—finding a job, finishing a project, finally doing what you want to do—is actually the problem to begin with.

How to Use This Book

You can, of course, use it however you like. The idea isn't that you follow it to the letter but let it nudge open the door to potential, curiosity, intuition, and exploration. I've packed everything that I thought you might want, need, and enjoy (including gluten-free beef jerky if you like that). And if you don't, that's cool—and you may not agree with me on everything that follows either. That's OK too.

But it's not just my stories and opinions that matter here. That's why at the end of each chapter I left room for you to have the last word with prompts for taking your own ideas and stories to the page—not because I'm your English teacher (wait, was I?), but because I know that the act of putting pen to paper is one of the most powerful discovery tools in your arsenal. Maybe you're a morning pages person. Maybe you're a *WTF are morning pages?* person. Doesn't matter. It helps to get your thoughts out here where you can see them. No one ever has to see what you've written. But I've led enough workshops with people who didn't consider themselves writers (financial advisors, sales reps, corporate execs, one woman with a PhD in chemistry) to know what amazing shit can transpire when you're willing to follow it onto the page.

The goal of this trip will be to show you what you *almost* already know: That your life is so much bigger, richer, and deeper than a single passion could possibly contain. The more time you spend pining or worrying about what you "should" be doing, the less time you have to enjoy your own rich potential, and the freedom of this very moment—which is the only one that matters.

In the wake of the pandemic, BLM, #metoo, and the 2020 election, hypocrisies and injustices are being exposed and shared like never before. We're waking up from the conditioning that for years we were told to sleep through. The last things we need are old myths, rules, and standards someone *else* set for what a good life looks like. And it's time to reinvent how we go about creating lives of meaning and value. That means it may not look like the picture you drew as a kid. But chances are, it's better than you imagined.

part one

unsubscribe

CHAPTER 1

How to Unsubscribe from Other People's Agendas

If you drink much from a bottle marked "poison" it is certain to disagree with you sooner or later.

—Lewis Carroll

Once upon a time, we were told what to think, what to do, what to swallow—whether we wanted to or not. Whether we liked it or not. And these things got into our bodies, our digestion, our DNA—ideas about who we were, who we could be, who's in charge. They grew in and around our very cells, so much so that it became difficult to tell what other people thought and believed from what we did. That's where influence won over independence, where fear won over freedom. And only by taking a good hard look at what we have swallowed can we begin to find our way out of the sometimes brutal, often well-intentioned, ways of thinking and seeing, and begin to tell the difference between what people want for us and what we want for ourselves.

Your life is not one big leap; it's a series of steps. Each one is an incremental move that determines your direction, the overall arc. Sometimes you know exactly where you want to go; other times you're nudged, encouraged, or railroaded. And while some steps are bold and definitive, others are trickier and require a degree of compromise to balance what you want, what others need, and where you draw a line. There's always a chance to course correct, but you can't adjust what you can't see.

Right now you might be at a crossroads, feeling pulled in two different directions, stalled out or stuck or spinning your wheels. Sometimes you'll take almost any advice, anything to dislodge the fear, worry, hesitation, and in some cases you may even be willing to do what someone else thinks just because it's better than nothing. Been there. There's plenty of you-go-girl advice, telling you just to follow your dreams and fuck everyone else. Oh, but if it were only that easy. Easy advice to give, but not easy to execute.

That's why we're not going to begin by burning whole cities to the ground here. We begin by questioning what we've been told and sold, check our sources. Do a full-on review of all the crap we've perhaps unwittingly subscribed to, which has the inbox of our brains teeming with lousy or ill-fitting advice. What *have* we been listening to, consuming, believing—and why?

So let's go back to the beginning: To the first time you did something, not because you wanted to, but because you were compelled. Because someone *expected* you to. You know the moment because it's where you . . . paused. Hesitated. Where the world slowed to a heavy tick and the ground started to separate beneath you and you had to choose a side: Go this way or that way. You decide you want to do the right thing, but you realize that sometimes what is supposed to be right doesn't feel right at all.

What I remember is that I was seven years old and bored. It was one of the straggly last days of summer, and I was, as my mother calls it, at loose ends.

"Why don't you go see if Leah is home," she said. It wasn't a question. Leah Pompeo lived a few doors down from me. She was a little thing but brassy and bold and never took no for an answer. I didn't want to play with her, or anyone.

Against my will or better judgment, I found myself knocking on the dark double doors at 11 Montrose Avenue, then admitted to the dark, air-conditioned foyer.

It wouldn't be the first time I did something because someone said I should do it. Sometimes you're glad you went against the grain of your own inclination, did something you might not otherwise do. But other times you resent being yanked along on the strings of other people's suggestions. And yet you do it anyway.

Leah came to the door wearing a tank top that tied into bows at the shoulder and led me to her bedroom, where we played with her half-dressed Barbie dolls. Then a button came loose from her elaborate bedspread. She picked it up and held it out to me in her chubby little hand, her sparkly pink nail polish chipped and bitten.

"Eat it."

While it might have looked like candy—shiny, round, red—I knew it wasn't.

"Eat it? Can you even eat this?"

When people in positions of power say things, it doesn't matter if they're true.

I wanted to believe her, that she had an edible bedspread, like the candy necklaces we wore around our necks and chewed at. You could be a necklace and candy, so couldn't you be a button and candy? Maybe.

Earlier that spring, I'd received the Eucharist for the first time. Holy Communion is the first sacrament you're really conscious for (I'm not counting baptism, which was very nearly like being waterboarded by a stranger holding a crucifix, and I'm glad I don't remember it).

What you're taught as a Catholic is that the Holy Eucharist isn't a *symbol* of Jesus; it *is* Jesus. I was almost afraid to chew it; I let it alight on my tongue like a butterfly. I wondered if I was different now that I had put God in my mouth. The day you receive this sacrament is the day you're given a seat at the adult table. You, too, get to swallow it whole.

I didn't understand how something could be two things at the same time: A body *and* bread, Christ *and* a cracker, a sacred thing *and* store-bought. There was what I was told and what my body knew to be true; I was taught not to trust my senses, but what someone said to believe. If you swallowed that idea, if you told yourself your body was not to be trusted, would you be able to trust it when you needed to?

Leah looked at me hard. Her mother called from the bottom of the stairs; Leah ignored her. The cherry-red button was rigid between my fingers. My face and neck flushed with an anxious heat. I put the button in my mouth and bit down, feeling the plastic crack against my teeth. It tasted like what it was, some kind of polymer.

Every religion or ritual you can think of involves swallowing *something*—unleavened bread, a sip of wine, a promise of abstinence. Or worse. Boys growing up as a member of the Mardudjara Aborigines of Australia undergo circumcision—and then are required to swallow their own foreskins. While it may be morbid, at least you're consuming something of your own.

The problem is that we're so often swallowing things that other people hand us: Their pointy opinions, hardened ideas, homemade beliefs they think would be good for you. But also: Ideas about you and what your life should be that simply aren't and don't have to be true. Hard-and-fast rules about how one should or should not behave, flavorless notions about who you can or can't be.

And sometimes it really is easier to swallow it, and maybe you cough it up later or it just sits there like a brick of lasagna in your gut and doesn't move. Take it from someone with a finicky digestion; I've learned the hard way what happens when you swallow the wrong things, even when they're seemingly harmless.

The question is, what are the consequences of swallowing things that you were given? Maybe it was easy going down and then the digestive turmoil hit later. Or it was really tough to swallow and you were glad you did (pride, for instance, comes to mind).

But think about this for a sec; think about all the things you're given and told to swallow that you (and I, and everyone else) swallow at some point, usually early. Beliefs about whether or when you should: Get a job, get a certain kind of job, make money, make a certain amount of money; fall in love (as if one can plan such a thing); get married, have children. Even when, left to your own devices, you wouldn't have considered such a thing. It's worth thinking about the fact that ideas you have about what your life should be aren't always hard rules but leaked in from movies and songs and images you liked, things people said around you.

Every kid has resisted swallowing a thing, sat there staring at a cold plate of food that they don't want to eat and won't, until they're dismissed with despair from the table. Maybe you think it's rude not to eat what's in front of you. But something in me also roots for the kid who holds strong to that boundary of what's going in and what isn't.

I felt the jagged pieces of button scrape their way down my throat, where they would get passed through each phase of digestion, each organ shrugging it along to the next.

"I want to go home."

"You can't," she said, raking a bubblegum-pink Goody hairbrush through her long brown hair.

"Yes I can."

"No, you can't." She slapped the brush down on the bed. "And if you try, I'm going to push you into that big pile of dog poop on the street."

I thought of my mother, five houses away, measuring rice into the rice cooker, sorting the silverware with the phone tucked under her chin, the kitchen soon filling with a sweet jasmine steam.

It was time to take Leah's dolls for a walk. When I saw my opening, I took it, slipping through a wall of bushes like a secret agent, stealing up my driveway, pounding the stairs, slamming the door where my mom was now filing paperwork, and throwing myself against it.

My mother swiveled her office chair in my direction. Her hair had started going gray in high school, but in 1980 it was called frosted, which meant she did it on purpose. "Who on earth are you running from?"

"Leah."

"Leah?" She laughed a little, shuffled a stack of papers before laying them back down on the desk. "Why did you need to run?"

"She might not have let me go."

My mother sat up straight and looked at me the way you do when you realize the person you're talking to is missing a critical step in logic and you must bridge the gap carefully.

"They can't *keep* you," she said. "You do know that, right?"

It sounded like the most obvious fact in the world once you heard it, like seeing how a trick is done, the hole in the back, the set of springs. I had all the information but still was not sure I believed it.

After all, people kept things that didn't belong to them all the time. They even kept other people. Years later I'd hear about a man who kidnapped a woman and locked her in a shed for years. She bore his children. They made a movie about it.

"I belong to you, don't I?" I asked my mother the next morning as she worked a comb through a challenging knot in my hair.

"I'm your mother. But you don't belong to me, or anyone. That's not how it works."

I had hoped that if I belonged to my mother I couldn't belong to someone else, that it was the belonging that kept me safe. But this wasn't even true. I don't know if I fully appreciated how critical a message that was, especially given that so many other people (mothers, spouses, lovers, cult leaders) have attempted to prove the opposite to so many women: *You are mine. I get to say what you do or don't do.* What it told me, in ways that had only begun to hatch, was that whether you want to be with someone or not was not the same as being possessed by them. Being safe and being sovereign were two different things. And no one could keep you safe.

I would be surprised if someone coerced you into swallowing a button off a bedspread (and yet part of me wouldn't be surprised), but you likely swallowed something along the way. Something you shouldn't. We all have.

But there was more than one moment in your life when you agreed to something you didn't necessarily believe or want to believe, or do, or take on. But you did. I did. Do you remember when that was for you? Was it a standoff between you and a pot roast? Was it what you wore or didn't want to wear? An assumption some asshole made about you that raised every hair on your neck? You might have wanted to just keep the peace and not make a fuss, or maybe you wanted to please or impress or join the club. Maybe it was way worse than that.

Swallowing is an act of trust, of acceptance, and of compliance. We do it for a lot of reasons, and I don't blame you for any of it. It's easier to swallow a thing than put up the fight, and even then sometimes you need to be taught to do it. I couldn't swallow pills until I was eleven. I had a mental block against it; the idea terrified me, to swallow something whole.

Your life and mine have been filled with people telling us, explicitly and implicitly, to say yes to things we wouldn't otherwise choose. To accept invitations we don't want, to say yes to people we neither like nor trust. We will have our own reasons for doing it, and sometimes they don't match. Maybe it's not that it's such a great opportunity or even a good idea, but sometimes we end up complicit because being complicit seems more important. No one can make you do things; you can only choose to go along. And that decision depends on what's worth risking.

Perhaps the most important thing, the most valuable thing, is to know what you're swallowing (what you keep swallowing) and why. To recognize that this awareness is the only way to be radically alive, rather than pretend that you can subsist on buttons, because you cannot.

I never had to play with Leah again after that incident. But I thought about it years, even decades, later, not without some shame. Because this wasn't "done" to me; I participated. Swallowing is a commitment that only you can make. No one can do it for you.

It's worth taking a good hard look at that boundary between what the world wants and you want and, well, making sure it's intact for one, but also that, regardless of what you decide to do, you know that it was a request you either granted or you didn't.

The goal here as we move forward is to keep bringing us back to this fact: That you are a sovereign person with the choice to do or not do—with your body, your mind, your soul. I'm certainly not interested in judging you, and rationalizing why we did what we did, if you ask me, is a waste of our very precious time. Because the mind is funny that way, and brilliant—it will make up incredibly sound reasons for what we did after the fact so it can remind itself it's still in charge. I don't care about excuses, and neither should you.

What you decide to take on, do, believe, swallow, has an effect on what you do next. And if you let your "executive function" run the whole show and your ego take credit, oh forget it. You'll be awash in horrible corporate memos on your brain's boring letterhead to explain to you Why We're Doing Things This Way. And fact is, all the reasoning in the world can't hold a candle to the moment your body tightens up around a thing and says no.

If you want to know what you "should" be doing, well, join the club. But the should is a made-up vision board that your ego threw together for reasons that serve only itself.

We've been taught to swallow all kinds of beliefs we never thought to question—including what's worth pursuing and what isn't, what job you should or shouldn't take, that you should hurry up and settle down before you're too old or unlovable. Who's saying that? And why would we take their word for it?

Think of this as a detox diet: You remove a bunch of foods and then, one at a time, start adding them back in, so that you can focus on how each one makes you feel. When you've swallowed so much it's hard to know what's what. So it's worth tuning in to the kinds of things we swallow every day. Pay attention to what the body, *your* body, is telling you. That's the first step of breaking free.

Gut Check: Some Things You May Have Swallowed

- A romantic relationship (or five) that someone else wanted more than you did
- The idea that you need a romantic relationship right now
- The idea that you need a romantic relationship later, ever, or forever
- A marriage
- A major
- A job
- An industry
- An invitation
- An apartment
- A whole house
- A product that you don't want, need, or enjoy
- The idea that you should look a certain way
- The idea that you should be doing certain things
- The idea that you should behave a certain way
- A trip you didn't want to take
- A compliment
- A flat-out insult
- A veiled threat
- A rule that doesn't, or never did, apply
- The notion that because you're "good" at a thing you should do it
- Someone else's life, or what appears to be someone else's life
- A goal someone thinks you should aim for
- An amount of money someone thinks you should earn

write your next chapter

OK! So here's your first prompt. Now if I were sitting there with you, I'd have you close your eyes and just rest for a moment. Climb out of the vaulted ceiling of your brain and down into your body so that you can write *from* your body, where your instincts and imagination and memories also live. Think of your feet, your fingers, the large muscles of your legs, the delicate structure of your spine rising out of the pelvis and arcing up toward the top office where you spend a lot of (too much) time.

You don't have to write an essay here, or worry about grammar or spelling. You're not preparing a document. You're simply going to uncap a pen or let your fingers alight on the keys and write whatever comes to mind when I give you this prompt. Whatever beautiful or horrible or nonsensical or ordinary thing. Just write and watch what unfolds. Follow it like a rabbit into the grass. See what happens.

Think about something you swallowed. Literal or figurative. Start with the concrete, as that is always easier to start with. Where you are, what is on your fork, your plate, your tongue. Your mind. Set a timer for ten minutes. Something you swallowed. Start writing.

grab a notebook

How was that? How did it feel to just write without worrying at all for a few minutes? Did the memory that surfaced surprise you? Upset you? Make you laugh? All of that is totally and completely fine. This, by the way, is all part of a specific approach toward creative work that I'll talk about later. Suffice it to say, the idea here is that throughout this book, you don't just wave at me and my stories on the page, but join me there, and actually write part of this chapter too—the most important part: *your* part.

CHAPTER 2

Why You Can Stay in Your Comfort Zone

Take us very far out of our comfort zones, and our brains stop paying attention to anything other than surviving the experience.

—Marcus Buckingham and Ashley Goodall, "The Feedback Fallacy"

Yes. You heard me right: It's OK to stay in your comfort zone. It's better than OK. The goal isn't to leave it, but to live *in* it.

You've been told the opposite, by everyone from motivational speakers and bloggers to people on TikTok to your friend who's starting a life-coaching business. They all preach that you must leave your comfort zone to do all the things you want—make money, make friends, make a difference.

Fact is, if you're reading this, you're *already* outside your comfort zone. We all spend way, way too much time standing in a semi-panic outside them, frantically searching for our keys. Or the opposite—what began as a comfort zone has now become cramped and insufferable. It shrunk or we grew, or both, and it's not so comfy anymore.

The goal isn't to get *out* of your comfort zone; the goal is to *expand* it. That's why it doesn't even make any sense to make discomfort the goal. If you make your Big Hairy Goal to get out of your comfort zone every single day, I promise you one thing: You'll spend much of the year . . . uncomfortable. Hey, that's your prerogative. You could also spend most of the year wet or sad or unshaven if you so choose.

You know when you're no longer in your comfort zone because you feel: restless, stuck, bored, tired, uninspired. Chances are you don't want to continue to be uncomfortable and you know that going smaller won't help—what you want is to stretch, to expand, to go bigger. When do things (animals, people, plants) get small? When they're cold, sick, dying, depressed. When we feel good, we take bigger breaths, stretch, make room. What does every decluttering expert tell us? We need to let go of shit so that there's room for what we actually want.

Your comfort level is going to be different from mine, which is why any two people can and will fight over a thermostat. Put me on a stage with a hot mic any day of the week and I'm thrilled, calm, focused. Hand my sister Kim a hot mic, however, and she may exit her body altogether. But stick her on the Rock 'n' Roller Coaster at Disney—to me the epitome of pointless discomfort—and she's right at home. If you want to go with her, I will absolutely hold your purse.

You may think that if you go through something uncomfortable but gain something as a result, then that must be attributable to . . . the fact that you were uncomfortable, right? That's like saying, "I got seasick on a boat to the Bahamas, but it was the best trip of my life. So whenever I want to have a good time, I make sure I'm good and nauseous first."

Discomfort isn't a guarantee, it's a *condition*. Just like cold on the climb up Mount Everest. You could decide to go, lose a few fingers on the way, and have a huge breakthrough about your life. But you could also return from the trip a few fingers short of what you left with and decide you're done climbing. Don't climb literally anything unless you want to—and certainly not because you think you need to do uncomfortable things (or, more to the point, *tell* people you're going to be doing uncomfortable things). Also, why go climbing at all when you can be just as uncomfortable in a cafeteria holding a tray with nowhere to sit?

Discomfort isn't an indicator of bravery; it's an indicator of . . . discomfort. In the act of being brave or courageous or ambitious, you will very likely encounter discomfort, but to aim "for" it, in my mind, is to miss the point and the goal. I feel the same way about "doing something every day that scares you." Being scared every day is a recipe for anxiety, not necessarily personal growth.

Fran Lebowitz has something to say about this (unsurprisingly). In her 2021 docuseries *Pretend It's a City*, in which Martin Scorsese essentially follows Lebowitz around Manhattan with a camera and serves as a one-man laugh track, she says this idea that we need to "challenge ourselves" causes people to do ridiculous things for the wrong reasons.

"Climbing mountains is a fake challenge," she says. "You don't have to climb a mountain. There are many things that people have to do and should do, that they don't do, because they're scared to do or because they're bad at it—those are challenges. A challenge is something you *have* to do, not something you make up. I find real life challenging enough."[1]

You know who *wasn't* trying to seek out new ways to be uncomfortable? The early settlers. War refugees. The people who lived twelve to a tenement on the Lower East Side in the early 1900s and worked in cramped, airless rooms. Or many millions of people, right now, who are so uncomfortable and itchy and unhappy and cannot imagine why on earth anyone would aim to feel that way. Which is another reason I hate this whole thing: Because seeking out discomfort is a pastime of the privileged.

The reason we "like" an uncomfortable experience in retrospect is because it serves as a clear and salient reminder of just how strong we can be. And that is a reason to be proud of doing something you didn't think you could. Beloved author, ultramarathon runner, and VP of Fitness Programming at Peloton, Robin Arzón—who was, in fact, born to a Cuban refugee—will tell you over and over, right when you're about to drop the hand weights and go eat a brownie, "Keep going. You can do hard things."

And you can. As one of many tens of thousands of people who got a Peloton during the pandemic, I will tell you I definitely feel challenged on that bike, but honestly, I didn't get one because I wanted to be uncomfortable every day; I wanted to feel *more* comfortable in my body (a body that barely left the house for a year). And now that there's a good ten pounds less of me, I am.

Take it from Marcus Buckingham, one of the world's most prominent researchers on strengths and leadership, who has two of the best-selling business books of all time and two of *Harvard Business Review*'s most circulated, industry-changing cover articles. He's made his mark calling into question entrenched preconceptions about achievement and success and, in the process, redefining them and the future of work.

In his 2019 *Harvard Business Review* cover story, "The Feedback Fallacy," written with Ashley Goodall, he questions the effectiveness of traditional criticism, and how helpful it is in encouraging growth and excellence in employees. Turns out, being told where you fucked up and how you might want to stop fucking up is not the most helpful. Few things will eject you from your happy place like negative feedback from a boss (or anyone):

"We're often told that the key to learning is to get out of our comfort zones, but these findings contradict that particular chestnut," Buckingham and Goodall write. "Take us very far out of our comfort zones, and our brains stop paying attention to anything other than surviving the experience. It's clear that we learn most in our comfort zones, because that's where our neural pathways are most concentrated. It's where we're most open to possibility, most creative, insightful, and productive. That's where feedback must meet us—in our moments of flow."[2]

In short, we're not only not at our best outside our comfort zones, but we're unable to access our best there either.

You only have so much energy and attention to spend in your waking hours. Are you spending it on the things that you feel you *should* do or that you've been told are good to do—or the things that really, actually matter to you? At what point does seeking out new "challenges" become a convenient way to hide from the actual hard things?

My bigger concern is that the discomfort-as-growth strategy is not only a waste of time but also a slippery slope. Because if you believe you must target discomfort to grow, you may *also* think you must suffer to do your work, or struggle to find love. Why would we agree to that equation?

Oh, you're worried that living in your comfort zone means you won't *do* anything? That things have to be hard to be worth it? OK. Then why are therapists' offices so cozy and well-appointed? Why do we meditate on a pillow and not a metal spike? Why is ski apparel so pricey?

Don't mistake my love of comfort for complacency or denial. I think of the comfort zone not as cold storage where you put your dreams on ice and go back to binging *Schitt's Creek* (again). The comfort zone is a greenhouse: Warm, sunny, protected from the elements—where living things thrive.

How Your Comfort Zone Can Keep You in Business

The word you might use to describe the three-hundred-square-foot studio I lived in for a decade is "cozy." It fit me like a glove. The day I got laid off, I came right back to it, and began to figure out what to do next. I reached out to the people in my comfort zone—friends, colleagues, not people who "challenged" me, but people who actually liked and supported me. And in the ensuing months and years, I took on gigs I liked and others I loathed, and the work that made me feel really uncomfortable? I ditched. I stuck with what I knew I was good at.

In short, I expanded my life and my work within a very small footprint, grew an entire consulting, speaking, and writing business without any shoes on. I learned to create and deliver virtual offerings via Zoom long before your mother ever heard of it, and, in a few short years, catapulted my income to more than five times what I was earning at my last job. Was I at times uncomfortable? Did some things not work out? You bet. I didn't need to scare myself daily to grow—not having a job was scary enough. I had no choice *but* to grow if I was going to stay in this very uncomfortable city that I never want to leave.

Taking a risk, trying something scary or new or something with very high stakes, is not about prioritizing discomfort, however; it's about *commitment*—committing to expanding your comfort zone so that you remain inside it. When I hit "send" on a big proposal, or stepped onstage to do a five-minute set at New York Comedy Club (you want to talk discomfort?), I wasn't doing it simply to be uncomfortable; I muscled through some of the discomfort to find ease onstage, to ride the rise and crest of laughter, because I wanted to get better at it and to enjoy being there, which I do.

My friend Laura Belgray has been in lockdown in her comfort zone for years. It's not only how she functions best; it's the *only* way she functions. She embraces what she refers to as her lazy and chickenshit nature. She said to me recently, "I like stasis." So you can bet you won't find her doing something scary just for the sake of it. Ever. Once, on a writing retreat we attended, a woman offered to top off her coffee cup and Laura got nervous that the woman might burn her. "I hate adrenaline," Laura says. "I want nothing to do with it."

The founder of Talking Shrimp and cocreator of The Copy Cure with her longtime BFF Marie Forleo, Laura is one of the most successful copywriters in the country. How do you know? She doesn't even *have* clients anymore. Why? Because after years of muscling through client work, she found it sucked all the energy out of her comfort zone. She compensated by raising its walls, and raising her rates higher to discourage business—*yes, she did that*—and it didn't work! You wouldn't believe how people were willing to stretch their *own* comfort zones to make the investment to work with her (something to keep in mind when you're thinking about pricing yourself).

Fact is, it wasn't about the money. It was about staying comfortable. She has since structured her business in a way that suits her far better, offering courses and masterminds for business owners who want to sharpen their copy skills, and partnering with colleagues to support their own launches. She's at the top of her game and running a seven-figure business, and she's also . . . on her couch.

"Rather than do things to make me uncomfortable, I look to bring more things into my comfort zone," she told me. That doesn't mean she's comfortable doing everything—hardly. As a high-profile writer and known personality in the world of online entrepreneurship, she gets invited to speak more and more—and that's not necessarily in her comfort zone. Yet. "One thing that inspires me is watching people who are comfortable up there, because that's how I want to feel."

If you follow Laura on social or subscribe to her emails (which I highly recommend), you'll hear all manner of personal stories about her life, and for some people, sharing all that would be really uncomfortable. But not for her. "TMI is squarely in my comfort zone, so that doesn't feel courageous." The key, she says, is to double down on things that feel comfortable and easy, because that is where your genius lives. When you must do something scary in order to expand your zone and get comfortable again, know that you do it with the goal of making it easier every time.

After ten years in my tiny prewar studio, I upgraded to a one-bed down the street (same zip code, new dry cleaner)—with an adult-sized dining room table and a kitchen that wasn't built for Barbies. The rent was a stretch; the trade-off was for *more* comfort, and more room in which to *be* comfortable—and to grow.

You can stretch your comfort zone, like you can your hamstrings with months of yoga. It's not sudden, but it does happen, and then you're more agile, less cramped, and more capable of taking on the things you most want to do. Not because you decide to scare yourself into them, but because you're really ready.

Tips for Staying in Your Comfort Zone

- **DEFINE IT.** Get real clear with yourself on how you want to spend your time and energy. For instance, I do not like open-ended anythings: meetings, events, contracts. I like start times and end times. What are your rules? When do you do your best work, and with whom? What kinds of things do you want to learn—and what do you not have an ounce of interest in getting any better at?
- **BE UNAPOLOGETIC ABOUT IT.** I find the whole explaining myself thing rather uncomfortable, for me and whomever I'm explaining myself to. If I can't or don't want to take something on, I send my regrets and that's it. No one actually cares and the more we try to defend ourselves, the worse we feel.
- **PROCESS IN THE COMFORT ZONE.** You build strength and confidence when you're feeling comfortable, not when you're feeling stressed, judged, and hating yourself. Find ways to make the risks you want to take more comfortable. If you've been through something that felt decidedly uncomfy, wait until you're squarely back in the zone to process what happened, why, and what you'll do about it.
- **LEAN INTO WHAT YOU'RE GOOD AT.** Prioritize that stuff—and procrastinate or delegate everything else. I do this. I know all work expands to fill time, and so I make sure that I am using my best energy and attention on the stuff I'm the best at, because that's how you can grow at a steady pace. And if you have to do something you're not great at for a bit? Be sure to end the day, the night, or the week with or on something you're really good at.

- **PREVENT HUNGER, NAUSEA, AND EXHAUSTION.** I don't go into anything remotely taxing feeling hungry, tired, or stressed. If I'm going to do something new that feels a little nerve-racking, I rest, eat something, exercise, talk to friends, listen to Stern, do whatever I must to get relaxed. If I'm going to be on a bus, boat, or other moving thing, I make sure I have dosed myself with OTC drugs so that I don't get nauseous. Because no one gets points for pushing from a weakened state, so avoid it if you can.
- **MAKE YOUR ZONE INVITE-ONLY.** Your comfort zone must be tightly policed and protected, and it is most definitely invite-only. You get to decide who comes in and shares that space and for how long. I have a friend who loves red wine and tends to spill things. I bought her a damn adult sippy cup so that when she laughs while holding a glass of malbec on my couch I don't get jumpy. I keep a pretty tight douche-proof filter in my friend circle, my programs, and don't tolerate problem people, including downers, nitpickers, negative Nancies, critics, and haters. Sorry. No admittance.

write your next chapter

Think about the last time you really felt in your zone. Where you had that sense of expansion and ease, where you were doing what you do best, in a way that felt natural to you. Doesn't matter where you were or what that thing was. OK. Set a timer for seven minutes (this is quick!) and write that scene. What was happening, what did it feel like? Really go into the body here. Relive it:

grab a notebook

What surprised you there? What came up that you didn't know you knew or even remembered? To reexperience that is to remind yourself, body and mind, of what it is to be in your zone.

Next, how comfortable do you feel right now? Today, this week, this month. But also: How comfortable are you in what you're doing, where you're living, who you're living with, how you're spending your time? What would it take for you to expand your comfort zone here? What feels too tight, too cramped? Where is the growth potential right now?

grab a notebook

Last, think ahead six months or even a year. What does your comfort zone look like then? What level of comfort are you aspiring to? What would you like to see yourself saying a year from now, "I love doing this"?

grab a notebook

CHAPTER 3

Unfollow Your Passion

Passion feels very democratic. It's the people's talent, available to all. It's also mostly bullshit.

—Scott Adams, *How to Fail at Almost Everything and Still Win Big*

At some point in your life, someone—a parent, a teacher, a well-meaning aunt—will tell you that as long as you follow your passion, everything will fall into place. Just find your passion and follow it. Forever. Sounds good and aspirational. Magic, even. We think it's what freedom must feel like—certainly this is worth leaving your comfort zone for, right? This one, sure thing that you're predestined to do? It must be the key to a meaningful life, right?

This sounds a lot better on paper or coming out of the mouth of a motivational speaker than it does when you try to execute on that idea. The problem isn't that passions are hard to come by—we have dozens, hundreds!—but that the minute we decide it has to be the center, the meaning of everything, the source of all motivation and pleasure and paychecks, the pressure is on.

In 2015, I gave a TEDx talk on this topic, called "Stop Searching for Your Passion"—why, because I was passionate about it? No. Because when a speaker dropped out of the lineup at TEDxKC, a spot opened up and I wanted it. I didn't even have my whole thesis worked out. I just had a few pointed opinions about advice I hate, and this was one of them. And so I told the TEDx producer Mike Lundgren on our first call that I thought the search for passion was a bunch of bullshit.

"Keep talking," he said. I told him the advice was unhelpful, unspecific, and made people feel worse, not better. Not because we are incapable of passion, but because we assume we're supposed to know precisely what to do because of it. We can and do feel passionate about a lot of things, but this pressure to find one deemed personally, economically, or commercially viable and ride it until the end of time feels like way too much pressure. I'd always known I loved writing, for instance, but feeling passionate about the act of writing didn't help me out of the postcollege slump I'd found myself in years ago, when I could barely bring myself to put pants on.

Telling someone to follow their passion is a little like saying, "If you want success, follow that car." *Which car? How do I know that's the right car? Because it's fast or my favorite color? Or looks like my old car? Because I like that car, but is it* the *car? You're sure? Where is it going? Do I need to know? Do you know?* This is limiting and restrictive, and presumes that you have to choose the right car to end up at the right destination—and if you don't, you're fucked.

Turns out, I was on to something. That talk hit a nerve, and at the time of this writing more than seven million people have seen it. Did I talk them *out* of following their passions? No! I relieved them of the need to wring their hands over the passion they think they missed like the last train out of town.

In *So Good They Can't Ignore You*, Cal Newport says: "Compelling careers often have complex origins that reject the simple idea that all you have to do is follow your passion."[1]

Why? Because *people* are compelling and complex. To believe you can be boiled down to one thing is not only unrealistic and uncommon; it's also dangerously reductive, and could lead you to abandon things before you fully discover their unique pleasures and rewards.

What if you don't know what you're passionate about, or you had one and it fails to do the job anymore? There's not a thing wrong with you. It doesn't mean you're "out" of passion forever. That's like saying you're bad at eating because every few hours you're hungry again. Our wants and desires, appetites and drives, move in phases and stages; they rise and fall, wax and wane. There isn't a human on the planet who doesn't enjoy that swell of emotion and energy, that cresting wave of motivation and focus that we associate with passion. So if we're talking about "choosing" a passion, let's start with the fact nobody *wouldn't* choose it. But passion is something we experience, not a thing we pick out of a pile like a cantaloupe.

Which means we just might have it backward.

Because more often than not, we get passionate about things that are working, not the other way around. In *How to Fail at Almost Everything and Still Win Big,* Dilbert creator Scott Adams talks about all his failed attempts at business ideas and how passion was not an indicator of forthcoming success. When it started to look like his comic strip *Dilbert* might actually work out, his passion for cartooning also increased. "Success caused passion more than passion caused success,"[2] he writes.

If that's the case, then there's no point in trying to find passion first. Why not let it follow you instead? That's essentially what Viktor Frankl says in *Man's Search for Meaning*; he's talking about success and the pursuit of happiness, but I think we can agree passion applies here too: "The more you aim at it and make it a target, the more you are going to miss it. For success, like happiness"—and we might add here "passion"—"cannot be pursued. . . . You have to let it happen by not caring about it."[3] I know this can sound like WTF advice, like when someone tells you that to get a boyfriend you should act disinterested and not text back right away. That's not what I mean. In fact, one of the worst things you can do is . . . wait for it.

Why You Shouldn't Wait for Your Passion to Show Up

The passion myth is a kind of fairy tale—which is what makes this whole approach *particularly* insidious for women. Think about it: It's the belief that your One True Passion is out there and that if you're good and worthy he'll come sweep you onto his steed and you'll live happily ever after, doing what you love and were meant to do. We have simply swapped out a romantic dream for a professional ambition, the prince for passion. We have fantasized that a singular passion or purpose must, like a glass slipper, fit *perfectly* in order to work—only to discover that it's unyielding, rigid, and impossible to walk in.

We actually *can* court passion—not by making it sign an affidavit, but by giving it room to move, and an opportunity to be discovered. What's far more critical than picking a passion is recognizing our *capacity* for it—which we all have. Each of us is capable of fire, but rather than picking up whatever sticks are nearby and rubbing them together, we keep looking for the perfect sticks. You don't need perfect sticks. What you need is friction. You need to start rubbing things together and generating energy yourself.

The way to experience and explore it is to invite opportunities for making things matter by investing time, attention, and ability to what's right in front of us rather than waiting for Prince Passion and milady Motivation to darken our door. When we act first, we switch on the circuits that give passion a place to go, a place to emerge. And there's literally no limit on all the ways you can do that, which you're about to find out.

Passion Can't Hold a Candle to What You've Already Got

There's another reason to give the passion hypothesis some side-eye: If we're so busy with our binoculars, craning to spot this mythical prince out there somewhere, we risk overlooking or missing altogether what you've already got: Your skills, which, like magical talking birds and chatty cartoon mice, are busy stitching ball gowns for you and getting zero credit for that effort.

Just ask *Shark Tank* fave Barbara Corcoran, founder of The Corcoran Group, if she followed her passion to get where she is. Someone did ask her that at an event I attended at the 92nd Street Y in Manhattan a few years ago. Her answer? Nope.

You could almost hear the crowd gasp (*What! No passion!*). "Oh, come on, Barbara," said fellow Shark Robert Herjavec from under his handsome head of hair. "You're the biggest name in the business. You have to have a passion for real estate!" She insisted she did not. I mean, the woman had had twenty jobs by the time she was twenty-three! She wanted to make money and earn a living and start her life beyond the small town in New Jersey where she grew up as one of ten (yes, ten!) kids. She got a job answering phones at Giffuni Brothers' Real Estate in Manhattan, looked around, and said, *I could do this.* She began where the opportunity was, right in front of her—and with a little spark and a $1,000 loan from her boyfriend started her own real estate company.

What she told the audience at the 92nd Street Y was that while she didn't give a pip about real estate, she loved growing and leading a team. And for a little while there she had to forego a salary to keep the wheels of that business turning. When things took off for her in a big way, she discovered she loved seeing her face in the media and throwing big parties. She loved it all! It didn't necessarily start with a ride-or-die love for real estate. But that's where it happened.

Now, lots of people answer phones at real estate companies and never once consider starting their own. Far as I'm concerned Barbara Corcoran was a lit match and whatever she touched was going to catch fire. It really wouldn't have mattered what she did. If she'd been answering phones at a shoe company, we'd all be wearing Corcoran boots right now instead of ogling her properties on Zillow.

The point here is that passion isn't limited necessarily to a topic, a subject, an industry, or even one specific goal. You don't have to choose one forever. Passion is not a whimsical fairy that blesses a rare few; it's the force of attention and energy you as a human bring to everything you do, even if you didn't plan to do it.

There's More to Life than a Single Pursuit

The expectation that passion will save the day is also a recipe for ruining your day-to-day life and robbing you of the pleasure of what does happen. We assume that once we achieve that thing, life as we know it will never be the same again and every moment will peak higher than the next. That is a very tall order indeed.

You know who learned that lesson the hard way? Joe Gardner in the movie *Soul* (please tell me you saw that). All Joe has ever wanted was to "make it" as a musician, to pursue his passion full-time. He gets his chance when he auditions for a famous jazz musician, Dorothea Williams. This could be it! He plays his heart out and Dorothea says, "Get a suit and be back here at 6:30 p.m."

This is the break he's been waiting for. This is the *life* he's been waiting for. Of course things go sideways when Joe falls through a manhole and into the afterlife and spends the rest of the movie trying to get back in time for the gig, which—spoiler alert—he does. And this performance is everything he imagined—immersive, exciting, received by waves of applause. But of course, that isn't where it ends.

Afterward, Joe is standing with Dorothea outside the jazz club after the show and he asks her, "So what happens next?"

"We come back and do it all again tomorrow night," she says. He looks crestfallen. Dorothea asks what's wrong.

"It's just, I've been waiting on this day for . . . my entire life. I thought I'd feel . . . *different*."[4]

This is a tough moment for Joe—and for all of us—when

something great happens and then things level out. *Is this it, then?* we think. Joe, like many of us, has been living another, fictional life in his head, about "what it will be like *when*." What he learns, of course, is that doing a thing well (what he deemed his purpose) isn't the same as meaning, as purpose. What Joe discovers is that the very thing he believes he's "meant" to do—music—has blinded him to the richness of his own life, and what it really means to live it. He's suffered from tunnel vision his whole life, and mistaken it for purpose. When he emerges from that tunnel, the world opens up, and he has an even bigger awakening about what his life *actually* means, the thing that inspires music itself (I'm not crying; you're crying!).

But before he has that final transcendent moment, when he's standing with Dorothea on the street, she tells him a story about a fish:

> *A fish swims up to this older fish and says, "I'm trying to find this thing they call the ocean."*
>
> *"The ocean?" says the older fish. "That's what you in right now."*
>
> *"This? This is* water. *What I* want *is the ocean."*[5]

This idea that passion will get us somewhere else, somewhere better, to that ocean over *there*, is an illusion; the water, however, is real. And it's not something you have to go find. It's all around you. The only thing to do? Start swimming.

write your next chapter

Think of a time when you believed that one thing, one activity, one goal, was the be-all, end-all. How old were you? What was that thing? Maybe it was a specific toy or trip you wanted to take as a kid. Or perhaps you were older and you got locked on to an idea and couldn't let it go. Maybe these were unique to you, and maybe they were milestones—graduation, job, even marriage. Start with one thing and give yourself ten minutes to write about that.

grab a notebook

OK, without overthinking, leap to another time in your life. What's another thing you became obsessed with doing, having, being? Dive deep into this memory and write out the details you remember about the time, where you were, what you wanted.

grab a notebook

Last, what are you excited about right now? Maybe it's something you want to learn more about or simply do more often. It might be a goal you set for yourself for six weeks or six months from now. It doesn't have to be a Big Hairy Goal. It could be something silly or small, but that you keep thinking about, something that fills you with energy, focus, anticipation.

grab a notebook

Now go back and look at all three. Do they have anything in common? Maybe, maybe not. They may be wildly different in terms of subject matter, but what resonates through all of them? What are the kinds of things that tend to draw you and excite you?

grab a notebook

The point is not "OK, now do that thing forever," but rather to become a keen observer of where and how your own passions rise and fall over time. You're certainly not less of a person because you were into one thing or because you aren't anymore. But what it shows you is that passion is a sustainable force, and will keep surging and rising to bring new interests and ideas to life.

CHAPTER 4

Dump Your Bucket List and Figure Out What (Actually) Matters

If you wait until the time's right, you'll wait forever.
—Denis Morton, Peloton instructor

I held on to my virginity so long I forgot what I was saving it for.

I'd known Liam my whole life; our parents were friends. His family owned a funeral home, so everyone knew the family and got to see them under unfortunate circumstances.

We'd dated intensely for a while, then broke up. And anyone could see that we were getting back together. The writing was on the wall—literally—the white marker board we used to leave messages before there was texting or Facebook. I came home one evening to find *Want to grab dinner?* in his shaky block print. And we snapped back together as if we'd never been apart.

My friend Jenni and I were dressed up as bumblebees at her Halloween party a few days later, discussing this new development, when she made a passing comment about makeup sex. That's when I let drop that we'd never had actual sex.

"What? Why not?" she said, her sparkly antennae bobbing inquisitively.

I didn't know why not. I was an everything-but virgin, a virgin on a technicality: You could put this there and I could put that here, just not *that* in *there*. What had begun as a principled decision was now a habit. I hadn't had sex, so I kept not having it. Liam knew the drill; his penis had long steered clear of the area like a dog trained on an electric fence. But in truth I had run out of reasons. It was like going into your wallet to grab a twenty and finding a few wrinkled singles, these poor excuses. I did some quick accounting: *God doesn't want you to? No. Mom doesn't want you to? No. Does anyone care? No.*

This is where firsts are tricky, and why they're worth talking about now. First-ever sex is a milestone, and it should be something you do on purpose. You're ready when you're ready, and really only you know. But that makes it like most things you do for the first time: The longer you wait, the higher the stakes. I was in no rush to have sex, clearly, and I don't recommend rushing. But the risk is that the drumroll gets longer, and louder, and your expectations rise along with it. And the higher they go, well, the farther they have to fall.

But another reason why this matters now is because if we get caught up in the mystical nature of firsts we might get precious about them, or more fearful than we need to be. This can in turn cause us to put things off that maybe we shouldn't, such as: Moving out, applying for a better job, booking your maiden voyage abroad—or, really, making any decision that you might hesitate to break the seal around for fear conditions aren't perfect. Because conditions are never perfect.

Plenty of people believe that their first time having sex should be perfect (oy). Or that it should be reserved for marriage, which is what I'd been told. And yet marriage as an ideal and/or goal had begun to feel farther away the older I got, and I felt less interested in trying to get there. Ever try to walk from the Luxor to Mandalay Bay? The farther you walk, the farther it feels. Is this worth it? Won't it just be all the same stuff inside a different building? (Basically.)

Once I got the idea in my head that it was time to have sex, a plan hatched fast—like when you go from not thinking about getting your hair cut to being obsessed with getting it done now now now. I was less concerned with "special" and more concerned with safe. So I didn't run out to buy candles and lingerie; I went to CVS with my (sexually active little) sister to get supplies. Condoms, check. Lube? Do I need that? "No," she said. I grabbed a can of spermicidal foam, the way you might jauntily throw in some Reddi wip when you've decided on sundaes.

I chose the night of a holiday dance. I told my friends; I didn't tell Liam. It was as if I were throwing a big surprise party for him in my vagina and everyone knew about it, but he was the only one invited. When we got back to my room, I went to the bathroom so I could fill myself with foam like a spermicidal doughnut. Then, rather than make any big pronouncements, I simply switched off the electric fence, and it was like a Labrador discovering he has the run of the place.

"Really?" he panted. "Are you sure?"

And while it wasn't scary or very painful, it wasn't what I thought it would be either. I don't know what I expected, but part of me hoped it would be like that moment in *Willy Wonka* when everyone's squeezed into an uncomfortable hallway with a miniature door and suddenly it creaks open to reveal . . . the Chocolate Room. *Notttt* really. Sex was what it was: Putting this part in *there*. I distinctly recall thinking that I was simply aware of it and that it wasn't unpleasant, like putting a Q-tip in your ear. And then it was over.

"So, how do you feel?" Liam asked the next morning. It was a new day, the first without my technical virginity intact, and it was like going outside without a coat and realizing with relief that you don't need one.

"I mean, I feel fine," I said. "I guess I'm glad I didn't wait until I was married for that."

"Gee, thanks," he said.

"You know what I mean." I didn't want to hurt his feelings, but it's the truth. I was relieved to discover that sex, though an intentional act and expression of intimacy, didn't have to be more than what it was. There was no cryptic door, and it didn't necessarily create, in and of itself, a fundamental change (and to believe it *does* is to subscribe to the patriarchal idea that you are "damaged" or "spoiled" afterwards, which is a bunch of bullshit). I certainly didn't regret sharing my first with a good man, but I also realized there was only one first for a reason. You didn't need more than one.

Sex, like most things (except, I imagine, crack), gets better the more you do it. Which is why it's unfair to expect our firsts to be the definitive experience. It can also set a low bar. Maybe you think a lot about the firsts you're dying to have: Your first time living without roommates or with a partner; your first job offer with the word "director" in the title; your first time traveling alone, just for fun. What are some of the expectations surrounding that first? Do you expect you have to be perfect or confident right from the jump? Can you give yourself some wiggle room to get better as you go?

Firsts are special by virtue of being first, so special that you almost don't have to do much else to it. Will you remember first things longer? Probably. First day of sleepaway camp. First time you failed a test. First boyfriend. First girlfriend. First breakup. First stunning betrayal. First oyster. It's just the way our brains work—all that wet cement, so many ways to leave a mark.

Firsts Are Often the Worst

We often assume firsts will be inherently interesting and important, even if they turn out not to be. The first is just your first; you have to pass through it to get to your second, and that may be its only point. You aren't defined by your first, especially since it's usually the least best way you'll ever have done it.

Take the first time I got behind the wheel of a car with my mother. I'd been in cars all my life, but being in that seat changed everything. I instantly lost all trust in myself and other people. I hit the brakes early and often and right in the middle of a turn, which of course made turning harder. You think brakes are safe, but that isn't always true; stopping short is just as dangerous. Maintaining momentum is critical, because it gives you more control; control and *stopped*, however, are not the same. "You actually want to *accelerate* into the turn," my mother said. "You need the gas to keep going."

I felt down about that first drive. "You'll get better," my mom said. "Someday you won't even think about it; that's how easy it will be." I went on to become a good driver, someone who enjoys driving. And she was right: As I'm cruising up the Merritt Parkway through Connecticut, I don't think about *how* to drive, any more than I think of my own spleen.

Does all this mean we shouldn't honor the firsts? Of course not. First man on the moon, first Black president, first female recipient of the Nobel Prize in Physics. There is power in being *the* first, but the reason they're lauded is not because they thought about maybe being the first, but because they did it.

How to Get Past the First

Here's some ways to reframe "firsts" so that you don't get hung up on them and you can move on past them to the next.

- **DON'T DEMAND A PERFECT FIRST.** In *The Creative Habit*, Twyla Tharp says if you believe conditions must be perfect to begin, you risk staying stuck. "You won't move on to that second chapter until the first is written, rewritten, honed, tweaked, examined under a microscope, and buffed to a bright mahogany sheen," she writes. "I know it's important to be prepared, but at the start of the process this type of perfectionism is more like procrastination. You've got to get in there and *do*."[1]
- **ASSUME YOU'LL BE BAD AT IT.** It goes without saying that you want to be prepared before you do anything for the first time. But having information in your head is not the same as having it in your body, and that means it takes a minute to do anything well, or at all.

The first (and only) time I've been wakeboarding, I watched my friends go first—and fall right on their faces. I could see where things were going wrong, so I visualized doing it the right way, and hoped my body got the message. Nope! Not even close. I clung to that board like a barnacle and never so much as got off my knees. I also don't own a boat and so have no reason to care or try to be good at it. Next.

- **LEAD WITH COURAGE, NOT CONFIDENCE.** We think that people who regularly do adventurous/scary/hard things are courageous, and that when we go to do a thing for the first time, we're supposed to be confident. Trying to be confident before you do a thing is like trying to get paid before you do the job. Courage, however, works on credit. You can bank on what you've already got, but you draw on courage *when you have nothing else*. You get paid for that effort—in the currency of confidence.
- **BEWARE OF BEGINNER'S LUCK.** Because it's not luck; it's a curse. Manage to bowl a strike, get a hole in one, or hit blackjack on your first round and you'll be temporarily pleased and then disappointed forever. I think of beginner's luck as the crack of first times, because you'll spend a lot of time chasing that first high, and we know how that goes. Instead, go in assuming you'll suck so you can enjoy the process of learning, which can be really fun, especially when you start to see yourself improve.
- **PUT IT IN PERSPECTIVE.** Putting too much pressure on or raising expectations too high is counterproductive. We'd all love our firsts to be special, which they are—even if they suck. They aren't who we are, nor are they an accurate reflection of ability; they're just how we begin. Don't wait forever for your first; blow through it on your way to sensational seconds, fabulous fourths. Don't linger at the door until things are perfect, or you are perfect. Firsts don't require much from you except that you do them. And they're really only firsts if you do them again.

The Problem with Bucket Lists

If you need more evidence of our obsession with firsts, look no further than the bucket list. I get the appeal and appreciate the sentiment of Things to Do Before You Die—a list of things you want to do exactly once. I mean, how many times are you going to walk the suspension bridge in Honduras or airboat across the Everglades? The goal is to do them, yes, but also to *say* you've done them—like, run a marathon—which, as a comic I know points out, you can say whether you do it or not.

There are things I have tried and liked, and tried and not liked, but I did them to see if I'd want to do them, or something like them, again. Take stand-up comedy, for instance. I'd been flirting with the idea for years, and told myself I couldn't do it because, well, of things I made up: "Real" comics were funnier or ballsier or smarter than me, and that turned out not to be true. What they were? Practiced. Honed. It's not just that they "were" a thing but also that they did a thing—over and over again. Endlessly. Comedy isn't some magical crazy gift—it's a skill. It's a craft. Which means it can be learned and improved. It's not so much that I thought I would "become" a comic, but that I knew that there were skills to forge in that particular fire that were worth knowing and practicing.

During that very first stand-up class, we went around the room to introduce ourselves, and one guy said he was there because doing stand-up was on his bucket list. That felt like a cop-out, like, "Oh, don't mind me; I'm not *really* here. Don't judge me! I'm not even really trying!" Perfectly nice guy. I applaud the fact that he showed up! But it highlighted for me the problem with the bucket-list mentality: It excuses your effort because you don't "really" care how it goes. But don't you? Don't we all?

I had no plans on doing comedy for a living, but I was all in because it's the only way to really learn anything. That means it requires risk. If you're just there to see what it's like, you don't quite have skin in the game like the rest of us do. If you want to create meaning and explore, you can't sidestep risk. That risk, of not knowing how a thing will turn out, of being *seen* trying, is the thing that separates someone who wants to do a thing, not just say they did it. You're capable of a lot more than you realize—it's not whether you were "born with it," but whether you've given yourself a chance to see yourself making progress.

When I did my first stand-up set in front of a live audience at Gotham Comedy Club, I bombed hard. Right out of the gate. My first joke didn't land because I hadn't finished writing it—I had this idea that the premise was funny enough, and I was wrong about that. I somehow saved the set with a quick redirect, and learned a valuable lesson (always write the whole joke). But this was just my first time, not my last. I got up the next week, and the week after that. Stand-up is not zip-lining in Costa Rica. Your options can't be "either I'm amazing out of the gate and make a living at this—or I try it once." What kind of choice is that?

What happened to the bucket list stand-up guy? Who knows. I'd bet you a million dollars he's not doing comedy. He wasn't there to "really" do it, after all.

Does this mean you shouldn't try new things? Of course not! And raising the stakes too high can give a thing more weight than necessary (see also: sex, above). I'm all for low-stakes efforts at playing and exploring. The risk of doing something once and only once means allowing that one time to stand in for the entire experience. So if you have a bad water-skiing experience, you may label it "water-ski = bad" and never do it again, or assume you're just no good at it. In the grand scheme, who cares if you don't water-ski again. But imagine if we did that with . . . sex. There's so much bad sex out there that if it weren't for a deep hardwired drive, we'd all have gone extinct a long time ago.

Writing a book is another bucket list item that puzzles me. Swimming with dolphins, OK. But a book? Given how much time and effort writing one requires, you'd have to be crazy to do it just to do it. Whom does that serve? Especially since the point of writing a book, unless you do it just for yourself, isn't actually for you; it's for the person who reads it. A book is a creative effort (underscore *effort*), and that means it's not a box you check, but something you undertake and put muscle behind, because you want to create something that matters, despite the risk that no one may read it. Sure, you could do a book as a kind of glorified vanity plate (many do). But honestly, if you want to do something that feels exciting, and requires a lot less effort, you're better off jumping off the Victoria Falls Bridge with a cord strapped to your ankle.

The reason you're even reading this book right now is because some part of you worries that you'll do the wrong thing or miss the right thing and then not have the life you were "supposed" to have—and that it won't thus be as good, or as meaningful. This idea, that there's a right and wrong way to do things, is evidence of a fixed, versus a growth, mindset. Just like the idea of having *one* passion. This is not only a limiting idea; it limits you—and assumes your life is set and ruled by a series of on/off switches or genetic lottery, rather than your ability to learn and change and grow.

I don't think it's bad if you have a bucket list. What I'm more concerned with is whether a bucket-list mindset is keeping you from exploring things that could change you if you gave them a chance. Because if you believe ticking off a list of to-dos adds up to a meaningful life, well, you may be disappointed. A bucket list, by design, places value on a singular experience over a recurring one, on thrill over stakes, and accomplishment over achievement. While you may experience bliss or eternity or release during those five (yes, five) seconds of sheer free-fall bliss off a bridge in Brazil, there's a catch at the end (there always is). You're yanked back (gratefully) onto land, onto your feet, and into your life, and when the buzz wears off, somehow, there you are, back to folding laundry, searching for the other blue sock.

My friend Becky Karush, a brilliant writer and host of the *Read to Me* podcast, quite enjoys trying things she has no intention of excelling in—like the time she tried making fried doughnuts, or naan, or roasting her own coffee beans. "There's pleasure in being a dilettante," she says. "But it would never be enough for me." What she points out, and which I hadn't even considered, is that even the most diverse bucket list isn't that diverse at all. "It may seem like you're doing a lot of things, but you're really only doing one thing, over and over, in different ways. You're always in the role of beginner. And that can be exciting, but it also means you're only using one set of muscles. And if you want to see what you're really made of, you need to use a different set of muscles, and keep using them."

To run a marathon, for instance, you'd better like running. And most people who run marathons, perhaps the most performative aspect of this sport, make running a part of their lives for a reason, and it's usually not just to cross a finish line once. It's worth thinking about this, to consider not just what you want to try but also who you want to be.

The Lure of Secret Genius

And this brings us to another reason why we may be tempted to bucket-list our way into meaning, apart from sheer novelty. If we're being honest, a tiny part of us wonders if we'll be good at it. Scary good. Will-Hunting-at-the-blackboard good, Beth-Harmon-in-*The-Queen's-Gambit*, seeing-chess-moves-in-her-sleep good. Competence is sexy, and so it's no wonder why we want to be good at something, and fast. I dated a Jewish man and shared a Hanukkah meal (my first!) with his family. They handed me a little glass dreidel and said, "Spin it." And I don't want to brag, but I spun the fuck out of that dreidel. It elicited much respect and praise (we're still friends and he *still* talks about it). I had a knack for this. I was good at it! They gave me the dreidel to keep. I still have it. I haven't spun it since.

The desire is to believe that if and when you discover a talent, or someone discovers it in you, maybe, just maybe, you will know that *that's* what you're supposed to be doing. That's the appeal of "I wasn't even trying and I crushed it" mentality.

Beginner's luck can strike when you approach something with no expectations, no stakes, and no real understanding of what's involved. But to believe that this means anything worth doing should come easily, immediately, and fully formed is perhaps one of the most limiting beliefs of all—and it doesn't hold up well in the face of challenge.

In a paper published in *Psychological Science*, Stanford psychologists Carol Dweck and Gregory Walton, along with Paul O'Keefe, conducted a series of experiments to explore whether people's belief in their passions as fixed or developed affected their interests.[2] What the psychologists found was that those who had a fixed theory about passion ("I'm into astronomy") were more likely to curtail interests in other areas ("I *said* I'm into astronomy and that's it!"). And get this: Those who believed passion was inherent or fixed were also more likely to anticipate "boundless motivation." Yup. They thought their passion alone would motivate them for *life*. Um, no. In one study, college students watched a fun, engaging video about black holes and then reported their level of interest ("Whoa, I'm way into this"). Then they were given a challenging scientific article about black holes written for scientists and asked to report their interest again. As predicted, finding the article difficult *undermined* interest in the fixed-mindset group more than the growth-mindset group ("Maybe I'm *not* really into astronomy, actually").

Look, you don't have to aspire to be a physicist to enjoy Neil deGrasse Tyson's TikTok (who doesn't?). But here's my point: Having a fixed mindset or tunnel vision around anything—passion, an industry, an idea of what you're good at and not (*I have to work in fashion* or *I'm bad at money*) may make it *tougher* for you to try, to keep going, when you face a challenge, not to mention less likely to seek or discover other things that would be just as, if not more, exciting and fulfilling. If you buy into the fixed mindset about talent or passion, you may give up too soon with little to show for it—especially if you believe that something is not worth doing simply because you're not amazing out of the gate, or it's not a thrill-a-minute experience. And if you quit then, you don't find out what it means to experience effort and reward in the longer term, something that doesn't end when the park closes for the day.

It's worth looking at your bucket list (if you have one) to understand what you think is worth doing once, or more than once, and why. Meaning: Are you using a bucket list to hide behind a no-stakes, just-trying, *I'm not really here* kind of way? Do you believe you have to be really good, scary good, at one thing to make it worth doing? Is there a part of you that wants to try comedy because you genuinely enjoy the spotlight and want to find opportunities to do more speaking and make people laugh? Do you have "write book" on your list because you want to literally write and produce a book, or do you want to simply do more writing, to express yourself on the page and connect with an audience, whether it's in book form or not? If so, why not explore that, not to "finish" a book, but to see what it's like to make that kind of creative expression part of your life?

If your bucket list is teeming with places to go and sites to see, that's great! Travel itself will change and expand you, transform you in ways you can't predict. Which is why visiting Ireland, for instance, will probably do more to create meaning for you than whether or not you kiss the Blarney Stone while you're there. Far as I know, no one's life changed because they laid their lips on the same rock as millions of other people (gross)—except for one man who slipped from his friend's grip and fell to his death.

Yes, explore. Yes, add to your list of things to do and visit and eat and try. But be wary of the tendency to see your life as a binary (that you were meant to do this or that or have to check x off the list).

Bottom line, sustainable satisfaction and pleasure and fulfillment, the kind we say we want, rarely comes from a thing you do once. An obsession with firsts can be a block toward momentum. It's not that they don't matter, but that they're not definitive, and not the only thing that matters. Firsts are humbling and relatable, and we tend to be vulnerable when we do them. There is a magic about firsts by their nature, not because we "make" them special or perfect. I think lots of phases and stages of your life should be special, and not just because they're your first. That's why, if you get married, your first wedding anniversary is paper and your fiftieth is gold. Things have to be earned. Stay in the game longer.

write your next chapter

Think of a time you did a thing you never thought you'd do. Maybe you were talked into white water rafting, or perhaps you entered a road race having never run competitively before. Maybe it was becoming a parent. What memory, near or far, rises when you think of seeing yourself in a role that surprised you? What was happening, what was it like, and what did you tell yourself after you'd done it?

Set the timer for ten minutes. Start writing.

grab a notebook

Boil Down the Bucket List

First: Turn over your bucket list and dump it all out. What's in there? No judgment! I swear I will not hate on you if you have "bungee jump in South America" on your list. Totally cool.

grab a notebook

Put aside the one-and-dones. Which of those things are legit things you really only need to do once (i.e., climb the Great Wall, dive with sharks in Bora-Bora, see the pyramids)? Put those aside for now if the only thing stopping you is securing the time and resources and buying a ticket. I don't mean to minimize your once-in-a-lifetime trip. My point is to separate out things that can be arranged via logistics versus, well, the other things on your list. Let's look at those.

grab a notebook

What is left on your list? Pick the top three, the things you're most committed to, and answer the following questions for each of them.

- **DOES IT HOLD UP?** Does this item still deserve a spot on the list? Or are you attached to the idea of it because you liked putting it on the list to begin with? Sometimes bucket list items don't age well, like attending a five-night nonstop party in Ibiza (though you can if you want to hate yourself). In some cases, you may age out of them altogether. Making the "30 under 30" list is no longer an option if you're 37 (maybe go for "40 under 40"?).

grab a notebook

- **HOW HIGH A PRIORITY IS THIS, MEANING IS THERE ANY URGENCY ATTACHED?** Is it the kind of thing you want to do in the next six months or year, or could you see yourself happily doing it, say, ten years from now? Can you put a time on when this would happen? ("Someday" and "later" don't count as times.)

grab a notebook

- **WHAT HAS TO HAPPEN FIRST?** What, if any, have dependent issues, i.e., you can't start a therapy practice until you're licensed; you can't go diving with sharks if you haven't been trained to dive.

grab a notebook

- **HAVE YOU STARTED ANY STEPS OR PROCESS THAT WOULD ENABLE YOU TO DO THIS THING?** Have you enrolled in a scuba-diving class, looked into applying to speak at a TEDx event? If not, why not?

grab a notebook

- **HOW DO YOU (HONESTLY) FEEL ABOUT THIS ITEM NOW?** And is there a reason why it's in this bucket, and not on your actual agenda as a thing to start or plan for?

grab a notebook

- **WHAT DO YOU RISK BY DOING IT?** What could happen? I don't mean just "lose a leg," but is there anything in doing the thing and, say, failing the first time out that would be more upsetting than not doing anything at all?

grab a notebook

- **WHAT WOULD MAKE THIS THING WORTH DOING MORE THAN ONCE?** What makes it worth the time, expense, attention, or effort to do this thing once, and would it be worth it to keep doing it? Why or why not?

grab a notebook

CHAPTER 5

Why You Probably Overpacked for This Trip

A good trip will ruin your life.
—Rev. Robert Barone

My friend Kim Vandrilla had been standing at the luggage carousel at the San Francisco airport for forty minutes when the last person plucked the last bag from the belt and left. Kim watched the mouth of the machine, waiting, willing it to spit up the two suitcases in which she'd packed her entire life. Nothing. She went to the claims office and filled out a form, the panic rising in her like a wave.

This wasn't a jaunt to wine country; she'd bought a one-way ticket here to start her new life, and it started tomorrow, at 10:00 a.m., at an interview for what she hoped would be her new job. She'd left her old job, her friends, and had whittled her belongings down to two things she could carry, and now those were gone too.

We've given some serious thought so far to the stories we're told (lies!), realized that comfort and growth are not mutually exclusive, dumped out our bucket lists, and pierced the veil on the passion hypothesis. And now it's time to take a good hard look at what we've brought along with us, and what we actually *need*. But to do that, it's worth looking at a word I really don't like: "baggage."

We usually use the term "baggage" to denote the unsorted emotional mess that follows us around. "Oh, she's a mess, too much baggage," or, "I can't date him! He's divorced and has all that baggage." It's a cruel blanket assessment of what someone else has been through, and what we assume it means. As if any of us gets through anything without taking some of it with us. What it also presumes is that baggage is something someone *else* has.

You've heard the saying "Wherever you go, there you are." Same goes for our memories, our impressions, our experiences. You take your life with you; there's nowhere else for it to go.

When it comes to actual packing, like for a trip, I'm not convinced lighter is always better. I don't trust someone who has packed *nothing*, who carries *nothing*, who strolls onto the plane with nothing but a magazine. Why would that appeal, this person who has left virtually everything behind? Also, don't tell me they won't need anything. They haven't eliminated their needs; they've simply delegated them. Likely, to you.

The person who overpacks—and I count myself in this category—may not be as trusting, and might have a bit more anxiety about leaving (check and check). I still think it's better to have more of what you need on hand than less. Poke all the fun you want at the fact that I travel with a veritable pharmacy sealed up in Ziploc bags, but we all know who you're coming to when you get the runs. (And yes, I got you.)

Ah, but therein lies the critical difference between luggage and baggage: Luggage we pack on purpose. Baggage is something others assume we have, not because we packed it, but because we're saddled with circumstance, namely, with what we've *lost*—a job, a parent, a spouse. The ability to trust. While luggage is designed to move with you (which is why it's on wheels), baggage is a burden; it's the reason we think we *can't* move on to the next thing. The irony is that we began our human journey as roving tribes; packed was our natural state. What's unnatural are the lives we have now, crammed with more things than we can carry. And not one of us hasn't faced something hard. In short, we all have some kind of baggage. What matters is what we choose to bring with us, what we leave behind, and all the other things that get lost along the way, most of which we didn't really need anyway.

What to Do When Your Luggage Doesn't Show Up

My uncle Bob, who loved to go places, hated getting there. "Jet travel is unnatural," he said. "It's hell on earth." Rev. Robert Barone, my mother's only brother, had earned his doctorate in Rome and was a theology professor at the University of Scranton. He was a large man with big hands and a booming voice; he laughed until he wheezed. He could speak Italian with priests in the Vatican, argue in Arabic with cabdrivers in Jerusalem. When he was done talking to you, he simply hung up. And if you were going to travel with him, he had a strict rule about bags: Nothing checked, and only what you could carry.

For more than twenty years, he led guided study tours of the Holy Land and Italy where he took clergy and laypeople to see the Bible in person, explore the roots of civilization, culture, art. Since I was a kid, he'd been promising me that I would someday join him. *Oh no, when do I have to do that?* I thought, slathering myself with SPF 6, drinking beer at a shitty rental on the Jersey shore. But when I was twenty-four, I was ready. I joined his colony of priests, a handful of nuns, and a few parishioners, most of whom were decades older than me.

He made an exception to his carry-on-only rule for me—once. And we both lived to regret it. We made it to Tel Aviv; my checked bag didn't. This was a lesson I could only learn the hard way. When you lose your luggage, you lose the one string tying you to anything and everything that you know for sure exists. And you're convinced you need it to survive. (You don't.)

For the first day or so, as I waited for my brain and body to catch up to the local time, I tried to push the luggage worry out of my head, thinking that because I didn't have my stuff, I couldn't be here now, which wasn't true. I was lucky to be here at all. I tried to assume a Buddhist posture of nonattachment, then went back to pining for my hair spray.

Meanwhile, Kim was luggageless in a new city with a problem to solve: What she would wear to her interview. She was camped at the entrance of Nordstrom before it opened the next morning and told her tale of woe to the employees, who, to their credit, seized on this Cinderella challenge. By 9:30 a.m., Kim was outfitted in a charcoal suit, a blouse, and heels to match, looking for all the world as if she were going to interview as a paralegal instead of a designer at a tech start-up, where everyone wore jeans and flip-flops. But what did she know? She'd never worked at one.

Kim had spent the past four years designing websites and emails for a Boston-based travel company, and had managed to expand her role to include a little content strategy. This wasn't the norm. Creative pros typically pick a track, design or copy, and tend to stick with it. But Kim resisted choosing. While earning her master's in publishing at Emerson College, she'd taken writing and lit, as well as every design class available. She wanted to do both.

When a new creative director came on board, however, she didn't approve of Kim's nontraditional design background, nor how she was straddling the line professionally. She told Kim that she'd hired her replacement and she could either move into a marketing role or leave. So she left. This wouldn't be the last time she butted heads with a boss who didn't know what to do with her (seems a failure of management, not of talent, but that's a discussion for a different day).

In a cab en route to the interview in her stiff new suit, she felt that old tug of insecurity around not fitting the traditional designer mold. She worried whether she should've just taken the marketing role like her boss said. While they'd only been paying her $39,000 a year—low for someone with an advanced degree—what if this job didn't work out and she never got a chance like that again? What if this was a mistake?

You Don't Need the Stuff After All

I was annoyed at not having the amphibious footwear I'd bought for the trip, but our daily schedule was packed: We rose early for mass on the rooftop before dawn, headed out on excursions ahead of the punishing sun—into ancient temples and churches, up the Mount of Olives, through the Damascus Gate, and into the tiny, rutted veins of the old city. Sister Margaret lent me her flip-flops for the hike through Hezekiah's Tunnel, an ancient, mile-long passageway dug by hand around 700 BC to transport water from the Gihon Spring to the Pool of Siloam in the southwest corner of Jerusalem. When the city was attacked by Assyria in 701 BC, that vein of water kept them alive and safe from destruction. It was all they needed to survive.

And it hit me: Here I was, agonizing over all the things I *thought* I needed, when I already had everything—great company, good food, adventure. I laughed with the priests and the nuns and the seventy-year-old retired nurse about how truly terrified we'd been walking through the pitch-black tunnel. And wouldn't you know, that's when my luggage showed up—like in a scene from a rom-com: The ex-boyfriend you had almost moved on from. Let's just say it was . . . anticlimactic (as such things are). Everything was just as I'd left it: socks, underwear, shirts, a hairbrush. What did I expect? The Holy Grail? Sometimes what you think you need is not all it's cracked up to be.

While Kim was (a touch) overdressed for her interview, it went even better than she'd hoped. The head of the department, whom she liked immediately, asked her what she wanted to earn as a visual designer, and Kim said $65,000, biting back a fear that it was too much. She knew she was worth it, but still. When she received the formal offer a few days later for $90,000, she cried. Within a year she was promoted to brand creative manager, and the woman who hired her remains one of her closest friends to this day.

Oh—the luggage? It showed up two weeks later, after she'd landed not only her new job but also a beautiful one-bedroom apartment, *and* a boyfriend (true story). The bonus? The $500 Nordstrom shopping spree was covered, compliments of the airline.

In both stories I just told you, luggage was lost and life went on. In fact, things went even better than expected. The hardest part wasn't not having the stuff; it was the idea that we needed something we didn't have, which turned out to be untrue. And this is how luggage, or the lack of it, turns into *baggage*—the thing you get so busy with *not* having that you miss out on what you *do* have.

Today Kim is a Head of Brand & Creative at a Fortune 500 company. I asked her if it still bugs her when someone questions her background. And she admits, it hits an old nerve. But does she regret her choices or worry that she doesn't have what she needs to thrive in her career and her life? No, she doesn't. She knows if she'd forced herself down one path she would've been bored. She's bored just thinking about it. "Design alone would have gotten old, real fast," she says. Her skills and interests evolved even more quickly than she anticipated—and she's since turned down several creative director jobs she would've killed for five years ago. She's not a junior designer missing a design degree anymore; she's a leader with a uniquely hybrid skill set. She's not prepared despite what she chose; she's prepared *because* of it.

That's worth thinking about, isn't it? What did you predict you might need to know or have, only to discover that wasn't the case? What have you assumed you'd love or hate doing, and how did it change? How many times have you looked back and thought, wow, I couldn't have known I would have liked doing this or that, but I'm glad I did it. As Steve Jobs said in that famous commencement speech, you can only connect the dots looking backward. We think we know what trip we're packing for, but we really have no idea.

What You Collect Isn't Just Valuable—It's Sacred

I was brought up Catholic (talk about an institution with baggage), and even though I haven't been a practicing Catholic for decades, seeing the birthplace of Christianity was fascinating: To touch the stones and smell their strange, ancient heat; duck through the low arch into the Church of the Nativity; attend mass at the Church of the Holy Sepulchre, trying to wrap my head around the fact that this was the literal site of the crucifixion. I bent down to touch the slab where they laid Jesus's lifeless body; then I stood up feeling woozy, like I'd been hit with a dose of holy radiation.

Bob explained that what made this place, and any place, holy was only partly what had happened there. Who knew whether this was the same stone, the exact stone? And did it matter? Not really. "A holy place follows a holy place," he said. In other words, it wasn't just about what happened once, but what *kept* happening. History was the record; *practice* made it holy. And the practice of people coming to worship in a place because they *believed* it was holy made it that way. Sacred traditions were built on other traditions—Catholicism on the roots of Judaism, which was built on the roots of other religions, to other gods, and on and on it goes, a long hall of mirrors reflecting all the places where humans have tried to find themselves.

A place can be sacred and not be religious at all. Take the T. A. Moulton homestead, the most photographed barn in America, a quaintly dilapidated structure built in 1908 in Jackson Hole. There's nothing magic about the barn; it's become a recognized symbol of America in all its pioneering spirit. It's famous because so many people photographed it. We share in the experience of sharing it (and if you overthink that you'll get caught in a loop). To that end, any place can become sacred—whether it's a table in a restaurant where Hemingway once ate, or on a rock where an angry mob murdered the son of God.

What's interesting here is that the very thing that makes a holy place "holy," and by that I mean sacred or special, is what gives anything we care about meaning and value, including the things we bring with us from one place to the next: They're accumulated and curated, over time.

The One Thing on All of Our Itineraries

Regardless of our particular faith, tradition, or practice, we're all looking for meaning. We *all* want to touch something that matters, if not create it ourselves, and we also want to know that what we've been through matters, too, which is why we might find ourselves clinging to things we've lost—out of a need to find meaning in them. But we don't have to drag our lives and losses along with us to make them meaningful, and there's nothing you can pack to fully prepare yourself for what's next. If a holy place follows a holy place, then the meaningful moments and skills and lessons follow too. You can't forget to pack it, and it can't get lost.

For Bob, what you packed didn't matter half as much as what you'd discover when you arrived. For three weeks abroad, I tell you, the man had one miniature suitcase that I couldn't fit two pairs of shoes in. What did he need? A change of shirt? Socks? That's it. The best part of going wasn't what you brought with you; it was what you saw when you parked yourself at a cafe with an espresso, walked through the piazza, gazed at fifth-century mosaics in a basilica in Ravenna. He loved teaching freshmen at the university, kids who'd just left home for the first time and were rigid with fear. At least they'd left home and were en route somewhere. "Most people in history stayed home," Bob always said. "But not us. *We* are fleet of foot."

Coming Back Is a Bitch

If the jet lag was rough going out, the transition home after my trip with Bob was worse. As the bus from the airport heaved into the church parking lot, I got weepy—not because of what I'd lost but what I'd gained. How could you come back to your life after a trip like that?

"A good trip will ruin your life!" Bob said, laughing. Though he wasn't kidding. He, too, would return to the same old grind, the same clinging parishioners, the students with their blank stares. How hilarious, he said, that people thought travel would make their lives better. The better the trip, the *worse* your life looked by comparison. The only way to cope was to plan the next trip. In other words, you had to keep going.

And I did. The following June, and several after that, I packed a single backpack and carry-on (I learned my lesson) and headed out to Kennedy to meet Bob and the crew to see Siena and Pisa, Pompeii and Rome. And after every trip, I'd come home again, brimming with things that I couldn't have packed or prepared for, feeling expanded like an accordion, unfolded like a fan. Maybe you've noticed that, or will—that every time you leave and return, you change a little, in ways that don't snap back, and that your life as a result might not fit the way it used to, and won't, that you brought home more than you packed to take with you. And you realize, maybe that is the point.

write your next chapter

What was the last thing you packed for? What do you always bring? Whether you were packing a suitcase, a daypack, or a purse, or boxes for a big move, what was or is the most important thing you bring with you, aside from the obvious (wallet, cash, ID)? Something perhaps that might not seem necessary, but something you wouldn't leave without?

grab a notebook

What comes up for you around the idea of baggage? Does it feel like something you're saddled with, and if so, why?

grab a notebook

What's something you're always afraid you won't have when you need it? I don't mean a toothbrush; I mean a skill, a resource, experience in a thing you fear you don't have.

grab a notebook

What's something you always think you'll need, and never do? This might be an actual object, and if it is, think a little about what that item represents for you. But it might also be a thing you're afraid you aren't or won't be equipped to do or handle. Has it happened? Write about it.

grab a notebook

CHAPTER 6

It's Not a Sin to Get Wickedly Curious

The urge to grow up is called individuation . . . the inner calling to push off from the shore of mother and father, to test limits, to know your worth, to speak your truth, to claim authentic selfhood.

—Elizabeth Lesser, *Cassandra Speaks*

We're nearing the end of the first leg of this trip. We've already sorted and checked our baggage, and if it gets lost we know we'll be fine. If we're always on the verge of arriving somewhere, then that means we're departing from somewhere too. And whether you bounce without so much as a look back, or worry for days in advance, leaving matters, yes, but not nearly as much as you think. It's not that different from firsts in that way; they're important, but not definitive. And what's worth doing is considering the stories we've been told about the consequences of leaving that can make it a lot harder than it has to be.

Let's start with the very first time you left.

From the moment you were conceived, you grew—like a fish,

a mushroom, a galaxy of molecular stars—in someone else's body. You were in her and of her, subsisted on the same blood, the same food, the same air. From the minute you exited your mother's body, whatever route you took, you began the long, painful process of leaving home. And nothing was ever safe again.

But what was the alternative? There was none. You had to go. This was not a decision you made; it was made for you. And life has continued to pull you along via a series of contractions and expansions, a wavelike peristalsis that propels you, and all of us, ever forward. That doesn't mean it's easy or that you don't have choices. But you can't make life hold still while you figure things out, because shit doesn't work that way.

It's in our blood to kick and scream when we have to leave, which we do from the moment we arrive. And some people say we never get over that first time. An early twentieth-century psychoanalyst named Otto Rank claimed, in his book *The Trauma of Birth*, that all of our anxieties spring from the devastation of being born, and that we spend our lives trying to find, create, or return to the womb in some way. Freud initially praised it, then changed his mind and kicked him out of the club, which I imagine *was* traumatic. (I'll add here that Otto Rank's original last name was Rosenfeld, which says a lot about his own feelings about where he came from.)

The last thing I want to do is get hung up on what a couple of old white dudes said a hundred years ago. But it's worth laying the theories about our original wound against cultural and religious ideas about original *sin*, all of which are intricately bound to what we're told are the consequences of leaving home.

Exit the Garden; Enter . . . Adulthood

We know the story of Adam and Eve backward and forward: They could enjoy the garden, so long as they steered clear of the Tree of Knowledge. But why? Eve liked the look of that fruit, grew curious and emboldened, got some intel from a garden snake, flouted the rules, and ate it. She then offered some to her partner, who also ate it, and blamed her for it later. And this, we're told, is why we can't have nice things. The decision to eat the forbidden fruit made them gods because they could see what they'd been blind to before (including each other, naked—yowza!). This got them expelled into lives of thankless toil and effort, marked by labor pains, illness, and death.

Cultural mythology is teeming with male heroes (Hercules, Odysseus, Moses, and more) who struck out for fame and fortune, power, profit, or just sheer adventure. Eve was really no different; she wanted to *know*. She made the decision to be noncompliant. Are there consequences for that? Always. Her story is told differently than any other hero's journeys, however. Rather than independent-minded, bold, or courageous, Eve is cast as the antihero, the source of original sin. Adam may have been a weak and impressionable idiot, but he's never blamed for breaking the rules; she is.

If you don't think this old story has any bearing on us today, you're nuts. Want a fun, lighthearted read on the topic? Check out *A Brief History of Misogyny: The World's Oldest Prejudice* by Jack Holland and your head will explode. It doesn't matter that there are more female executives in the C suites, or that a female doctor operated on your foot once. While women are making huge strides and may earn more than men in many cases, don't be fooled, says Holland. Misogyny persists unchanged and "comes back to haunt our ideas of equality . . . a ghost that cannot be exorcised." This prejudice is as "up to date as the latest porn website and as old as civilization itself."[1]

These stories have become part of our collective DNA. Could the ingrained belief that women are to blame for all bad things have something to do with why we tiptoe around saying "sorry" all the time? Isn't it ironic that Eve is credited with goading mankind into sin when most of the time women can't get a word in edgewise? Do you think it might have something to do with why women feel guilty about, well, everything?

Elizabeth Lesser, cofounder of the Omega Institute for Holistic Studies in Rhinebeck, New York, argues in *Cassandra Speaks* that Eve isn't a troublemaker or a corrupting harlot; she is, in fact, humankind's first grown-up. "The 'temptation' she succumbs to is the most fundamental human yearning," Lesser writes, "to know oneself, to find one's own path, and to courageously engage with the big world beyond the garden of childhood."[2]

As for their punishment? Labor pains and lifelong toil? Welcome to . . . adulthood. "To grow up is to admit that life is challenging," and this urge to grow up and go off on your own is called individuation, or "the inner calling to push off from the shore of mother and father, to test limits, to know your worth, to speak your truth, to claim authentic selfhood."[3]

You can decide to see Eve as a bad influence and the source of sin, or as heroic as the men who did similar things; as an example of what it means to follow your curiosity toward freedom, at any cost. For Eve, that was better than staying compliant and confined within the garden wall. (Though are we surprised in the least that Adam wanted to just chill at his Dad's place rent-free? No, we are not.)

My friend Nicole has moved sixteen times in nineteen years. She left the Texas town where she was raised by her adoptive parents to a house with a man she married, and then divorced, and that was just the beginning. She likes to immerse herself, really learn the place, and then she's ready to try somewhere new. She broke her own record when, in 2020, she moved two times—once when a tornado tore through her Nashville neighborhood, to a rental house across town; then a new job took her to North Carolina, where she bought a home on her own for the first time, and she knows this isn't her last.

When she was four or five years old, she had a little red suitcase that said *Going to Grandma's* on it and one of her favorite games to play was runaway, where she packed a few things (a doll, a set of crayons, her dad's old wallet) and walked around the house like she was going somewhere. This game infuriated her mother. "Are you playing that game again, Nicole? Because I don't like it," she fumed. "It's not a nice game to play when you're in a house with people who love you." The last time she remembers playing it, her mother became unglued. She took the little suitcase and put it out on the porch. "If you want to run away, go ahead. But don't come back inside if that's what you're gonna do." Wow.

Nicole understands now that her mother was deeply afraid that her birth mother might come and take her, or that she might simply leave, which, ultimately, she would. Think about the impact a message like this can have on a kid, especially someone whose wanderlust didn't have as strong a pull as Nicole's, someone who might have believed from then on that to leave is a form of betrayal.

If you're a woman, chances are good you've been schooled, scared, threatened, and cajoled into staying where you are, regardless of whether your parents let you go to sleepaway camp or spend a year abroad. Ask a man why he's frustrated and he may say he's not getting what or where he needs to fast enough. Ask a woman why she's frustrated and she'll tell you she feels . . . stuck. Women talk all the *time* about how they're stuck—in their work, their relationships, their lives. And they often blame themselves—for being lazy or indecisive or not motivated enough. Are women prone to getting stuck? Is it a design flaw? No. This phenomenon points to the friction between wanting to move and being afraid to. And gee, I wonder why! If we weren't flat out beaten, beheaded, or burned at the stake for attempting to leave throughout all of human history, we were gaslit into madness, coddled, and kept close, told that to step out was to be unsafe, unwise, or unkind. The son who holes up in his parents' basement is a failure to launch; a woman who stays home to take care of her parents is a good daughter. Go ahead and think back to every scary story you were told, or flip through the horror section on Netflix right now, and you'll see a familiar allegory: tale after tale of Bad Things That Happen to Women Who Go Out There—and, well, they were warned.

What are women who feel stuck told to do instead? Take a bath, get things done, try a new hairstyle, shop. But don't rock the boat, test the limits, or question the rules. In short, *don't get too curious.* The consequences for doing more than risking a bold lip color are dire, from getting hurt to getting murdered, from being distrusted to being dismissed.

The one way to avoid being stuck is to *stay* wickedly curious—about what could be, what might be, what you just might do, or where you might go next. This is not easy to do when the world is working hard to snuff out what it deems a dangerous flame. Curiosity gets the wheels turning, and wheels that turn are not stuck.

I urge you not only to get curious but also not to talk yourself *out* of being curious. Don't clip those adventurous new stems down to the nub. The idea of forbidden fruit has been co-opted by tawdry affairs, dalliances, all of them sexual in nature. But remember Eve didn't pick fruit from the Tree of Porn. It was the Tree of *Knowledge*. You, too, possess that same natural curiosity, intelligence, a deep desire to *know*.

Contrary to what you've been told, curiosity will not kill your cat or anyone else. That tingle, that itch, that rising wonder, is critical to your next move, your next decision. It's a reminder that you've got a mind and body of your own, and that you can go from thinking a thing to doing it.

Look, you don't have to be a rabble-rouser. Maybe you like living in the town you grew up in, happily followed your mother into politics or took over your dad's business. You don't have to burn the place down to start something new.

I say this to you as the kid who *never* wanted to leave home, who was reduced to tears when leaving for *day camp.* Who a year before graduating high school began a yearlong descent into mourning at the thought of moving away. By October of my freshman year, I'd lost my boyfriend, my appetite, and far too much weight. I was a fragile husk moving across campus, caught in a riptide of homesickness. And as curious as I was and am, I wasn't immune to that part of the process, the deep sadness and fear that I would never find my way back or come home again, which turned out not to be true.

What you may not know about riptides—I didn't until much

later—is that they aren't always an endless one-way pull out to sea. Eighty to 90 percent of riptides move in a circle, and if you let them take you for a bit, they will inevitably arc around again, where the breakers drop you back on the shore. It's as good a metaphor as any for leaving home, because while we must depart from what we know, we are, in fact, always on the verge of returning. When the homesickness ultimately lifted, I thought, *Oh good, that's over with. I'll never be homesick again.* But what I didn't realize was that the bone-deep longing didn't end after you left your home of origin; you simply rack up more places to leave, and long for.

Don't worry that what you left or will leave will vanish, because it won't. Just because you aren't there now doesn't mean you can't or won't return. And don't fall prey to the notion that curiosity is a dangerous door, when it's the only way to open one. You don't drop off the face of the earth once you exit the garden gates, and closing the door to your own wondering and wandering comes at a far greater cost.

Wouldn't you like to know what you might do next? Aren't you curious what it could feel like, be like, taste like? It's time to find out for yourself.

Things You Will Leave

- Your mother, in one way or another
- Your father
- Your first boyfriend
- Your first girlfriend
- The comfort of your first bed
- The comfort of someone else's bed
- Every place you'll ever write down when asked to "fill in current address"
- School
- Countless friends, some for a while, some forever
- Your first job
- Your second job
- Your third job (and you'll be sad about that one)
- The bar, when it closes
- The restaurant, when you're paid up and full and there's no other reason to stay

- The party, because it's time to go
- The train, because it's going farther than you need to
- Your apartment, to get coffee
- Your apartment, for a bigger apartment
- Your spouse, many times or just the one time
- Your old idea of how things would turn out
- The old version of you
- The most recent version of you
- The time you loved most
- The town you lived in
- 472 projects you thought you wanted to do, which you will leave unfinished
- The shop you came to for a specific thing, which you'll leave empty-handed
- An animal
- A car
- A group of people you really like
- A group of people you loathe
- A dream you had
- A nightmare

write your next chapter

Something you're curious about. I invite you to explore, in particular, something you're quietly curious about. A thing you may not be ready to air or discuss, since you're not even sure what you think about it yet.

grab a notebook

Something you're thinking of leaving. What about this decision feels scary, exciting, perhaps even a relief?

grab a notebook

part two

uncover

CHAPTER 7

You've Got Mad Skills

Without skill, all the passion in the world will leave you eager but floundering.

—Twyla Tharp, *The Creative Habit*

We've spent a good amount of time now challenging the ideas that we've been given, handed, or heavily encouraged to comply with. Ideas that do us little to no good in the make-your-life-matter department. And look, it takes considerable, even a kind of muscular, effort to unseat those ideas, whether you find it hard to let them go or can't be free soon enough. Dislodging them can change how you move through the world.

Now that we have cleared the cultural clutter a bit, we can start to see what's what—and can move into the what *now?* What do we do instead? If we let go of the binary that we're either good or bad at things, have to be complacent or uncomfortable, passionate or bored, what then?

What I'm going to say next will come as no surprise: I can't tell you what *you specifically* should do right now. So I'll save you the trouble of DMing me to ask. It would not only be incredibly arrogant of me to assume I could, but it would also be an abdication of your role as sovereign ruler of your life to assume someone else knows better. Plus, you probably wouldn't do it anyway! Not because I'm ignorant and you're obstinate, but because if you really believe someone else can tell you, then why would you ever trust yourself? All the advice in the world can never replace what you need more: The ability to make a decision on your own behalf.

I've said it before, but it bears repeating: *No one knows anything.* Not me, not your mother, not your friend who just earned another degree. We are all making it up as we go, checking ourselves against our gut, our parents, our peers, our faith, and what's been done already. And we're trying to do what we can without fucking things up royally for ourselves or other people. And yes, it's harder than it looks. But no one *isn't* trying.

Here is where skill comes into play: Because despite all the talk about values and intention and mindset, fact is, in order to make something meaningful for yourself or others, you need to actually do something. And you don't need confidence first, because no one starts with it; they end with it. No one can hand it to you (though plenty of people will try to sell it to you). You can fake it, but in a world where "authenticity" is de rigueur, faking it doesn't feel on trend. Plus, it never felt good. My friend Ilise Benun says that you don't "need" confidence to do things, to speak up, to try. What you need is courage. And you don't get it by waiting until you're confident; you get it by practicing things you're *not* confident in. Wait to have confidence and you'll never do anything at all.

Oh, but wait. You're looking at that other person and wondering how they got to be where they are, how they move through the world on wheels greased with ease and self-assuredness? You admire how smoothly they cast a fishing line, poach an egg, give a speech. The answer: *Practice.* We give "talent" far too much airtime. We believe it's a predetermined, immutable, mystical thing that's visited upon the blessed few. If you believe that, then what would be the point of doing anything if you could "see" that someone has talent and you don't?

I mentioned earlier that I've studied and performed stand-up comedy. One of the teachers I studied with was professional comic Jim David, and one night, under piss-colored fluorescent lighting, he dismissed this whole notion of scary talent and big personality—two things we thought we needed to do comedy—with a wave of an irritated hand. "No you don't," he said, listing the names of very popular comics who he didn't think had much talent at all. "You just need to know how to write a joke."

What that means is we're far less served by an obsession with talent and better off dedicating ourselves to skill, because while talent is a slippery, immeasurable thing, skill leaves evidence.

In his book *The Practice: Shipping Creative Work*, Seth Godin says: "It's insulting to call a professional talented. . . . Many people have talent, but only a few care enough to show up fully, to earn their skill. Skill is rarer than talent."[1] We need to be willing to trust ourselves enough to be the kind of person who builds skill, he says, a person who engages with the process and practice of doing a thing.

This is what we're diving into next: That it's about not just what you learn but also how to *use* what you learn. Skills transfer. If you ask me what skills are worth learning, then I'm going to have to grab you by the shoulders and give you a firm but loving shake. Because that's the binary part of your brain, which sounds a lot like a dad from the 1950s, assuming that some skills are worth learning and others aren't. The point is to devote yourself to the skills you have an opportunity to learn—some of which you may seek out, but others may be right there in front of you. And to get good at something matters, even if you don't "intend" to make a living at it.

Right after graduation from Boston College, I found a

paid internship with a book publicist, a delightful, smart, soft-spoken man named Victor Gulotta. He set me up in a spare room with a computer that ran on DOS, a green banker's lamp, and one of the largest private collections of Longfellow books, manuscripts, and artifacts, which he owned. This was an English major's world. In Victor I learned that art and business did not have to be at odds; you could be a bibliophile and a successful business owner.

I learned to do all kinds of things—from reading books to packaging them up and mailing them out to calling editors to see if they received the books ("Honey, if you sent it, we have it") and if they plan to do anything with them ("We'll let you know"). I felt chastened by these very busy, important people. I said, "I wouldn't be rude like that." Years later, when I was a busy editor with a stack of unopened mail, I made sure when publicists called me I wasn't a dick bag.

The skill that I apprenticed myself to was the art of the press release. I spent hours on them, as if I were crafting a sonnet commissioned by the king. Press releases don't have bylines; no one frames them and points to them and says, "I did that." No one cares about press releases! But for a while, they were my life. I studied their tautness and craft, rewrote the headline five times. It mattered when Victor walked into the room with the draft in hand and said, "This is really good."

It was not high art. But when it was good, it got used. Editors might lift the copy directly from the release for the write-up and that was a win! We encouraged this kind of plagiarism! Victor said, "You know, you could be a freelance writer." What? He might as well have said that I should be a famous physicist or fashion designer, like you had to be someone to do that (when really you must be tough and tireless). When I left the internship, Victor called to ask if I would like to continue to write press releases for him for $200 a pop—in 1997. And that's how I started doing freelance work.

Where Skill Meets Passion (Sometimes in a Dark Alley)

Twyla Tharp wrote: "Without passion, all the skill in the world won't lift you above craft. Without skill, all the passion in the world will leave you eager but floundering."[2] So while passion can provide heat and energy, it's skill that grounds your ability, your focus. And one does not precede the other in linear fashion. You could learn a skill without any real big plans for it; you may even learn the skill out of necessity and survival.

I never worked in book publicity again after that, though I built on those skills. Yes, I learned how to write a press release; in doing so I learned a skill I still use: Taking large, complex ideas and distilling them down to key points that keep someone reading. I'm using it right now.

Your skills are reincarnated and repurposed throughout your life in ways you might not expect, and give you the ability to make useful and meaningful contributions. Heat up a skill, and passion can rise, whistling like steam from a kettle.

In the next few chapters you'll see how that plays out and can yield meaning in interesting places, and give you a leg up later in ways you won't recognize till it happens.

How Skills Keep You Afloat

We all want ease and flow, to be held aloft with very little effort or struggle. I know of no better skill where you can experience that more directly than swimming itself. It's also not optional like fly-fishing or roller-skating; you need it to save your own life. And yet swimming for me was the source of incredible angst and dread.

Water is not my element. I'm an air sign and a land animal. I loathe water parks and boats in equal measure. I don't like to be wet. Even my showers are short. Water covers three-quarters of the planet, so it's safe to say that most of the earth is outside my comfort zone. And that's OK. I don't need the entire world to be inside my comfort zone (as I mentioned earlier). But you have to learn to swim. There's a good chance that you will, at some point, find yourself in or near a body of water, whether it's the ocean, a lake, or the town pool, and you need to survive your encounter with it.

My mother used to be a synchronized swimmer; today she can still bliss out for laps and laps. I always got the sense that she understood my fear of the pool the way you understand someone's fear of the color yellow (yes, that's a thing: xanthophobia). She tried to show me that the water was gentle, friendly. Yet even she got caught in a riptide at the Jersey shore one summer and was nearly pulled out to sea.

Swimming lessons were like rehearsing disaster and calling it fun. I didn't want to do this.

I could not put my head underwater without panicking, or stand the clatter and chaos of other children's limbs. I couldn't be lured into diving for quarters, let alone pennies (ugh, who cares, keep your money). I thought I could get by just fine with inflatable swimmies, but this kind of dependency was discouraged. By seven years old, you were supposed to learn to float on your own.

"I think you're going to like Doris," my mom said. Entering the swimming pool area of the Ramada Inn off Route 10 in Livingston, New Jersey, was like walking straight into someone's mouth. You could feel the air drag its tongue against your skin. It was like being swallowed whole.

Doris stood in the pool to her waist in her white bathing cap, and waved to me. She didn't wear a bathing suit, but a *swimsuit*, which meant she was there to *do* a thing, not look like a thing. She had a kind, plain face that wrinkled into a smile when she saw me. I don't think I ever saw her hair. She was exceedingly kind and made no sudden moves. She specialized in tough cases like me.

I stepped down into the water, which was warm as spit. There is a kind of pleasure in submerging, in being blissfully relieved of your own gravity. But I knew I'd always be a tourist, awkward and careful and clearly only there for the day.

"Let's practice breathing," Doris said. We laid our ears in the water, took a breath, before turning our faces down and blowing out. Since I didn't like putting my face in the water, Doris suggested goggles, which gave everything a cheery, egg-yolk glaze. Soon I couldn't swim without them. Even the sensation of water on my eyelids made me feel like I might drown.

I've struggled to let go of things like anyone—old grudges, criticism, bad friends. But one of the hardest things I ever let go of was the edge of a pool, knowing that to do so was to put myself in the hands of sheer physics, and I was dubious about whose side it was on. I can still feel the curve of the concrete edge under my cold fingers. But you can't stay there.

Doris taught me the strokes, each one like conjugating a new verb. She showed me how to use the water's weight to my advantage, to do more with less effort. She taught me to trust my own buoyancy, that I would rise to the surface, each time. Panic was the real danger, the flailing and breathlessness, the wasting of precious resources, which happens when you rely on fear instead of skill. Ultimately, it was how I responded to the water that would determine whether I would survive it—and enjoy it.

There was a lot more I absorbed in the water with Doris, too, that was never part of the lesson. When Doris's daughter Carolyn was twenty-one, she was hit by a drunk driver and suffered severe brain damage. Doris didn't lose her daughter, technically, but she did lose the daughter she had. Carolyn spoke in grunts and wails, had to relearn basic skills, like how to walk and eat and dress herself, sit upright in a chair. My mother explained that Carolyn would always be like a baby. I knew people's lives could be cut short at any point, including my own, but it never occurred to me that they could be rewound and paused at another point.

Doris taught her to swim again, and while Carolyn would

never be independent, she could swim lap after lap, her round body rolling like a whale through the water, the occasional spout of rough breath. I'd learned that year that whales weren't fish at all, but mammals who breathe air just like me. The whale can't breathe water, but it also can't walk around. It lives between worlds, in an environment that cannot wholly sustain it but is the only place it will ever be. What was that like, to live where you cannot breathe, where your next breath is something you had to wait for? I was afraid of her in ways I couldn't articulate.

After our lesson, as I put on my flip-flops, Doris would swim over to Carolyn and they'd move through the water soundlessly together, all the time in the world between them, all the air they needed to breathe, their arms synced, rising and falling through the water with a steady, easy rhythm.

Today you can take me anywhere and I can and will get in that water and likely survive it. I'm also well aware that regardless of how well I can swim, anything can happen. The difference is that I'm capable of getting in there, thanks to Doris, who not only was an excellent swimming instructor but also had faced the worst possible fear a parent can—and survived that too.

It always helps to have a teacher, coach, or mentor, not because they know better, but because the best ones teach you to trust yourself—which is the very *definition* of confidence: "a feeling of self-assurance arising from one's appreciation of one's own abilities." This is why skill building *is* confidence building: Because learning a skill gives your confidence a place to show itself. Feel good about one thing and it will change how you approach other things too.

I not only learned the basics of swimming from Doris; I also learned what it is to be in and out of your element at the same time, that skills were a currency, a touch point, and something you could return to. Skill itself was what allowed you to stay afloat. And here's the thing: It feels *good* to improve a skill, to mark your improvement and have something to show for it. I felt a tremendous sense of achievement when, the following summer, I moved up the ranks in swimming at camp from "sunfish" to "barracuda." Look the fuck out.

And while a skill in itself may not automatically spark passion for you, it can show you something more useful: How to not just do but also enjoy a thing you didn't think you could. And because of what Doris helped me see and try and trust, I can quite happily bliss out doing a breaststroke, or take pleasure in the feel of my own body moving seamlessly through the swell of an afternoon tide.

Skills Withstand All Kinds of Chaos

The frustration of school was learning things you didn't think you'd need. What was the *point* of having to memorize this, to master fractions or theorems I'd never touch again? Because it's not what you learn, but that you learn *how* to learn. To flex those muscles lest they atrophy, muscles that you might use in geometry one day, but then another day in the future you'll use to master something called an iPhone, or use the "If . . . then" math problem to structure a critical argument with your boss. Skills give you something to do and to draw on, and return to, when life takes a hairpin turn. Your skills can get you through.

When the world locked down in March 2020, every one of my speaking gigs evaporated and, with them, swaths of potential business. Of course I panicked. I flailed. I splashed around in my own self-pity, knowing that while I had it easier than most, I was still scared. But flailing is wildly unproductive.

One thing Doris had told me, over and over: "The water is heavier than you are. It naturally holds you up. See?" She'd roll onto her back and let her arms dangle there, lightly, as if off the edge of a chaise lounge. I took comfort in the notion of water as one big heavy thing and me as a water bug, weightless and skittering along the surface. The only risk to my own survival was exhausting myself with wasted effort.

Forty years later, I tried this again. I stopped crying and

slowed down. I breathed. Rolled over onto my back and floated for a moment on my couch.

I had spent the past few years paddling comfortably along in my business, mastering the strokes, gaining speed and confidence. And even though it felt like the floor had dropped out on March 13, I reminded myself that all I had done and made was still there; the only thing that had changed was what I had *expected* would happen. My skills, my relationships—those weren't going away just because the world changed.

I took a hit in 2020, though nowhere near as badly as those who lost their livelihoods and businesses in one fell swoop. Given the kind of work I had been doing virtually for years, I could pivot more easily than most. What did I do? I went back to the strokes I knew. I launched a series of webinars and online programs to help business owners rethink brand messaging in this new age. I gave writers a place to write in a supportive environment, somewhere they could go to create, and be heard. We all just kept swimming. And so can you.

What You'll Do Next

Are there things you've been wanting to do, try, or explore that you hope to someday make a living doing? I'm sure there are. There may *also* be opportunities that come up that may not "look" like the dream job. Working at a wig company hadn't been on my list of dream jobs, but when it came up I took it, and it also changed my life. I have drawn on the skills I learned there throughout my career.

You may have been born with certain predispositions and innate abilities. But skills are things you learn. You picked them by chance or on purpose, in class or outside of classes. You found teachers, or, in some cases, they found you. Skills in and of themselves are an achievement, because they're evidence of what you are capable of learning and doing, creating and contributing. And you have more to offer than you might think.

write your next chapter

Write about a skill you can do with your eyes closed. Could be how to tie a rock-climbing knot, handle a customer service issue, or sell your boss on an idea. Maybe it's something you do every day; maybe it's part of your job that you know you excel at. Take me into this skill the moment you're doing it, and use plain language and metaphor, rather than jargon, to explain it. Write for ten minutes.

grab a notebook

What was it like to write about that skill? What occurred to you in writing about it that maybe didn't occur to you before? What did you remember or discover in the process of writing that surprised even you?

grab a notebook

Skill Inventory

Now that you have that skill fresh in your mind, let's unpack it further. Because there are several skills involved in performing *that* skill. Make a list of those skills. For instance, let's say the skill you wrote about was "handling customer service requests." There are other skills you use to perform that skill:

- Greeting people cheerfully, regardless of how you actually feel
- Showing empathy and concern

- Asking the right questions
- Coming up with a creative solution
- Getting buy-in from the customer

If you wrote about building furniture in your woodshop, then likely that skill involves:

- Operating heavy machinery
- An attention to detail
- An aesthetic eye
- A knowledge of how to work with specific hard materials
- The ability to turn an idea of a thing into an actual, usable household object

Write out all of the skills involved in the one you chose.

grab a notebook

Your (Not So) Secret Skills

Let's widen the lens of skills and look at things you do well that may or may not appear in a job description. Because when people discover you can do them, they ask you to do them all the time. These might be job-related skills, or they may be totally random.

I know a psychologist and author who *loves* untangling necklaces. I know this because I was cursing at a knot in the green room at a TV station with her. "Give that to me," she said. That's a skill she has: Patience and persistence in loosening knots other people give up on—not a bad description of what a psychologist does too. Give yourself a few minutes to write out everything you can think of, and again, use plain language, not résumé speak. Might be things like:

- Finding lost things

- Tracking down information online outside of a straight Google search
- Saying the right thing in an awkward moment
- Explaining things to children
- Repropagating house plants
- Picking out gifts
- Getting your money back

Create a Skill Cloud

What you need for this next part are Post-it notes in different colors. Doesn't matter what color you use, obviously, but for the purpose of clarity, I've assigned colors below.

- **ON YELLOW "SKILL" NOTES**: Look at all the skills you've listed and written about, and write one skill per note.
- **ON BLUE "APPLICATION" NOTES**: Looking at each of the yellow skills, write one area of your life—one project, one application, one situation—where you use that skill. So if one of your skills is "listen without reacting," where else does that help you at work, home, or otherwise? One idea per sticky note.
- **ADD SKILLS**: What other skills come to mind that you use in those areas? Generate a few more yellow skills.

The goal here is that the skills and the places where you use said skills inspire one another, so that your Post-it notes are spreading across the wall. You might have twenty; you might have thirty-five, or more. You can also get creative about how you color-code them if you like.

Find the Connections

You now have a wall filled with at least two colors of Post-its (more if you got creative): skills and the places where you either already apply them, or could. Now comes the fun part: You make like a human Ouija board and let your intuition drive. There is no one "right" way to do this as it's individual and unique to you. The purpose of this tool is to break out of linear thinking and allow you to see how movable and flexible your skills are, and make it easy to see new connections between the many things you do.

- **START MOVING THE NOTES AROUND THE BOARD.** You don't need a rhyme or reason; maybe one reminds you of another or feels like it goes with that one. Or maybe you find most of your skills hovering around one blue note.
- **LOOK FOR PATTERNS.** See what skills seem to call to each other, what surprising ways they connect.
- **FEEL FREE TO ADD MORE NOTES** as you go through the process, as one might make you think of another.
- **MOVE THE NOTES AROUND.** See what comes to light when you move one here and that one there. You might like moving them quickly to see what connections rise. Or you might prefer to go slowly, staring at the pieces like a chess player. Watch how these clouds can take shape.

Extract the Genius

At this point you probably have a cluster of Post-its over here and some over there, following a kind of intuitive logic or structure that makes total sense to you but wouldn't to someone who just walked in the room.

While there's no point at which it's "done," there is a point when the thoughts come. This is when you grab a notebook or your laptop and start writing to capture the ideas you unearthed in this process. You can write on your own, or use the questions below as a guide.

- **DO YOU HAVE MORE OF ONE COLOR POST-IT THAN ANOTHER? (TOTALLY FINE, BTW.)** Maybe you have nearly twice as many skills as you have places to use them. If so, you can use that as a prompt to come up with more places and ways you can use some of the skills, especially the ones you like doing.
- **WHICH SKILLS HAD THE STRONGEST PULL FOR YOU OR SEEMED TO "LEAD" THE GROUPINGS, AND WHY?** Are they the most valuable to you or to others? Or do you simply love doing them?
- **WHAT NEW CONNECTIONS DID YOU DISCOVER** between skills you use and where you use them?
- **WHAT CAME TO LIGHT** about what you love doing and want to do more of?
- **THINK ABOUT THE THINGS YOU MIGHT LIKE TO LEARN OR DO NEXT—IN YOUR CAREER, IN YOUR LIFE.** I'm not talking job titles. Stick with the plain language we've been using. Is it that you love doing a certain kind of skill and want to explore how to do it in a different industry or for different people, or with a different end goal?
- **ARE THERE SKILLS YOU WANT TO LEARN SO THAT YOU CAN SERVE THE SAME PEOPLE OR INDUSTRY, BUT IN A NEW WAY?** What might those be and how can you build on what you already have?

grab a notebook

This is a powerful exercise to use anytime you want to make sense of something in a tangible, intuitive way or synthesize thoughts. I use it all the time to create talks and workshops and even when I was creating this book. You can use it to take stock of what you have, to explore new ideas, and even decide a plan of action. The more you can draw connections between what you know and can do, the more things click together—and the more you can apply what you know to the opportunities right in front of you.

CHAPTER 8

Practice Makes Purpose

Practicing an art, no matter how well or badly,
is a way to make your soul grow, for heaven's sake.
—Kurt Vonnegut, *A Man without a Country*

When I was twenty-two, I got my first full-time job as the executive assistant for the Center for Quality of Management, a small firm in Cambridge, Massachusetts. They knew what they were getting: A kid out of college with zero experience, someone who could be trained from the ground up because there was nowhere lower to start from. I hadn't done an online job search because that didn't exist in 1997. The woman who recommended me had tried to hire me previously for a work-from-home position (which weirdly *did* exist), and I didn't want it. After many months of feeling alone, aimless, and sad, I had one prerequisite for a job: That I leave my house.

The work they did at CQM, which I didn't even really understand yet, didn't arouse passion. It didn't need to. My goal was to beat back the WTF Do I Do Blues with a daily shower and a steady paycheck, people to talk to besides my cats. I didn't just miss having a place to go; as someone who thrived in school, I missed having something to be *good* at. At this point it almost didn't matter what it was.

We just talked about your skills, and how they feed all your efforts, even the ones you don't know you're going to make yet. And the way you get good at anything is through practice. The willingness to keep doing, keep trying, keep practicing, is what contributes to what Angela Duckworth calls *grit*—and which she says is far more indicative and predictive of who will achieve and succeed, beyond sheer talent. Purpose doesn't always predate that effort; it often arises from it.

We think that a desire to do a thing—music, math, urban planning—will rise naturally and purposefully with clear inclination and without any effort, that it will point to a clear destination, at which point your job is to follow it, excel at it, and do that thing as long as you can. That's not what happens for many (most) people. If it did happen for you that way, amazing. You should write a book about it (it just probably isn't this book). But there's also nothing wrong if it doesn't all happen in precisely that way. The fact that our lives unfold the way they do, and not the way we think they should, says more about what's wrong with our expectations, not us.

No one tells you this, but you can and do learn a tremendous amount doing something you're not particularly passionate about, and not the best at. Some things worth knowing aren't always discovered in the blazing sun of white-hot passion, but in the quiet shade of learning and doing, of curiosity and competency. And practice. Of doing a thing over and over again.

The reason I took the office job was the same reason I'd signed up for school band. "You need something to *do*," my mother said. After a year of tooting "Hot Cross Buns" through a recorder, I chose the sax. The sax! I was a bespectacled fourth grader with wrists the size of a number 2 pencil. It hung like a metal albatross around my little neck, and came in a case so big, I could fit in it. When I left for band practice on Tuesday mornings, I looked for all the world like I was headed to LaGuardia for a month abroad.

While I quite liked its raspy, golden tone, there were two things I hated: licking the reed to get it "nice and wet" (gross), and practicing at home, so I didn't. I practiced complaining about it instead, a long scale of minor notes that irritated my mother no end. "Why are we doing this?" she said. I switched to flute, and went from wrestling with a large metal bird to playing a silver soda straw. My posture improved.

I was not an "inspired" music student. I didn't wow people with my scary talent. I didn't have a famous flautist taped to my wall. I had Kirk Cameron taped to my wall. Also, I was ten. I did most things because it was strongly suggested that I do them, or because they were something to *do*. I picked up music the way you learn beginner French: a word, a phrase, at a time. And yet it also never occurred to me to quit. Band was actually a lot like going to mass: You sat quietly in rows while someone at the front waved their arms around. I figured I wasn't going to be playing in a band forever, and that was true—making it not unlike any job you or I sat through for a few years.

The offices at the CQM were small. My desk was huge. Did I know how to do the job? No. But sitting down at that desk wasn't all that different from sitting down to play an instrument. I practiced the office work like sheet music. I simply looked at what was in front of me, and breathed into it. This note, then that one, then that one. I mastered a few bars at a time, found a rhythm, found my step. Once I got going, I found I had a flair for things no one ever told me you could have a flair for, like PowerPoint slides or charming the gatekeepers who jealously guarded the calendars for the CEOs of Raytheon and GE.

Most important, I learned I didn't have to be scary talented to enjoy the experience of doing a job well. I've found that to be true of most things I've done. And the job itself didn't have to be exciting to be engaging. Plus, the perk of hearing someone speak your name out loud every day, even come to depend on you for things you did, showed me the value of contributing something, anything, to a collective effort. My own life, which for months had felt as if I'd been dragging it through the sand like a weather-beaten boat, started to rise under a slip of tide, and I felt the friction ease.

And while I didn't aspire to be a management consultant, just being there changed me and what I saw, and how I saw myself. I bumped up against ideas and concepts and people I wouldn't have otherwise. It was like someone flipping lights on in rooms you didn't know were there.

By the time I was twelve, I'd been playing one night a week in regional band (one step above school band, one step below state). One night, we were given the chance to audition for state band. *Why not?* I thought. *I mean, I'm here.* I felt uncharacteristically cool about this, given what a nervous kid I was, prone to stomach cramps. Why? Because the sun did not rise and set on school band. I worked hard and played my best, but I knew my life wouldn't change much whether I got in or didn't. Honestly, I wish I could have *bottled* how little I cared about it so I could take a swig literally every other time I worried about impressing anyone ever again. Auditioning for state band felt like putting in for a promotion in Jersey when you were thinking of moving to Denver anyway. And the irony, of course, is that I made the cut.

There Is No Career Template

I do a lot of public speaking and have for years. But early on, I didn't know I wanted to be a professional speaker because I didn't know that was a thing. And there really is no one right way to be a speaker, except to start speaking, to seek out places where you can stand in front of people and do it.

In 2004 I found a call for speakers online from an education company—no experience necessary. I forget the name of it now, but it was something with an exclamation on the end, like You can do it! or Make it count! They were training regional speakers to hype up high school students about going to college.

They gave you a script and encouraged you to "put your personality into it." The talk ran a full forty-five minutes. I made the first round of cuts and flew to Minneapolis to audition. It was a good way to learn to practice speaking because I didn't have to give a thought to content at all. They'd written it; all I had to do was commit it to memory.

You don't memorize a forty-five minute talk in one go. You have to literally rebuild that script in your head, line by line like a layer of bricks in your brain; once the cement is set on the first row, you lay a new row over that, and on and on until you have a big, sturdy structure that is so grounded in your body and mind nothing can knock it over.

Some aspiring speakers might say, "But I need it to be *me*, my ideas, what I'm *passionate* about. I need it to be authentic and something I believe in." Nope! It could have been a talk about rotating your tires. I did not care. This was a chance to practice the work of speaking without any of the other stuff that I would ultimately have to learn to give talks of my own. I had the luxury of that one focus. Memorization is often looked down upon, but it's a powerful tool when used well. There is a kind of freedom in knowing something cold.

I got the gig. I was beyond excited. The only real bummer it turns out? Actually *doing* it. What I didn't realize is that I would be sent to room after room of bored teenagers who looked at me the way you might at a sleepy panda at the zoo. They were not set ablaze by my oratory. Sometimes they pretended I wasn't even there and the moderator had to step in to shush them. It was humbling, to say the least. But I'd learned this skill: Memorize a talk and give it, and by the way, here's what it feels like when your audience checks out. I now had a practice to build on.

Later, when I started getting invited to speak at conferences as an editor at Martha Stewart, I had a new challenge: Come up with things to say that were worth listening to. Gauge the audience's response; think on your feet. Did I do it for the money? If that were the measure of success, I would have quit a long time ago. Because I didn't get much or any at all for a while. Once I prepared a talk to give at a gym at Columbus Circle in Manhattan. *And not one person came.* So they sent me home. I'd had the experience of having a built-in talk and a built-in audience, and now I knew what it was like to make up your own talk and have no audience. The magic would happen when I could line those things up: a talk I could give to an audience who wanted to listen, or when I could create something worth listening to, in which case the audience would follow. And did.

On the back of practicing how to deliver a talk, I learned how to create a talk in lots of low-stakes situations (this alumni event, that dinner) and then, over the course of years, how to get people to invite you to speak. When the TEDx opportunity came up, obviously, I was beyond excited. And that was the first time I remember thinking everything had come together—I got it based on the idea I pitched; I wrote it myself, and then committed it to memory. I was not taking a damn chance in this high-stakes situation. I knew that thing backward and forward, and the moment I stepped onto that stage I was ready.

Today that talk has more than seven million views, but it wasn't some viral hit right away; it grew a little, and then it grew exponentially. And while it absolutely supercharged my speaking career, I'd still be a professional speaker, whether I got that chance or not. Simply because I knew it was something I wanted to do, so I kept practicing at it, every chance I got. I also worked hard at nurturing the relationships that ultimately led to speaking opportunities. The practice was cumulative and has grown over time. You might be tempted to look at the numbers alone, to see how many millions of views that TEDx talk has, and assume, *Oh,* that's *how she did it.* As if it were all part of a master plan. But it wasn't. The minute I left that stage in Kansas City, I had no idea if anyone besides the people in that room would ever see that talk or care.

You might also look at this book and say, "Oh, she got the TEDx talk, and then of course a book deal." But those things hardly happened the way you might think they did. What you don't see are hours and days and years of writing, unsure of where it would go or what was worth sharing.

Careers are not monoliths. They're woven from whatever threads you happen upon, find, or create in your own life, which is why yours will look very different from someone else's, even if you grew up in the same town, went to the same school, majored in the same thing. Yours may be a series of shorter loops, connected through circumstance, or relationships, or wild-ass opportunity. It may be a series of outrageous, uncanny leaps. Some loops are abandoned—because this job or that opportunity goes away, or the economy shifts, the world is shaken by a global pandemic, or you just get bored. Whether it turns out to be a short loop or an elongated one, that work leaves an impression and helps you hone something you might not have otherwise.

Sometimes you practice at a thing not knowing where it will lead or what you might use it for. The Karate Kid spent hours waxing Mr. Miyagi's car or painting his fence, only to discover later that he'd trained himself to respond in ways that would make him a champion. The thread that connects any and all your efforts is your willingness to *practice*, to do a thing over and over, not just because you think this is The Thing You Should Be Doing but also because practice is what enables us to maintain skill, build confidence, and maintain that confidence. Because, as Seth Godin says, to create anything of value, you have to decide to be the kind of person who keeps showing up.

The Motivation Myth

But what about motivation? Don't you have to be motivated to practice? Sorry, but no. I don't say this to bum you out, but to free you of the tyranny of this racket: Motivation is a luxury. Like passion, it's a feeling; it's mutable, evolving. It rises and falls like atmospheric pressure, and so rather than stand outside with a bucket waiting for it to rain, you need to set up pipes and get water moving through them so you have it on demand.

Just ask Mel Robbins, whose book *The 5 Second Rule: The Fastest Way to Change Your Life* has made her one of the most popular life coaches on the planet—not to mention made her a top-tier speaker, host of a nationally syndicated talk show, and, for a while, the face of a big-ass billboard over the mouth of the Lincoln Tunnel, which was just as impressive to me.

Robbins writes about how she saw a TV ad late one night featuring a rocket launch during a particularly depressing and difficult time in her life. She decided that's what she needed—to literally launch herself out of her bed, out of her rut, out of the mess she was in, and into a new life. And the 5 Second Rule was born.

Here's how it works: The moment you have an instinct to act on a goal, count down 5-4-3-2-1 and *move*. Physically move before your brain has a chance to stop you. That's it? Yup. Now try doing it. Because understanding it doesn't count. The point: Thinking is your enemy; action is your friend. The minute you stop to think? You're cooked.

As for motivation? "It's complete garbage," she says. "If you want to improve your life, you'll need to get off your rear end and kick your own butt."[1] Now a rocket launch is a big production; it's eventful, but that doesn't mean every action has to be. What practice lacks in excitement it makes up for in power. "It's not the big moves that define our lives," Robbins writes. "It's the smallest ones."[2]

Decide on a Thing to Practice Now

I watched an episode of *MarieTV*, in which the ever-charming Marie Forleo, founder of B-School, author of *Everything Is Figureoutable*, and reigning queen of coaches and business owners everywhere, tackled a question she's probably received no fewer than seventy-three thousand times: "How do I stay motivated when I feel so stuck?" And after recommending self-care, meditation, and a healthy diet (in that order), she shared a line that is sheer genius in its simplicity: "Ambiguity is the enemy of execution."[3]

You can't say, "I have so many things I want to do," and then ask us to believe that when you've made no progress in any direction. The point? Decide—not what you want to be, but what you want to *do* right now, what's worth doing.

Don't Count on Medals to Mean Much

Popular columnist Jeff Haden, author of *The Motivation Myth*, asked Lance Armstrong what he missed about being a pro cyclist. Was it the fame, the glory, the medals? Nope. He missed the process, the effort that went into earning that spot on the podium. "I don't miss the result," he told Haden. "I miss the work."[4]

Getting there isn't as fulfilling as becoming what you most want to achieve. And that's why there's no shortcut to motivation, as that misses the point. Try to "hack" motivation and you've just cut off the legs of what makes something worth doing. So while we all get a rise out of rousing speeches and riveting reads (ahem), I'm under no illusion that reading this book alone can create a change for you, because that's on you.

"Motivation is a result, not a precondition," writes Haden. "Progress provides lasting motivation."[5] So if you would like to get into fighting shape and feel fit and energized again and are looking for the right dose of motivation to get you there? Then you're not going anywhere. The people who are "motivated" to work out typically feel that way because they've had a taste of progress.

So the question is, where are you allowing yourself to experience progress? To see for yourself, to bear your own witness to find out what you're capable of?

Remove the Prize Altogether

Seth Godin learned to fly-fish in Wyoming with some friends. But he had no interest in actually catching a fish. So what did he do? He asked for a rod without a hook. No hook! He watched his friends spend the day trying so hard to catch a fish. Since that wasn't his goal, he could focus instead on the practice, the art, of fly-fishing. It's not that we're *not* trying to catch fish, make a living, get paid, win awards. "But the catch is the side effect of the practice itself," he writes in *The Practice*. "Get the practice right, and your commitment will open the door."[6]

After a year or so at the Center for Quality of Management, I'd dramatically improved my skill set. I'd learned to coordinate travel for three different people, set up the board meetings, and build slide decks from scratch, which I still spend an inordinate amount of time doing. I also had the distinct privilege of being the only one who knew how to use the newfangled, state-of-the-art videoconferencing machine, which in 1997 was less good at capturing video than it was of people sitting very still in real time.

Another thing I taught myself to do was not in the job description: Write and perform skits and funny poems for staff parties, which were a hit. I learned how much people delight in being written into stories and how good I was at creating them. Making people feel seen, heard, and in on the joke? That's a skill I've built my business on to this day.

You Don't Need to Do It Forever and Ever Amen

I found an old picture from state band recently, everyone wearing sashes and looking a little like the Hitler Youth, a sign behind us that says "Future Musicians of America." I think they overshot a bit. In that picture everyone is looking in one direction and I'm looking in another. I was searching for either my mother or the nearest exit.

Very few people proceed directly from school band to career

musician. Does that mean we shouldn't have bothered? That it was a waste of time because you didn't end up in the Philharmonic? Of course not. Will it be useful? Maybe not in a linear sense where you learn a thing and then spend your life doing it. But that's not the point of everything. It's not the point of most things.

There is no end to practice, wherein the "real" stuff begins. Practice is as real as it gets. *Everything* is practice. And while my school band life was not a high-stakes situation, that doesn't mean that the things you do as a kid aren't or shouldn't be. I don't mean to imply you should just take all your shit lightly. The opposite: Take it seriously, even if you don't intend to do it for very long.

There is one—one—band moment that stays with me, and it was during my very first state band rehearsal. We were playing the hardest piece of music I'd ever seen, "The Liberty Bell." It started at a note so high I didn't know it could exist, a B that waved far above the staff like a flag on the helm of a pirate ship. And it didn't work up to that note; it started there and cascaded down, so you had to give it all you had. The conductor raised her arms and cued us to begin. I tightened my hands-fingers-throat-eyes-lips, my whole body gathering force to reach that note. And I did—but rather than hear myself, I found myself deliciously lost in the middle of the making of the song: air and pressure transformed by metal tubes, splashed off high hats, a muscular, soaring, percussive rumble. It was nothing short of extraordinary, this stunning collective effort. I'd been playing in band for years, but this was the first time the lift and soar of what it sounded and felt like took me off guard.

Everything up to that point I had done believing that the value of my individual work was in what was counted and recorded: a perfect score on a spelling test, an A on a project, an acceptance to regional and state band based on my solo audition. And I would continue to reach for personal achievements, and still do. But I felt then what it was when your effort and skill folds into a larger thing, when you realize that your small contribution doesn't have to be especially noteworthy to matter, but practice does. That each single action lent a depth and complexity to something else, the whole of which you could not claim. It was a relief too—to discover that regardless of whether you had a lot of talent or a little, big aspirations or none at all, it mattered to do a thing, and to do it well, to be part of something wondrous—even just for the moment, even if it wasn't something you would keep.

write your next chapter

Think about a time you practiced. What was it that you practiced? Maybe it was a formal lesson or discipline like piano or soccer, but maybe it wasn't. Maybe you practiced braiding hair or roller skating or doing tricks on a skateboard (those guys practice *hard*). What's something you did over and over again, twenty-five years ago, yesterday, somewhere in between? Describe it in as much detail as you can, the sensory experience of doing it, and, if you like, how you ended up using that later or not at all. Let your mind and pen wander deep into that practice, and wherever it takes you next.

Set the timer for ten minutes. Start writing.

grab a notebook

Now zoom out on that experience.

- What did you learn from doing it that you might not have realized at the time?
- What did you learn about yourself and what you were capable of?
- How do you exhibit the same strengths, skills, or abilities now, or in other seemingly unrelated areas of your life?

grab a notebook

CHAPTER 9

No One Was Given a Script

People want to be told what to do because they are afraid (petrified) of figuring it out for themselves.
—Seth Godin, *Linchpin*

I was laid off from my job as features editor at Martha Stewart Living Omnimedia in October of 2011. I'd say I "lost" my job, but I didn't lose it. I knew exactly where it was when I left it.

A tidal wave of phone calls began in HR that day, leaving few departments untouched, and one employee after another washed up on the banks of unemployment to damply gather their things and leave.

For a few tense hours, every time a phone rang a collective muscular spasm gripped the room. Then the phone on my desk sprang to life. Everyone turned and looked at me with a mix of pity, horror, and dread.

"It's OK," I said. "Seriously, it's going to be OK." I felt two things at once: A cool leak of adrenaline that made me feel hot and cold at the same time. And also, relief.

No one ever knows what will happen. Which is why I think

it's weird when people refer to a certain period of time (the pandemic, for instance) as "unpredictable." *All* times are unpredictable! What's rare is not that shit happens, which it always will, but that we *ever* see it coming. This was one of those moments. What I was about to learn was that even when my life took a hard left, I was able to hug the curve and hang in there based only on the information I was given at the time. And you can too.

I walked into an office where my boss was sitting alongside an HR person I'd never had reason to meet. They looked grim. I realized with gratitude that I only had to do this once; they had to do it all day.

"I'm getting laid off, aren't I."

"Have a seat," they said.

I'd been working for the magazine for the better part of a decade, during which time it had undergone several iterations. What began as the hippie mag *New Age Journal* in 1974 (think Deepak Chopra before everyone knew Deepak Chopra) went mainstream as *Body+Soul* in 2002, and was snapped up by Martha Stewart in 2004, not long after I joined. It was a Cinderella tale; we were sweet but broke, hardworking but overlooked. We had (actual) fleas. And then Martha strode in on a white horse and gave us an instant upgrade. We now had a bigger national reach, a shiny new look and feel, and my own résumé stock shot up on a much more visible masthead. When the company announced they were moving the magazine from Watertown, Massachusetts, to New York, we were invited to reapply for our own jobs there if we were interested.

So, I applied for my job, and got it (again!)—no small feat, given that bringing editors to New York City is like bringing sand to the beach, and I was the only editor they kept. It helped that I wasn't just a print editor but had been hosting a daily radio show for the brand and doing TV hits in morning media for years. I couldn't believe I'd made it there, even as I zipped up the elevator in the monolithic Starrett-Lehigh Building on West 26th Street, stepped into an airplane hangar of an office with windows so big it felt as if all of Manhattan were leaning through them. I was beyond thrilled, and yet while I was working in the city and sleeping there, it didn't feel like I was *living* there. Because all I did was work. The only people I knew were at work. I would leave around seven or eight at night, and zip up the West Side Highway in a cab, blinking at the skyline feeling as if I'd been living with a stranger. And when I looked at the editors who helmed the publication, hunched endlessly over their desks, one crucial fact became blazingly clear: I didn't want to be them.

The executive editor was in her chair when I got in every morning, and she was there when I left, engaged in the Sisyphean task of muscling drafts uphill, only to be hit with a new stack. The editor in chief, ironically, didn't seem to have much time to do any editing at all. In short, the upward rise at a magazine seemed to be: work really hard on what you do well, so that you can either do more of that work, for longer hours, or land the top job where you wouldn't get to do any of it. That's the tale of any managerial rise, perhaps, but in publishing it was not accompanied by jaw-dropping leaps in salary. It didn't seem like a great trade.

When you look up and realize you don't want to go where this train is headed, it's worth asking why you're still on it. By that fateful day in the fall of 2011, I had been wiggling in my seat like a loose tooth for months, thinking I could simply leave one moment, thinking I couldn't the next. I knew either I was going to get yanked or I'd have to extract myself.

The terms of my severance were explained to me patiently by this woman whose job was to deliver bad news. I was told to sign here and there and everywhere, and then I went back to my desk to start the process of disentangling what was me from what was not me. I left that desk with dozens of unopened emails, drafts I hadn't read, piles of books I never got to. It had been my job, but now it wasn't me anymore. I hadn't just been given a (measly) severance (and boy, was it), but a real opportunity to start something new.

I made some weepy goodbyes, and then went directly to my

dentist, where I'd already had an appointment scheduled. It was a get-laid-off-and-head-to-the-dentist kind of day.

(And when I was invited to join a Facebook group of former Martha employees who'd been laid off and wanted to stew and kvetch and rail against the unfairness, I declined.)

OK, so now what. Having interviewed and been hired for my *own* job twice and laid off once, I wasn't interested in getting back on that particular horse. I flipped through job listings (content producer, senior editor) like a rack of clothes I know won't fit me at a sample sale—lots of cool things that seemed like they'd be great for someone else, and which, like a one-off Alexander Wang jumpsuit marked down to forty dollars, a bitch would cut you for. And no, I don't think a job is a luxury item. But I also knew that this was my chance to *choose*, not scramble or scrounge or squeeze myself into whatever I could find. If I believed I was desperate, then I'd believe I had to take whatever someone gave me.

And what I wanted, really, was the opposite of what I'd wanted when I was twenty-two. I didn't want to show up at a job anymore; I wanted to work from home. To decide what projects I'd take on and not what a boss handed down to me. I was willing to bet that if I could be a contender at a full-time job based on the skills I had, then maybe I could do some of the work for a sliver of someone's budget and get paid by several people at the same time. What I couldn't afford to do was worry about whether I was as good as someone else or not good enough, because what mattered was letting everyone know that I was capital *A* available right now.

Along with my job and my daily routine, I had also lost the connection and community of people I'd spent every day with for nearly two years in the New York office. I knew I needed to get out and meet people. I signed up for an improv class at the Magnet Theater. Of course, I had no intention of pursuing a *career* as an improv actor, which made about as much sense as trying to make your living as a traveling bard. (Even the improv teachers don't make their living doing improv. One of them was rumored to live out of his car.) But what I would do was stand in a circle with other adults and pass around an invisible ball, memorize their names, and build a whole scene around one simple suggestion. Which, it turns out, is how everything begins.

"Yes, and" Is Not the Same as "Yes Man"

Every improv scene starts with a suggestion. A person, place, or thing. A nongeographical location. A color. A word.

"Who's got one?"

"Banana."

Ken and I jump up at the same time. Neither of us knows what we're doing, but we've decided we're all in.

"How much for a banana?" Ken asks. Ken is six feet, four inches of blue-eyed gorgeousness with natural comedic timing and a pleasant, nontoxic masculinity. He is no more aware of the effect he has on a room than a Labradoodle does. He's thirteen years younger than me, and I wonder if or when I might sleep with him someday (and, years later, I do).

The relationship, the setting, comes to life, like any game of make-believe you ever played. If he is asking me for a banana, I must be selling one, so I have to believe that I am. Improv is essentially one long trust fall with an audience, with just enough conflict to give it some heft, something to lean against. It's essentially what your life is and mine: A series of suggestions, and how you respond to them.

"They're seventy-five dollars each," I say (he makes a face), "but that's because they aren't regular bananas. They're *magic* bananas."

The signature rule and guiding principle at the heart of improv is "Yes, and"—meaning, whatever assumption, suggestion, or leap your scene partner takes is a ball tossed your way, and the goal is to keep it in play. So when I tell you I have a magic banana for sale, the very worst thing to say is, "That's not a magic banana."

Ken would never do that. The world has already said yes to him in so many ways, he has no problem saying *yes, and* right back.

"A magic banana! Cool!" he says. "What can it do? Make me invisible? Make me fly? Make me good at math?"

Of course it will.

"The world of yes may be the single most powerful secret of improvising,"[1] writes Patricia Madson in *Improv Wisdom: Don't Prepare, Just Show Up*. It's what allows total strangers to create a scene together, and there's safety knowing that your scene partner will go along with your suggestion.

To be clear: "Yes, and" is not synonymous with submission or pandering. It's not about being quietly complicit while people run roughshod over you. "Saying yes is an act of courage and optimism; it allows you to share control," says Madson. "Yes expands your world."[2]

"Yes, and" keeps a scene moving; it's also a way of choosing, the decision to gain momentum. You can't steer a bike if you're not pedaling it. If you've ever had a friend or coworker say no to everything you suggested, then you understand the magic of "yes, and." It doesn't mean "do what I say"; it's about getting someone to play with you, because without a little yes, there's no forward movement. It's all dead ends and whirling eddies.

Let's take a scene you may find yourself in at work. Boss says, "Hey, we need to do this thing." Instead of "No, I don't want to and can't anyway," you might try, "*Yes*, I can see why that project is critical *and* we should talk about the best way to put resources in place to get it done" (subtext: I'm not doing it without you paying me more or hiring someone else to help me).

Because if you start leaning on the *but* too much, you sound like this: "Yes, *but* we don't have the resources," "Yes, *but* people won't like it"—and if you say it enough, people tune you out. They literally can't hear you because your but is too big.

Of course, you have to suss out a situation or an obligation. You "yes, and" a conversation—not a huge commitment. Meaning: You don't "yes, and" a job offer off the bat, but you use it during the interview ("Yes, and I can see why this role is critical to the work you're doing"). Do I say yes to everything? *Hell no.*

But I do try to lead with "yes, and"—just to see what happens next. Because what do I know? What does *anyone* know? When you say yes, you allow something to develop that you might not have seen coming.

What I was doing in improv class was not unlike what I was trying to do in my real life: Turn suggestions into real paying gigs; get people to remember my name; say yes to what people needed and figure it out as I go (which is still how I do things 99 percent of the time). There wasn't some preconceived box for me to fill or check. Part of what made my work possible, and ultimately in demand, was because I was able to make suggestions that appealed and encourage conversations I was in to keep going.

How I Made It Up as I Went with a High-Stakes Opportunity

Around this time, I'd been getting to know a brilliant woman I'd met at a conference, Pilar Gerasimo, who was the founding editor of *Experience Life*, a health and wellness magazine owned by LifeTime, a leading fitness-club company. I'd been confiding to her about how I felt a serious shift coming. The day I got laid off, she was one of the first people I called.

"Well," I said, sighing. "I've been cut loose."

"Good," she said. "I have an idea." Those are four of my favorite words.

Pilar had recently learned that the sales team had a new problem to solve: They needed more things to sell. They already sold full-page ads in the magazine; they sold signage at their gyms—but they wanted to offer something more to their corporate clients and didn't have the resources to do it. While sales teams sell content, they don't often make it themselves. What they needed was top-notch editorial for some sponsored content by someone who was not also employed by the magazine.

"Get on a plane to Minneapolis," she said.

And that's what I did. I improvised. The key players and I walked into the scene (a nice conference room with recessed lighting and ergonomic chairs) with no idea what might happen. I've come to love these kinds of meetings. I'd been given just enough intel to know who the players were, what they wanted, and who they were beholden to, and that was enough. I didn't have a slick proposal because I needed to listen first. I was going to "yes, and" my way into a project that hadn't been invented yet.

In other words, I was going in there with a magic banana.

After we talked for a bit, I could see it clearly: Where their road stopped and mine began, what they wanted, and what I could offer. I went into what-if mode, to feel out what made them excited: What if this wasn't a one-off but a six-month campaign, a full-page spread in the next six issues? What if it wasn't just print but also video broadcast on their closed-circuit TVs?

Yes, yes, yes, they said.

I left there realizing that very real work could come out of a simple suggestion. I went home and gave a lot of thought to that proposal. I got creative with compensation too—what if I got a percentage of the sales made on this project? *Wellll,* they didn't love the idea of cutting the consultant in on commissions, and I wasn't surprised. But while the head of ad sales said no to that, he followed up with a "yes, and": "Why don't we just up your monthly rate?" I almost fell out of my chair. And that might be one of the most powerful lessons of improv: That you teach yourself the skill of saying yes because the most interesting, curious, funny, or fortunate things can happen when two people decide to . . . agree.

That single project taught me listening closely and using what you have outweighs nearly anything else. We "think" things are set in stone, that there are "jobs" that either are or aren't available. And yes, there are measurable jobs out there and we know when they become more, or less, available. But a job is just what someone thinks they need filled because they needed it before. What about all the other needs that have yet to be filled and ways to fill them? You'd be surprised at what companies can find a budget for when it makes them money, or makes them look good, or solves an issue that's costing them. Thinking literally outside that box, and expansively, about how to serve has turned into very real work for me.

Granted, this is how I make my living, and that's not to say that it's the only way, or that you have to be a consultant to think in an expansive way about work. In fact, it can serve you anywhere. Because you *also* have a magic banana, and it's all about how you use it (OK, this is getting weird and I know it). It's not so much what you're "able" or "allowed" to do; what matters is where your own evolving skill set, ideas, and ability to execute on those ideas meet the needs of another. That is where work can come from.

Opportunities for work and life don't always come barreling through with a horn section and baton twirlers. If they did, they'd be easy to spot. They come through small asks, offers, requests. They come from that initial flicker of a light going on when someone says, "Wait, I have an idea." They don't always strike like lightning but can drift around the room like a stray feather; you have to be tuned in to notice and seize it.

Stop Trying to Write the Ending First

There's a point in every interview with anyone you've ever admired where the star/athlete/magnate/demigod says that if someone had told them they'd be doing what they're doing right now, they wouldn't have believed them. They wouldn't have believed their own story if you read it to them ahead of time. Even the people who *had* big goals (write book, win prize, guest host on *Saturday Night Live*), and who believed they might be able to do it, were *still* surprised when it happened.

On even our brightest days lurks a shadow-belief that in order to have the life we want, the one we're "meant" to have, we're supposed to know something we don't already know, have something we don't already have. If we had that one thing, that one answer, our lives would instantly become whole, perfect, complete. That we missed the day they were handing out code words and now we're fucked.

There is no code word. There is no secret knowledge. There's knowledge and wisdom and resources, and it's on us to seek those things out as we need them. But while we are all born into (wildly) varying levels of privilege, exactly no one is given the answer sheet before we begin.

"In creative endeavors," Twyla Tharp writes in *The Creative Habit*, "luck is a skill."[3] Just as a skilled improviser doesn't write a scene on her way to the theater, we can't plan everything either, if we want to take advantage of what's in front of us. Those efforts "can never be thoroughly mapped out ahead of time," she says. "You have to allow for the suddenly altered landscape, the change in plan, the accidental spark—and you have to see it as a stroke of luck rather than a disturbance of your perfect scheme."[4] None of that can happen if we're not open to possibility. If you try to write the end of your improv scene, you close yourself off to potential developments. (And later we'll get into how an attachment to plans can block us big time.)

Say "yes, and" because you want to see where something goes, because you want to lead with curiosity and courage and an open mind. Because you want to see whether this thing might grow legs or wings or a tail or anything else that might move you through the world in ways you wouldn't have on your own. It's also the way you discover what you have to offer; what makes you stand out; what gives you *distinction*.

Why do you need distinction? Because as Seth Godin puts it, "average is over."[5] It's not enough to just show up and do your job, to check a box—even if you have a good job, one you like and perform well. (Also, job security is an oxymoron; a company will eliminate your job or anyone else's to protect profits. No hard feelings.) As he says in *Linchpin: Are You Indispensable?*, jobs that can be measured, controlled, and predicted can also be replaced, optimized, and found cheaper somewhere else.

Here's the rub: There is no instruction manual for standing out. "There are no longer any great jobs where someone else tells you precisely what to do,"[6] he says. To be clear: Those jobs are available, sometimes more than others. But you are not that job, and that job is not beholden to you. You have it for a while, and while you're there that job takes on the shape of you—your skills, your personality, your actions. And even though the job title may stay the same, the next person who has your job will bring something different to it altogether, just as you did.

A résumé is a record, not a scene partner (at least, not a very good one). Titles are fleeting and mutable; companies change hands, are sold, or collapse altogether. What I'm telling you is that the places where you will find and create meaning will come from what *you* bring to the job, you as in you specifically, not in what someone told you to do. "Leaders don't get a map or a set of rules,"[7] says Godin. If there were instructions to be a leader, anyone could do it. And most people don't.

How I Know You're Already Good at This

You know how I know you can improvise? Because you already do it. Every. Day. You do not have a script. You have a loose plan, a sense of what could happen. You make it up as you go.

And you don't need an "ideal" scenario; you need to spot your options. A skilled improv actor doesn't pick and choose between which suggestion she feels "aligned" with. The best improvisers take anything you lob at them, any shaggy, silly, weirdo suggestion, and turn that into something worth watching. The key, says Madson, is not how prepared you are for what you think will happen, but how present you can be, right in this moment. Only then can you take advantage of what is actually happening. A good improviser (that would mean me and you) is "someone who is awake, not entirely self-focused and moved by a desire to do something useful and give something back and who acts upon this impulse."[8]

We walk through our lives in a kind of daze, she says, half-awake and caught up in what we think or worry or imagine might happen. Meanwhile, "the detail of each day takes place in front of us, moment by precious moment. How much are we missing? Almost everything."[9]

Say "Yes, and" to Yourself

But here's where this skill goes beyond "how to work with a scene partner" or "how to get along with your boss" to something far more critical: *How to learn to say yes to yourself.* Because if you don't, you will be forever stuck in a cell of your own making—and you also will be unable to make, share, or do the thing that sets you apart, that makes you distinctive. "Yes" opens a door. Not just because you need a way *out* of where you are but also because you need a way *in*—a way to find ease and comfort even in situations where you have no fucking idea what comes next. And to seize the opportunity to create, say, share something that only you would.

write your next chapter

Think about a time when you made do just with what you had. That might have been starting an actual fire with two sticks, entertaining a group of kids with nothing but a wig and a beach ball, or making magic in a meeting where you didn't have the information on hand that you had hoped to. A time when you had *no* idea what would happen.

A time you improvised, in other words. Set the timer for seven minutes and start writing.

grab a notebook

What surprised you about this moment? Did you remember more details than you thought? Do you think differently about that time now than you did then? Do you see how you have made this magic happen before? I bet.

grab a notebook

Your Next Scene

With that memory fresh in your mind, let's think about what else you can do and want to do, using what you have right now. Make a list of things you might like to try or do or explore. It may be that you've had a taste of it and want more, or you're curious about doing it. Maybe you want to find your way into groups of people (or even into meetings) that you might not normally be part of. What are some of those things?

grab a notebook

Use Your Magic Banana

A skilled improviser doesn't just have witty things to say; they listen and respond in real time to what's right in front of them. Want a better, more engaging, more fun scene? Dial into what's happening—because that's where the most interesting and unforeseen opportunities are. So let's step into the scene. Here's how.

Plug into the moment. Who's around you right now? What's happening? What do you find you're spending more or less time doing than usual? What have you been doing a lot of, or what habits or actions have you stopped doing? What's the mood of the environment you're in? And how do you tend to respond to it? What are you tired of? What are you hungry for?

grab a notebook

Eavesdrop. What conversations have you been privy to today, yesterday? What did you overhear? What have you noticed about either interactions or conversations you've been having? Start to take notes on that stuff as you hear it. Or take a moment now to jot down things that have occurred to you, just as you go about your day.

grab a notebook

Look for patterns and trends. What have you noticed in the larger conversations that are happening around you and maybe without you; say, trends you're observing in whatever you tend to pay attention to, be it fashion, or pop culture, or food, or website design? Doesn't matter. What has been catching your eye? And, as we know, based on what you're saying and searching, your phone is also populating your feed with those things. In my feed: A lot of water-resistant gold jewelry. Because guess what I'm shopping for.

grab a notebook

Who needs help? They may not have asked you for help directly, but you may have become aware, indirectly or otherwise. Maybe someone did mention a thing to you in passing or you saw them post about it online. What are people wishing for, wondering about, and wanting to know or do, and how can you help?

grab a notebook

What's one thing that has bugged you recently? Say a customer service issue, or a UX problem on a website, or something that just made you think, *There has to be a better way to do this.*

grab a notebook

"Yes, and" your way to your magic banana. Write down one way you might like to offer help (whether you're looking to volunteer to gain experience or charge for it, that's up to you to decide). Where is the intersection between what you know how to do and how you might provide all or part of a solution? How can you become a resource for that person or problem as you see it?

You might feel those buts rising—i.e., "But they probably already have someone for that," or "But they wouldn't want me to help," or "But I don't have the experience that someone else might have," and on and on your critic can go. Go ahead and write out the but, and then I want you to "yes, and" your response.

If one of your buts is "But they probably already have people for that," your response might be "Yes, and they may be overwhelmed with work and those people are busy. They might appreciate the offer for outside help."

If the but is "But I feel weird asking when I don't know them or what they need," you can respond to that with "Yes, and it would be an opportunity to get to know them and what they need. So that even if they need someone else, maybe I can be a resource and help them find the right kind of support somewhere else."

grab a notebook

Now that you have "yes, anded" your way and seen for yourself all the magic bananas you have to offer, what are some next steps you can take?

grab a notebook

CHAPTER 10

Why You Didn't Miss Your Calling

I don't ask for the full ringing of the bell. I don't ask for a clap of thunder. A scrawny cry will do.

—Wallace Stevens

I wanted to know why Sister Terry became a nun. Or rather, how she knew she was supposed to become one. So I asked her. We were in the classroom facing the swings, in the small parochial school that extended like a limb from the belly of Our Lady of the Blessed Sacrament Church. The school was one long hallway; I started at one end at seven years old and would exit the other end the day of my eighth-grade graduation. From there the distance between me and the church would only lengthen.

How did Sister Terry, or anyone else, know what they were supposed to do or be? Though it sure looked like people knew: Kids grew up into adults who married each other and had kids of their own, and on and on it went. But what about the nuns? Hmm.

Sister Terry had smallish teeth, scrubbed skin taut over

her cheekbones, a few freckles. Her lips were thin and bare. She seemed old and young at the same time.

"You just know," she said. "You're *called* to do it." And that was that. There wasn't much else she had to say about it.

It was an answer, but it wasn't. Because I didn't know what that meant, to have Jesus call you directly. And I wanted to know so that I could avoid answering it.

Now I had a new thing to worry about. I had quite a collection at this point: That spiders would crawl on my face while I was sleeping, that the neighbors would let their dog off the leash, that I wouldn't finish my homework, that I'd lose my mother at the mall, or forever. And now, that I'd get The Call.

What a Calling Is (and Isn't)

Earlier, we talked about why the follow-your-passion-and-feel-it-forever advice falls short. And how as convenient as that theory is, it isn't how passion works; it ebbs and flows, spikes like a fever, goes away, shows up somewhere else.

A calling, however, is different. Whereas passion is born of emotion, a calling is most often associated with higher purpose—not one we chose, but one that chose *us*. It also implies that you're "meant" to do or be something, that it was predetermined—which certainly makes for a great story, validating our existence while simultaneously letting us off the hook, and absolving us of error. Unless of course, you don't answer The Call, and ironically, that's often the way we talk about them—as things we should have been. ("Oh, Sheryl! You really should have been a comedian. You missed your calling!")

Remember the study that showed how having a fixed mindset about passion made people less likely to stick with one? Callings are *defined* as fixed. People who believe they must be called rarely say, "Yeah, I had a calling, but then another call came through, so I hung up." Make no mistake—that *is* how life works, but not how we think "callings" do. The problem is, if you believe that you must be called to do a thing, you might end up sitting by the phone a long time.

The notion of tracking your passion through life like a snow leopard through Nepal sounds dreamy and adventurous. It also verges on elitist—as do callings, because this assumes someone is on the short list for calls and you're not. Attributing your choices to having been "called" to do it always seems to me like a cop-out, a convenient explanation of why and how things happened that you can't learn from or do anything about (and neither can we). It obscures circumstances, choices, and chance behind an ethereal cloud and stops the conversation short, just like Sister Terry did when I inquired about her vocation. She was *called*, and that was that. What I was left with was really an unanswered question that bordered between terrible and mystical—as good a way as any of summing up Catholic school.

Nuns as Badass Career Women

All I really knew about the nuns was that they weren't married, didn't have kids, and lived together in a brick house at the other end of the church parking lot. I was told that the nuns were all married to Jesus, which made sense, I guess, because didn't everyone have to marry somebody? Could you marry someone you never saw? It made about as much sense as Lisa Volkmann believing she would marry Michael J. Fox.

It occurs to me that the nuns were the first career women I ever knew. They were the only women I wasn't related to who had opinions and authority and clout, who could command respect, pass or fail you, and whose attention you both feared and craved.

Who would want to be a nun? To wear the same black dress and (back then) a veil pinned to your head—which they called a habit, I figured, because they put it on every day. I once saw the principal Sister Margaret at the ShopRite piling Diet Coke into her cart. I almost didn't realize it was her because she wasn't wearing her habit. I was shocked at how shorn she looked, the cropped white hair, her neck narrow as a bird's. I wondered when she had gotten The Call, and whether it caught her off guard or if she'd been waiting for it. My father was an anesthesiologist and lived his life on call. It might come at any time, and you had to be ready, whether you were dead asleep or halfway through a bowl of spaghetti. I don't know if he wanted to go. I never asked.

I respected the nuns, strange breed that they were. Some warm and quirky, others sharp as vinegar. They never broke ranks. They held us to higher standards. But who held them? I figured the priests must be in charge (weren't men always in charge?), but for the most part, the priests were large and sleepy as bears. They moved through the hallways on silent rubber soles, performed sacraments, finished whatever was left in the chalice, then loped distractedly out the door toward the rectory, while the nuns called after them—"Father? Father?"—chirping at their sides like a clattering of jackdaws.

Why didn't Sister Terry say, simply, that she'd made a choice? That she wanted to live with other adults and have her own room and read when she felt like it? That a life of faith mattered more than a life of family? Or that she didn't want to be married or a nurse and those had been the options, which was likely closer to the truth? But I'm disappointed in her too. This was her chance to tell a girl about choice, initiative, the role we play in our own decisions about work and life. She could have been honest about what life was like for her, that it wasn't magical or weird, but more like other people's lives than we thought; that she and the other sisters wore regular clothes around the house and washed dishes and took out the trash, called one another by their first names when we weren't around.

Sister Terry might've sold me on that path, or one like it, if she'd told me I had options, that I could do what I wanted and mind my own business and care about my work more than other things. If she'd said that she hadn't just been "called," but that she chose this life, and there was a lot to like about it.

Do You Have a Job, a Career, a Calling—or All Three?

Amy Wrzesniewski and her colleagues at the Yale School of Management wanted to know what determines whether people see their work as a job, a career, or a calling. In a study they published in the *Journal of Research in Personality*, they defined a *job* as a means to an end (you do it for a paycheck and that's it); a *career* as a path to advancement (you trade up one job for another, better one); and a *calling* as meaningful, fulfilling, socially useful work that's integral to identity and self-expression.[1] That doesn't mean, however, that it calls you first.

Now, one might assume that, say, someone who works as an administrative assistant would see their work as a *job*, whereas the director of a big agency or CEO of a culture-disrupting start-up has a *career*, and someone who does good works, say, to promote literacy or feed hungry children, would have a *calling*. Of course that might be true for some. But that's not what the researchers discovered.

What they found was that the way people defined their work wasn't necessarily determined by demographics or occupational differences. At all. The researchers found that satisfaction with life and work may be more dependent on how an employee *sees* their work, more than any other thing. In a subset of the study, which involved twenty-four administrative assistants (people who all had essentially the same office job), one of the most notable differences between those who considered what they had a job, career, or calling? *How long they were in that role.* The admins who saw themselves as having a calling spent on average *more than double the amount of time* in the role than those who saw themselves as simply having a job. Meaning: The ones who saw their work as a calling versus a job were those who, by and large, spent more time in it.

Huh.

It wasn't the only factor. But it was significant enough for the researchers (and lots of other people) to take note. You might say, well, the people who are called to be admins stayed *because* they were called. OK. Do you know anyone who woke up one day and felt called to be an admin assistant? To assume that it has to work that way assumes causation, rather than correlation. And, turns out, you don't have to feel called to do it to experience your work as a calling.

There are people just dying to quit their admin jobs, or simply holding out for a promotion, sure. While this was not stated in the study, I'd bet my hat that there are others who didn't intend to stay but did. And the longer they stayed, the better they got; people came to depend on them, respect them. They became more connected with the company and mission. They didn't just have a job anymore; they had a critical role where their skills were used and appreciated and their work mattered.

What this suggests is that a calling, as inadequate a term as it is, may have less to do with the titles, roles, or job descriptions (a lot of which, let's be honest, is a mutually agreed-upon fiction) and more to do with what you—you, specifically—do while you're there. That means experiencing your work in a meaningful way isn't about whether God beamed your brain the right instructions, but whether you gave yourself a chance to explore what it is to do something and to do it well. Because you get better. You do things faster, more intuitively. You see yourself improving. You might get a promotion or a raise. Great! The real satisfaction and sense of accomplishment comes from watching yourself in the act of growing and achieving.

There are other perks too. The researchers found not only that those who deemed their work a calling see and experience work differently (that it's more than just a job) but also that they reported significantly higher life and job satisfaction and ranked work satisfaction higher than those who described their work as a job or career, and even missed fewer days of work—regardless of their status or salary.

How I Followed the Thread from One Job to Another

After a year or so of working as an executive assistant, I found myself getting weepy at the fax machine. I knew it was over and I had to find a way to break up. I'd fallen in love with the idea of going back to school and was flipping through course catalogs on the train. Later, after I'd completed my master's and was in year two at the wig company, I took to closing my door in the afternoons under the guise of "getting some copy editing done," and instead put my head down for a nap. I figured it was just me getting adjusted to my antidepressants, which was probably true. But I was also flat-out bored. There just wasn't anything more to do there, and I knew it.

Jump ahead a few years to the end of my tenure at the magazine. I'd sneak off to the lactation room around three o'clock on many occasions (when no one was scheduled to use it of course; I'm not a monster!). It was the one place in the whole office without a goddamned sliding glass door. I'd drift blissfully for twenty-five minutes or so before returning to my desk, pretending I'd been at a meeting. Sleeping and crying at work were two pretty consistent signs for me that it was time to move on.

When I lost my radio gig at the Martha Stewart channel on SiriusXM, my replacement was none other than Martha's niece, a lovely woman who said she was struggling a bit on the air, and did I have any advice? After swallowing my ego, hard (have you ever been asked to train your replacement *after* you were let go?), I did help her—and it was then that I realized just how much I had learned about broadcast. *Wait a minute*, I thought. I might not be hosting a show anymore, but someone is, and maybe they need help too.

So when I met the owner of a small talent agency, I offered to media train their clients. And here's what I discovered: Brilliant people of all backgrounds wrestled with how to communicate their insights sharply and effectively—not just on TV but also everywhere else. I developed an approach to coaching that went beyond media training, helped them dig down into the marrow of who they were and what they were actually trying to do.

And *that's* how I got into brand consulting. I'd never tell you I was "called" to do that work because, quite frankly, I didn't know what to call it! You can ask five different brand consultants what they do and you'll get five different answers. Nor did I choose that work because I thought it would be meaningful; I discovered what it meant by seeing the results. The people I worked with didn't just appreciate what we did together; they felt empowered by it. And I, in turn, felt energized by them. That—*that!*—is where the meaning emerged. Because for me, there was a direct line from the effort I made and the skills I applied to someone else's progress. If I'd made a series of wildly different career choices, I have no doubt I could find a similar sweet spot in my work as an interior designer or English language professor or cognitive behavioral therapist. And I might be very happily styling your three-bedroom loft right now.

Look, everyone wants to feel they're "meant" to do a thing. What we want is to feel in *flow*, to know that our work is seen and appreciated, that everything isn't a thankless uphill toil. That's not career dependent; that's a human desire. And no one job provides it. That also means your most meaningful contributions need not be preceded by a "calling." That feeling, that sense of making your work matter, is something you discover for yourself.

After a while I didn't need the media-training gig anymore, because what I learned I took with me to the next thing. I knew by then that there was no one coming to save me, or to call out to me over a celestial megaphone. Armed with my own experiences and abilities and the curiosity to see what's next, I could head in any direction at all.

Callings Aren't Limited to Career

What about the call to do things that have nothing to do with career? Some people will tell you they feel called to be parents.

Many don't but have kids anyway. And some just roll the dice and say, if we have kids, great; if not, great. Really? The biggest decision of your life and you'll just . . . see? We don't even leave *entrees* to chance. You sit down at a restaurant and you choose. You can't say, "Bring me whatever, or, nothing. Doesn't matter if I eat."

You have made choices. Regardless of what you think of them now, they were the best ones you could make at the time. You didn't mess up. You didn't choose the "wrong" thing. You didn't miss your calling like a phone you couldn't get to quick enough. Just as you may not feel one way about one thing forever, you don't need to divine a Singular Higher Purpose to give your life meaning. You might feel drawn in one direction or repelled by another. But be wary of using the language of callings, which almost *always* reflects agenda and bias, implying that some things are worth pursuing and some are not. What's far more important than trying to suss out some faint calling in the wind is dialing directly into what's happening right now and what you decide to do about it.

Make no mistake: The world will spam the shit out of you, calling at all hours from an unknown caller ID, calling with its own needs and with no regard for yours. The challenge isn't that you're *not* being called, but that you've got so many things ringing you can't hear yourself think. And your own fears and doubts are static on the line. But to see yourself as the one who must be called—to be a marketing manager or a dentist or to go back to school for your master's—is to deny yourself the chance to call the shots yourself.

What I couldn't possibly have known or expected was that my life would, in fact, resemble Sister Terry's more than those of any other women I grew up with, most of whom went on to marry and mother. And while I don't live a religious (or celibate) life, I crave my own company and a quiet room to return to, rather than the loving tumble of family. While I have no interest in sharing a house with half a dozen other women either, I do maintain a kind of convent of solitude that I wouldn't trade for the world.

I wonder if Sister Terry went home and laughed about the question with the other nuns that night, as they stirred Coffee mate into chipped mugs and muscled through our math homework. If she thought about it later, by herself, and marveled at it, the wonder of how any of us ends up where we do, and comes to love it. That the questions were perhaps the most interesting of all, especially when they came from unlikely sources, from a kid like me—skinny ponytails, Orphan Annie glasses—and how we never quite know what life was waiting for us, what life we might choose.

write your next chapter

List jobs you've daydreamed about. Write down all the things you've *ever* considered doing or being—whether it was an astronaut or fashion designer, a teacher or a dairy farmer, or when you very seriously considered the military. Just dump a whole list of things you ever considered, whether they were "serious" or not.

grab a notebook

Pick one that jumps out at you from the list. Which one seems resonant or meaningful, whether you had real intentions, never did, or still do? I don't mean the one that matches what you do now. Don't think about whether it's practical or realistic—none of that. The one that you still get a kick out of, that seemed fun or interesting. Maybe you do some version of it now.

grab a notebook

Write about what you imagined it to be like. Just freewheel a bit about it—what appealed, what you pictured or pretended it would be. What you think you would have liked or disliked about it. Set a timer for seven minutes. Start writing.

grab a notebook

Explore the themes that rise to the top. In writing about it, what came up? Are there things about that work or profession that still appeal to you on some level? Are there elements that actually *have* found their way into your life? For instance, you might not be an actual rocket scientist, but you may love coordinating launches for businesses. Perhaps you're not a foreign diplomat, but part of your job now is brokering agreements between people who speak very different languages.

grab a notebook

Think about a time someone told you what they thought you should do or be. It might have been a compliment, a shared joke, or even a directive (that you either heeded or ignored). Chances are, lots of people have opinions about what you "should" spend, do, or be. Think of one time or suggestion that stands out (or one that kept coming up), whether it was good, bad, or neutral. See if you can remember the circumstances, maybe how it came up, and most important, what it made you think about. Did you agree with them? Did you hope it was true? Or did you pray it wasn't? Set a timer for ten minutes and start writing.

grab a notebook

Compare what you dreamed of doing versus what you were told or encouraged to do. What themes or topics or similarities emerge between what you thought you might do and what other people thought you should? There is no one right answer to this. As I've said, no one knows more than you do about how you'd like to live your life. What I'm interested in here are either the things that resonate—or where you see a striking difference.

What are some of the things you're glad you didn't do, advice you didn't take, and what does revisiting these ideas and memories tell you about what you might want to do next?

grab a notebook

CHAPTER 11

Making a Living vs. Living Your Life

Be sure there's at least a tiny part of you that's off-limits to the marketplace. Some little piece that you keep for yourself.

—Austin Kleon, *Keep Going*

There's a scene in Irving Stone's *The Agony and the Ecstasy*, the famous historical novel about Michelangelo's life, that I love.

The great sculptor is fourteen years old. He has been released from his painting apprenticeship and admitted to work in Lorenzo the Magnificent's sculpture garden, which is where he's been dying to be (and which, I imagine, would be like getting a pretty cool writing job but then being tapped to join the writing room at *SNL*).

One of Michelangelo's peers, a kid (unfortunately) named Soggi, suggests they ditch this gig.

"Michelangelo, let's you and I get out of here," he says. "All this stuff is so . . . so impractical. Let's save ourselves while there is still time. . . . They're never going to give us any commissions or money. Who really needs sculpture in order to live?"

"I do,"[1] Michelangelo responds.

Soggi then lays out an argument that is as real today as it was in the 1400s. He says (I'm paraphrasing), *Oh yeah? Where will we find work? What if Lorenzo dies? What if the garden closes? Who the heck needs a marble cutter? We can't feed ourselves with that! It'd be much better to trade in pork or wine or pasta, things people need.*

Michelangelo declines, of course. He says sculpture is not only at the top of his list; there is no list. That's it.

Soggi quits. Their teacher, Bertoldo, says he knows people like Soggi, people who aren't driven by love or affinity for the work, but by "the exuberance of youth," he says. "As soon as this first flush begins to fade, they say to themselves, 'Stop dreaming. Look for a reliable way of life.' "[2]

Those people *should* leave—because the very fact that they see the work as optional means they're not really there to do it.

"One should not become an artist because he can," says Bertoldo, "but because he must."[3]

Michelangelo needed to make a living like anyone—he had a family to support, including a father who berated him, took his money, and demanded more. Michelangelo wasn't running a get-rich-quick sculpting scheme. He just knew what he had to do, and in his mind there was no other choice. There was no contest between sculpture and painting, and he wasn't trying to decide between sculptor and business consultant. We choose from the options we have, and while a great income is nothing to sneeze at, ask anyone who's gotten paid exceedingly well for a job they despise whether it's worth it.

This is nothing new, this tension between doing a thing you love and doing a thing that pays, the wish to combine the two things. There are people on both sides of the argument: Some say that it's a crime to try to wring a profit from every last ability, or to "force" your passion or art to pay for itself. And there are those who argue it's a damn shame not to.

Am I telling you that if you follow your passion to be an underwater basket weaver, the money will follow? No, I most certainly am not. Should you quit everything and try to subsist by being a sculptor? I mean, do *you* think that's a good idea? Because the world doesn't owe any of us a living, let alone a profit for feeling good about this thing we like doing.

It's not a question of talent or whether we're good enough. It's not a question of who is more devoted than someone else, or more deserving of success (debatable). The only question to ask is: *What do you value?* If you only want to do your own art, and that's it, no one says you can't, but you're probably going to want to keep your overhead low. If you're like me, and a skin-care snob who likes having her groceries delivered, well, you need to find ways to subsidize that life. There is no one way to do it; you get to make the trades you want.

Soggi didn't value the artist's life. He didn't value the work or the risk. Now, granted, we don't go to Florence to see what Soggi created. But Michelangelo didn't create his art because he thought a bunch of tourists in the twenty-first century would want it. *He* needed to do it, for *him*, and of course his work was praised and paid for too. He found his audience and made a living (and don't tell me he didn't sometimes loathe his clients).

Who knows what became of Soggi? We don't know if he would have turned out to be a world-famous artist if he'd stayed in the garden with Michelangelo, and that wasn't what he was after, anyway. Maybe he turned out to be one hell of a pork salesman. Or fell in love ten times, or died in his own vomit on a cobbled road at midnight. Michelangelo made the choice that was right for him (and which we were the beneficiaries of). Soggi made his own choices too—and so do we.

The Risk of Trying to Profit from Every Ability

The world doesn't owe us a living to do what we want, yet we seem to be under the illusion that we're supposed to be doing, and profiting from, everything we like doing.

This is part of the opportunity, and the problem, of the world we live in right now. In *Keep Going: 10 Ways to Stay Creative in Good Times and Bad*, Austin Kleon (of *Steal Like an Artist* fame) says that it's not enough to just be good at something—making scarves, baking scones—just for fun, anymore. "The minute anybody shows any talent for anything, we suggest they turn it into a profession. This is our best compliment: telling somebody they're so good at what they love to do they could make money at it."[4] Hobbies have become side hustles; our personalities have to be "brands." And the things we used to do to relax, to unplug and add meaning (outside of what pays the bills), aren't just things we like to do but are "presented to us as potential income streams, or ways out of having a traditional job."[5]

This can come as a risk, he says. "You must be mindful of what potential impact monetizing your passions could have on your life," he writes. "Be sure there's at least a tiny part of you that's off-limits to the marketplace. Some little piece that you keep for yourself."[6]

Fran Lebowitz has said many times that she loved writing—*until she got paid for it*. Then she hated it. And she hasn't written a book in thirty years.

For some people, what they do and enjoy is so precious to them that they refuse to turn it into a living. Take my sister Lori, for example. She's a *supremely* gifted and skilled singer. When I hit puberty, I got feathered hair. When she hit puberty, she got the big, smoky, sonorous voice of a thirty-five-year-old Broadway songstress. She even seemed bewildered by it. When she played Mabel in *The Pirates of Penzance* her sophomore year, it got people's attention. The music director called a friend from NYU's Tisch School to come hear Lori sing, and he did—and told her if she wanted to pursue that path she had a chance.

It was thrilling and flattering—and terrifying. Because not a bone in her body wanted to go do that. So while Michelangelo may have been all in on Lorenzo's sculpture garden, Lori really had no interest in diving into a life on Broadway. She wanted to do what her older sisters had done: go to Boston College and major in something like human development (which she did), sleep in a dorm, go to tailgates with friends. She loved singing, and reigned during her undergraduate tenure as one of the superstars of her a cappella group. If she wanted to pursue a career as a performer or recording artist, she might have had a chance, as harrowing as that path might be.

On a whim her senior year, Lori joined every college kid within fifty miles of Boston at a public casting call for *The Real World*. And . . . she got called back. Then she got called back again. And again. What started as a funny thing to do became real. We started to think, *Holy shit. Is this happening?*

And then *she got it*. She did the impossible and got cast in the ten-year anniversary season of MTV's *The Real World*, which remains the first, and longest-running, reality TV show, bar none. This wasn't a singing audition; they picked people based on a mix of personalities and potential for compelling on-screen drama. And she was precisely what they were looking for. She had no idea of what she was getting into; none of us did. It was a taste of fame that shocked her when it happened, and which she quite honestly did not love.

"The day after the first episode aired, a few girls stopped me in a parking lot for my autograph, and that threw me," she said. "Then we did a bunch of press for the show and all of a sudden my face was in *Seventeen* and on the cover of *TV Guide*. It was sudden and scary." What she learned was what she already knew: She's a very private person who did not thrive in the celeb spotlight. "I said to myself, this sucks, and I don't want it."

When she thought about what it might look like to even consider a professional singing career, even the best-case scenario wasn't appealing. "Oh God, it just seemed like a nightmare to me," she told me. "Even if it worked out the way you'd hope—and there was no guarantee it would—and if . . . *if* . . . I had the opportunity to make a living as a recording artist, I would have been miserable." She'd have had to travel, stay out late, live on a tour bus, or go to the theater seven days a week and twice on Sundays. "None of that appealed to me. I wanted to be home and in bed early. I wanted kids and a dog and a house. I'd have to want that career so badly that I'd sacrifice literally everything for it, which I wasn't willing to do—plus stress out about my voice, afraid to shout or drink or get a cold. If I depended on singing for a living, I would have come to resent it."

So, she sings when she feels like it. But here's the thing that irks her: When people press her or, worse, judge her on why she didn't pursue it.

"I know people mean it as a compliment, like, hey, you've got a great voice, you're as good as anyone I've heard on TV. But what I don't get is when people say, 'You should have gone professional,' or even more puzzling to me, 'Why don't you do it now?' Um, because I don't want to?" she says. It's not like it never crossed her mind. "But I'm also a grown-up and made my choices on purpose," she said. "Frankly, I resent the implication that I should have done something else, or worse, that I'm crazy or stupid for not pursuing a career as a professional singer. You can have a gift, a talent, and not have to make a living from it."

What this all comes down to is that it really isn't about what you do, but what you *value*, and what you want your actual life to look like. So maybe you have a gift and you'd like to pursue it—ask yourself why. So that it would feel validating, that you "could" do this? Do you want the life that goes along with it? Turning something you feel passionate about into a profitable business is not necessarily everyone's goal, nor should it be.

Saying you should turn something you love into a business is like assuming that if you're best friends with someone you'd also make good roommates—or good business partners (I can tell you from experience, this is an emphatic *no*). Just because you have shared a room at the Ritz for so-and-so's bachelorette does *not* mean you should share a lease or a bank account.

In fact, what better way to use a gift than to make a gift *of* it, and use it in ways that enrich your life and others'? You don't have to work strictly with oil paints or Carrara marble to call yourself an artist. Seth Godin defines artists as "people with a genius for finding a new answer, a new connection, or a new way of getting things done."[7] They don't do the work because they have to, to check a box or to comply, but because they want to do it. If you're getting paid for it, he says, it's not a gift anymore; it's a job.

Today my sister works at a pharmaceutical company, doing something that even she has trouble describing. When she first started working there, she became friendly with the people who sat nearby, and couldn't help but overhear that they were drowning in work and completely overwhelmed. So she offered to help. And the more she helped, the more interested in the work she became, especially when she realized she had a knack for it—for spotting problems, analyzing data, identifying opportunities for improvement.

It wouldn't have sounded like a dream job on paper, but she finds it incredibly satisfying to do the job well, which she does. She's earned promotions, bonuses, and some of the highest honors her company awards, and the fact is, the job suits her. "I wouldn't say I'm 'passionate' about my job," she says, "but I do it passionately." And she gets the life she wants, which includes piling onto the sofa at night in a house she loves with her kids and dogs to watch TV. You might think the life of a professional singer would be more glamorous, and it might be. But easier? Better? Not a chance.

write your next chapter

The Sweet Spot

What are some things you do simply for the joy of doing them? Could be anything: cooking, singing, doing puzzles, taking apart computers and putting them back together again. You may teach for free but learn languages for fun. Literally anything you will make time to do for no other reason than you like doing it.

grab a notebook

OK. Choose one of the items from your list at a time, and walk through this with me:

- WHY YOU DO IT. Let's leave money out of the equation for a moment. So the "why" should have nothing to do with what it can get in the marketplace, or because it pays the rent, or because you think you could make a lot doing it. Why do you do, and enjoy doing, that thing? How does it make you feel to do it? How do you feel before, during, and after said activity?

grab a notebook

- WHAT IT COSTS. I mean cost to *you*. Meaning: the investment of time, supplies, equipment, education. This is not for budgeting purposes; I just want to look at what you give *to* this thing that gives something back.

grab a notebook

- **WHAT IT PAYS (IF ANYTHING).** Again, we are not measuring the value of what you do or its worth by what someone will pay you to do it. That's not our goal right now. Do you trade on this activity or skill in the marketplace (whether for cash, credit, trade, or access; i.e., if you sing here you can use our piano for free)? List those things.

grab a notebook

- **THE EFFECT OF BEING PAID.** If you have been paid to do it, how did being paid affect the work? Did it make you feel good (which isn't a given, by the way; see: Fran Lebowitz). Did the validation make the work something you wanted to do more of or less of? Did it draw more work to it and you—and, here's a critical question, was that a good thing? How has being paid changed your relationship to that activity, including how often you do it, how you feel about it? And is that change a good thing?

grab a notebook

- **THE EARNING POTENTIAL.** If you're not living off said activity, is that a real goal? We all think it would be better to be paid than not to be paid, but I'm not sure I agree. When you agree to terms with someone who will pay you, you're not always as free as when you do it on your terms, regardless of or without payment. You may not want your living to depend on it but might like it as a side hustle. What would you gain by doing it? What would you have to give up? How would the cost/investment on your part change if you were going to do that? Does it appeal?

grab a notebook

- **WHAT YOU VALUE MOST.** Apart from this or any of the skills or activities on your list, what do you value most? Maybe it's free time. Maybe it's money. Maybe it's time with specific people, or time alone. The ability to travel—or to stay home. Or time to do the thing you don't get paid for but that you couldn't live without. Take a moment to write out some of what no one could pay enough to keep you from doing or having.

grab a notebook

You don't have to earn your living from just one thing, and who you are is not dependent on where one big check comes from. In the end, your life will become what you spend time on, not who paid you. Finding that happy mix of things you do, things you invest in, and the ways the world invests in you looks different for everyone. What matters is that you choose it.

CHAPTER 12

How to Stand Out When Everyone's Peddling the Same Shit

Selling is not just a job or a career; selling is essential to the survival and well-being of every living individual.

—Grant Cardone, *Sell or Be Sold*

For a while, I worked for a multilevel-marketing organization that sold sterling silver jewelry to suburban women who often purchased it under the influence of chardonnay. I was aware of the bad reputation MLMs have, preying on the weak with dreams of effortless earnings and then there you are with a garage full of dish soap that you can't move or afford. The good news is that there just wasn't much damage I could do with jewelry. The worst that could happen was that you wore too much and gave yourself a cramp.

Filmmaker Mark Vicente, former member of Albany-based sex cult NXIVM led by psychopath Keith Raniere, said in his documentary, "No one joins a sex cult."[1] No one joins an MLM either. Someone tells you about a cool way to earn money on your own terms, on your own time . . . and then they tell you why it's *not* a pyramid scheme. While statistics and surveys consistently show that only about 10 percent of distributors make more than $100 a week and as many as 99 percent lose money in their MLM business,[2] some make quite a bit of money doing it. But what I appreciate most is the opportunity it gives women to build their own teams and learn to lead them.

You may not see sales as a job, career, or calling for you, but a lot of people do: CNBC reported on research by Glassdoor that more than fifteen million people work in the sales industry in the US alone.[3] That's about 5 percent of the population. These are the people who make things happen, because sales is the engine that keeps the wheels of business turning.

And yet lots of people have a deep aversion to sales. In fact, sales is one job that someone will be proud to tell you they're *bad* at—the implication being that they're simply too honest to do it well. Even people I've met who are really good at sales will sometimes even *apologize for it*, in an attempt to prove that they're a good person even *though* they're in sales. Do you know any plumbers apologizing for being plumbers? What about teachers? Tailors? No.

Even if you never hold a traditional sales role, you're lying to yourself if you think you're not in sales, simply because you actually can't get much of anything you want in your life without it. Sales is not the opposite of authentic or reliable or real. It's not even limited to an industry. It's a skill that can be used for good or ill. There are bad salespeople just like there are bad teachers, bad mechanics, bad boyfriends. And make no mistake: You *do* sell. Just like you improvise: Every. Single. Day.

In *Sell or Be Sold*, entrepreneur, real estate investor, sales deity, and bro king Grant Cardone writes: "Your ability or inability to sell, persuade, negotiate, and convince others will affect every area of your life and will determine how well you survive."[4] Sales is not a specific career track or a department or a type of person; it's something we do and *must* do to survive. Maybe not always for monetary reward; we sell people things we don't personally profit from all the time. The reason I have a Peloton in my apartment and ILIA's True Skin Serum on my face is because my sisters sold me on it. And they didn't make a dime. You sell your friends on a movie. Sell your kid on going to bed early. Sell your boss on the idea of having an off-site retreat. There's no shame in that game. "A sale is made in every exchange of ideas or communication—there are no exceptions,"[5] Cardone says.

The MLM I was part of didn't require that I hand over collateral or my life savings or cut off all contact with my family. All you had to do was fill out a form and buy your starter kit. There wasn't a master plan or really any intellectual rigor there; it was jewelry, not juju. It was shopping as entrepreneurship. We put signs on our tables that said: "Your husband called—he said get anything you want!" (which is wrong on so many levels #patriarchy). I didn't make millions, nor was I coerced into sex acts with anyone, least of all the company's founders, two women in their fifties with spunky haircuts who lived in Kansas City and were more obsessed with accessorizing than world domination.

There was not, however, a shred of evidence in my life up to then that would have given anyone, including me, the slightest clue that I'd be good at or ultimately go into sales of any kind. I'd just earned my MFA in poetry, and was working in the creative department of a wig company. I often wrote catalog copy in iambic pentameter. The jewelry was a fun way to make a little extra money and upgrade my wardrobe. What I didn't realize was that this hands-on training would help me bust through my own mental block around sales and competition, around what it means to sell a thing when you know for a fact other people like you are selling the same thing.

The Hero's . . . Jaunt

You've heard, perhaps, of "the hero's journey"—a commonly known story structure that comes from mythology, in which a hero (usually male) strikes out on a journey, undergoes an ordeal, reaches an epiphany, and returns home with this new truth or wisdom. I have scaled down the Odyssean tale here and adapted the journey for our purposes, let's call it the Hero's Jaunt, to take you through the phases of almost anything you sign on to do or offer. This isn't necessarily how *your* Hero's Jaunt will go, but the general strokes of it are hardly unique to me.

Step 1: A Shiny Object Snags Your Attention

"That's a beautiful ring," I said. My friend Karen worked in production at the wig company. She paid fine attention to detail and chose very tasteful, interesting jewelry. The ring was simple but elegant, with a blue stone in the center.

"Oh, thank you," she said, admiring her hand. "Chalcedony."

Chal-*what*-dony? I wasn't schooled on semiprecious (as a rule, I really don't like to get precious about anything). I was thirty and it had only recently occurred to me that every piece of jewelry I owned came from Claire's at the mall. It was time, I thought, to invest in myself in ways that matched my age, by owning things that would actually last. I was selling myself on this idea, which is really all selling ever is.

"I'm actually having a jewelry party next week, if you want to come," Karen said. "What does that even mean?" I asked. It meant that she was having friends over to hang out, drink margaritas, and look at jewelry. A trunk show, she called it. And I went.

Every surface of Karen's living room was teeming with shiny objects. The sales rep, laden herself—stacked bangles, concentric necklaces—was eight months pregnant. Once she finished setting up, she parked herself on the couch and watched sleepily as we swarmed the merchandise. A pair of peridot earrings caught my eye. A silver ring crowned with a chunk of blue-green labradorite. A tiered necklace studded with lapis and pearl. I picked them up, tried them on. They felt dense. Weighted. Real.

Everyone knew the Tupperware "party plan" model, which is what this was: gather women into a room like a school of groupers, whip them into a bait ball, and then make a dive for their disposable income. But that rep wasn't whipping anyone into anything. And I was surprised, especially when I knew that the job that paid the most wasn't selling earrings, but selling the "opportunity" to the right people. People like me, manhandling her display and asking a lot of questions.

The pieces were moderately priced, anywhere from $29 to $200. There were nine people in the room. I did the math: An average night of sales could be anywhere from $300 to $1,000. A 30 percent commission meant a take-home profit of $90 to $300 for having women shop your personal jewelry collection.

"You should do this," the rep yawned. That was the extent of her pitch.

Step 2: You Sign Up

If she'd been smart, or interested (and she may have been neither), she'd have followed up with me the next day, and every day after, to tell me about my earning potential. But she did not.

Instead, I called the 800 number—they picked right up—and said, "I think I might want to do this, but can you stick me with someone with a little ambition?" And they did: a stern, no-nonsense woman named Anne with a square jaw and a Protestant work ethic.

I had very little in common with the other reps: I wasn't married, I didn't have kids, and had no interest in either. I wasn't looking to get back into the workforce: I was already in it. Soon after I started selling jewelry, I left my nice copywriting job to be an associate editor at a magazine—a career investment that would cost me quite a bit; to take it, I also had to take a $15,000 pay cut. It was jewelry or bust.

The sales reps I met had very different lifestyles and lived in three-bedroom homes, but like me, they loved the idea that potential was both recognized and unlimited. It wouldn't have mattered what we were selling: soap, candles, skin care, durable plastic containers, or silver jewelry. This was the dream, right?

Sell something you like to people like you. And make 30 percent commission.

Step 3: You Hit Your First Roadblock

Ever thought you were all in on something and then realized you didn't know WTF you were doing? Been there.

A coworker hosted my first jewelry party. I painstakingly set up the display as I'd been shown: Velvet boards strewn with chains, a dish of stacking silver rings. Hoops and studs and silver cuffs laid out like rows of stunning punctuation.

And then you know what I did? Not a goddamned thing.

I left that gorgeous display standing there all dressed up and neglected like my prom date in 1990. I felt a creeping awareness—like when the crotch of your tights starts to fall—that while I wasn't unwelcome, I had an agenda. And I wasn't sure how I felt about that.

It became clear to me then just how far *liking* a thing was from *selling* it. You might as well say you wanted to be a doctor because you look stunning in a white coat. It's not about the coat. Show me someone with a lot of passion and zero skills and I'll show you a lousy salesperson. I froze up and committed one of the greatest sins of sales (and a lie you're told): I assumed that if the product was good it would sell itself. Nothing sells itself.

That party was a bust. I sold a single pair of hoops to a woman who had recently lost one of hers. And my hostess got 30 percent of zero out of the deal.

I packed all that jewelry up and rolled home.

Every new rep had Velveteen Rabbit dreams of making their business real, meaning you sold things to strangers and didn't always have to ask your cousin for a favor. So even though I worried that I sucked at this, I kept booking parties. I was in it now. Next goal: move beyond your immediate circle of influence. A month or so later, I did a party for someone's sister-in-law—and that's when things changed.

Step 4: You Have a Breakthrough Moment

A pretty, silver-haired woman sidled up to the table, looking less like she was shopping and more like she was taking in a live butterfly exhibit. When she got to the showpiece known as the Silver Cascade, sparkling on its own headless display, she leaned in closer.

"Would you like to try it on?" I asked.

"Well, OK, why not," she said. She slid it off the velvet bust tentatively, then clasped it behind her neck. She picked up the handheld mirror (pro tip: always keep one on the table).

"Oh, isn't that beautiful." She ran her fingers along the tiered chains. "But I couldn't wear this. My sister could, but not me."

In truth, I never expected anyone to buy that necklace. That was a bar-setting item, the most expensive one ($225!). ("Don't sell out of your own pocket," my mother would tell me later. "You have no idea what people will buy.")

"Look," I said. "Since your sister isn't here, I have no idea what she would wear. All I know is you can wear it. You *are* wearing it, right now. So why couldn't you wear it any other day too?"

She bought that necklace. And a few other things.

The moment the sales game turned was the moment I realized this had nothing to do with me. Sales wasn't talking people into things they didn't want; it was helping them see they could have what they *already* wanted. It had everything to do with who—and how—the person in front of you wanted to be in the world. And that we were all the same people we were as kids, which meant you could be a full-grown adult and still be hamstrung by the belief that your sister was better than you.

I also learned that sales weren't wholly dependent on the goods themselves, no matter how good they were. Sales were fueled by emotions (why do you think we sold at parties full of friends and stocked with wine?). People wanted more of the things that made them feel good, and they felt good based on what they told themselves. Cardone says "salespeople, not the prospect, are the ultimate barriers to every sale."[6] And so I got out of the fucking way.

Was I into the jewelry? Was I *passionate* about it? I can't say I was. I was interested enough, but honestly, if Karen had hosted a sex toy party I might have been hawking dildos instead. I discovered a taste for running my own show, which, unbeknownst to me, then a contented W-2 employee, would serve me later in the many 1099 years ahead. But most important, I didn't have a latent talent for jewelry sales; I had an innate ability to connect and I applied it to a hard skill. You can do the same, no matter what you're interested in doing, making, or offering.

Step 5: You Start Cooking with Gas

In *The Motivation Myth*, Jeff Haden says it's really tempting to assume that successful people have some "special" quality that makes them successful, something that, well . . . you don't have. And this idea, he says, is simply untrue. Success "looks inevitable only after it is achieved," he writes—and talent "reveals itself in hindsight."[7] No one would have said to the poet with an MFA and a job in publishing that she clearly had a strong future in jewelry sales. But did I discover I could do it, once I knew how to do it, and experience the rewards? You bet.

I was on a *roll*. I sold so much damn jewelry I earned the free, all-expenses-paid trip to Saint Thomas. "Wow, this is fucking sweet," my boyfriend said on our veranda overlooking Magens Bay. "Good job." I had also started building a team, and enrolled six other reps in my very own adorable downline, including a woman I met at a bar, another I met at Staples, and someone else who followed me around a party in Rhode Island for four hours. While I was still entry level at my day job, I'd essentially promoted myself to manager in my side gig.

I had upped my game—and also mastered the art of layering. You needed to *wear* your inventory for opportunities to find you. It can't sell itself if it's in a box in your house. And since we reps were literally all wearing the same jewelry, layering was how you made it your own. You could spot a newbie on sight: They were wearing one necklace, a single bracelet. The most successful among us didn't pick up their dry cleaning without at least ten to twenty pieces on at a time. We all jingled like a set of janitor's keys when we walked into the room. We tried to outdo and impress one another at regional meetings. *Whoa! Check out Gail layering the locket with the beaded double loop* and *the silver choker. Damn! Well played, Gail.*

And this is how sales begets sales: because the more I wore the jewelry, the more conversations I was having with people about the jewelry, and the more interest I was seeding, and that interest turned into parties—and sales. There was a confidence and security in sheer numbers, in worrying less about individual customers or leads and focusing on keeping the interest coming.

Step 6: You Go from Breakthrough to Needing a Break

My boyfriend is a New York City cop, and he won't wear his uniform on his way to my apartment (much to my dismay) because if he's wearing it, anyone at any time on the streets of Manhattan can drag him into a situation he wants nothing to do with. I, too, had fantasies of removing my metal armor. The comment, "Wow, I love your necklace! Where'd you get it?" was sometimes music to my ears, but they were also the opening bars to a song you knew and had to dance to every time, even while you were in line to buy super plus tampons at CVS.

Remember, I was doing this in my free time, after hours. A girl gets tired. Just when you were wondering if this was worth it, it was time to head to Kansas City for the annual conference, where thousands of jangling women wearing their weight in silver descended on Kansas City to recharge their batteries and to see the brand-new collection the moment it launched. The night of the reveal, our anticipation rose like carbonation in a bottle of prosecco. When the auditorium doors finally opened, we poured in, fizzy with excitement, to Shania Twain's "Man! I Feel Like a Woman!" Balloons fell from the ceiling. Ice sculptures of mermaids towered over tiers of silver trays loaded with mini cupcakes.

"Oh my *God*, there's a chocolate fountain!" one woman squealed. This was *Willy Wonka* for middle-aged women.

Step 7: You Identify Your Role Models—and Eye Your Competition

At the awards ceremony, the prize for the biggest everything—sales, downline—went (of course) to Lana Larraday (not her real name), a woman from the Cape who looked genetically engineered to showcase silver. She stood five-foot-ten, with a glistening mane of jet-black hair and a year-round tan (rumor had it she was part Cherokee). She'd been a waitress prior to her sales success, had four sons, a daughter, and a husband with a blue-collar job, and wore her humility softly around the edges like her Boston accent. Lana had been taking nearly every top award for *years*. She'd risen like a rocket through the organization; they had to keep inventing titles for her: She shot past Silver Manager and Sterling Leader in two years, and they were like OK, now you're Star Director, now Duchess of Sheen; I think they finally crowned her Queen of the Galaxy.

Lana had done more than a half a million in sales during her jewelry career (about six years by then)—which seemed like a lot, but what I didn't realize then was that that came to $150,000 in commissions total, or about $25,000 per year, of course not counting what she must have earned from her team. Still, all any of us could say was that Lana had earned six figures in her business. Six. Figures. The holy grail. She might as well have been a millionaire.

I'll add (proudly) that Massachusetts, where I lived, was leading the nation in jewelry sales. And Lana had everything to do with it. She had personally recruited more than one hundred representatives, each of whom had reps of their own, and on and on it went. You could trace your upline to Lana like in the King James Bible—Lana begat Gail, who begat Denise, who begat Methuselah, who begat Methuselah's sister-in-law, who begat Anne, who begat me. We were all basically related.

Step 8: Scarcity Thinking Sets In

As the success in our corner of the Northeast market grew, so did the scarcity thinking. Fear of the regional market getting too "saturated" and that too many successful reps meant no business "left" for anyone else. This is where "we're all in this together" turns into doubt, fear, and scarcity thinking.

The sales leaders, our uplines, told us that those fears were unfounded. We were part of a thriving group who generated the most sales in the country for this organization—and for ourselves. We did have more reps than other states, but that still wasn't many when you considered *the entire population of Massachusetts.* What I noticed was that the complaints came mainly from those who weren't doing as well. It was not a coincidence. These were the ones who seemed to think that being a leader was circumstantial; that if they had simply been earlier they would have naturally been Lana Larraday. Doubt it.

I could have decided to join the scarcity or the abundance club, and I made my choice, simply because the smaller, more fearful mindset was not where I wanted to hang out. I also believed that more sales and salespeople signaled *more* interest—and, if anything, created *more* demand for the product. There were only so many days in a week and hours in a day, and you couldn't *be* everywhere all the time, nor would you want to be. There was enough to go around, I said. Second, I knew that anything worth doing was going to be competitive. Period. Good luck trying to sell a thing no one knows they want. You have to do *twice* the work; you have to sell the idea and yourself as the one to provide it.

This all seemed to stem from, and promote a falsehood

about, women and competition; namely, that there's only room for a few women to do well. This is internalized sexism, something that's been in the water so long we don't even taste it anymore. I realized I could assume the party was crowded and get out or I could keep going and find my own opportunities, and that's what I did. Where other reps contracted in fear, I expanded, because of what I saw the leaders above me doing—and they were never skimping or gripping or greedy with other reps; they knew there was more than enough for everyone. They saw themselves as leaders. And you can't lead if you're the only one in the room.

This perspective helped me years later when I started making a living selling my wares as a writer, speaker, and brand advisor—in New York, where you can throw a rock out my window and hit another person who does the same thing. And it can help you too. Because it doesn't matter if it's jewelry sales, or consulting clients, or anything else you can compete on: People get fearful and jealous when they're confronted with other people doing similar things. That's a natural feeling, but you get to decide how to respond to it.

What I've found as a business owner and consultant in New York City who finds herself around more women than men is that those who, like Lana Larraday, offer, extend, and support without fear are the ones who do far better—they have a strong and supportive network, a steady and reliable source of clients and income. When times get tough, they don't pull back but give more, support more, and it comes back to them in ways they couldn't have predicted. They're the ones who see themselves as leaders, and you can't hoard information and knowledge, be suspicious of everyone, and call yourself a leader. At least, not a good one.

Look, we all feel the squeeze from time to time. I get jealous and nervous and competitive like anyone. It's normal and fine. But whenever I feel that contraction, that tightness that makes me worry—that I'm behind, or that there's not enough for me or everyone's better and I'll never (blah blah fill in the blank)—I make it a point to push *against* that contraction. I take a big, gulping, loose-lunged breath. Because when you're feeling tight/scared/worried, you end up sipping air through a straw, which only makes you feel more panicky.

Just feeling more expansive inside your body, letting in all the air, more than you'll ever need, is the first step. Then, rather than give in to the clench, I take an action, any single action, that runs counter to what my fear is telling me. So if I'm having an "I'm behind on everything" day, I do something to push someone else forward. If I'm having an "I don't have enough" day, I find a way to give, freely and without restraint, to somebody who needs it. Why? Because I'm some kind of saint or martyr, or a ridiculously nice person? No, actually, I'm none of these things. It's not an act of kindness or self-denial either. It's an act that counters the squeeze, that pushes back—hard. And I do it because I don't let anyone else tell me how to live or what choices I have, so why would I allow the squeeze to have that kind of power? I do it to remind myself that I decide what to think and how to respond, and because if I believe there isn't enough for me then there won't be. When you act as though there's enough, and give as though you have plenty to give, things change.

I had a very nice friend for a while. She liked being nice and being known for being nice. She excelled at thoughtful, well-timed notes and flowers. She had a memory like a steel cage. And yet I found, over years of observation, that when it came down to real generosity, when the act of giving required bravery, not just a handwritten card, she came up short. I don't put a lot of stock in nice because people tend to be nice when it's easy. Generous has far more to recommend it. Spend too much time with people who are proud of being nice and you might learn better manners, but there's often a calculation beneath it, a metric that must be measured to be appreciated, and I don't work like that. I'd rather spend my time with someone who gives recklessly than carefully. And I'd also rather be one of those people.

Step 9: You Go Out on a High Note

Back at the annual conference in 2004, the jewelry company was on the rise, breaking records, and so were its reps—even me.

I was halfway through a devil's food cupcake at the awards ceremony when I heard my name.

". . . And the second place for Rookie Recruiter of the Year goes to . . . Terri Trespicio!"

What! I was not expecting that. "Me?!" I got excited and stupid and couldn't find the stairs like a giddy actress on the Golden Globes.

The award was announced by the company's CEO, the husband of one of the founders. Why the founders *weren't* the CEOs I have no idea. The more I think about that, the more it bothers me. Because Girl Power is not handing over the business decisions to your husband. ("Larry, you handle that stuff. We need to curate the new line!")

Once I got my award and my picture taken, the CEO said, "This surely isn't the last you've heard from this young lady."

And yet they never heard from me again.

I'm proud of having earned that distinction early on, but even though I am pretty competitive, it wasn't the goal. Remember what Lance Armstrong said about missing the work, not the medals? Remember sweet, couldn't-hurt-a-fly Seth Godin with his hookless fly-fishing rod? The prize is not the point. At the same time, what it teaches you is that you can achieve distinction on the way to becoming someone you're proud of being.

Step 10: You Take Your Skills to Go

Just as Keith Raniere moved on from his initial illegal pyramid scheme, which collapsed under the weight of its federal investigations in 1996, so that he could start his sex cult, I, too, moved on to new goals. I focused on my work at the magazine, where all kinds of new opportunities were popping up and required minimal accessorizing.

The party plan industry has shifted for several reasons: more women working longer hours, and the steady migration of our businesses (and shopping) online—making meet-at-Susan's-to-shop tougher to do. COVID-19 was of course a party killer. People still sell in that model, and MLMs continue with varying degrees of success—but now the method and format have changed, and reps find themselves having to reinvent how they do business virtually. And as with every team or organization, you'll see a few rise to the top.

It was around this time that the magazine I'd been working for was attempting to sell itself—to Martha Stewart. And she bit. That changed things considerably at the magazine, and new opportunities opened up. So instead of selling birthstone rings, I sold *myself*—first as a senior editor, then as a radio host, as TV talent, as someone equipped to promote the newly branded magazine. Soon I was doing regular national TV appearances, and hosting my own daily radio show on SiriusXM. When Martha decided to move the magazine to New York and the new editor reinterviewed me for my job, I'd call that one of the greatest sales of my life—and I closed it. I got to move to New York and keep my job. It didn't happen because I sat still and waited for people to notice me, either, but rather, because I had learned how to position myself the way you might a necklace—by showing how it would make someone else look good.

Years later, when I got laid off, I had my own wax-on, wax-off moment, when I realized I could use what I'd learned in my side gig, that the skill of selling transferred from chalcedony to consulting contracts. Being a successful solo business owner means you have to be as versatile as a solid silver cuff—dress it up, dress it down, pair it with everything. I found there was no limit to what I could do if someone thought they'd look better having hired me to do it, whatever it was. I realized I could do and liked to do a lot of things, and the fun part was making it work for the people who wanted to work with me. It doesn't actually matter what I sell anymore, as long as I enjoy it and it works for the person who needs it.

It's worth honing skills and getting better at what you like to do. But the sooner you realize it's not just about jewelry or job titles, the faster you free yourself up from being a one-trick pony; then you can start finding opportunity wherever you go. That way you can stop looking in the mirror and saying, "Oh no, I couldn't do that, but I bet my sister could." You start to realize you can wear this or that or whatever you want, and pull just about anything off.

write your next chapter

What's on Sale? (Literally Everything)

The word "sell" is polarizing, and most women I know, even the ones who own their own business, are terrified that someone will think they're trying to do it. We don't have to love sales any more than you have to love your toothbrush to use one; our success relies on how well we apply that skill.

Think about the last three things you sold. Maybe it was a set of deck chairs on Craigslist. A consulting package to a client. You may have convinced a company to give you a full refund, or your boss to give you a promotion. You might have gotten the entire crew to agree on a movie or restaurant, and that is not easy. Maybe your biggest sale was getting your partner to go all in on a trip to the Bahamas. List as many as you can think of—no fewer than three, in the past year.

grab a notebook

Pick one you're *most* proud of. Why that one? What did you do that worked, and how did you know it was working? If you bumped up against resistance, how did you pivot? What ultimately worked? What surprised you most about it?

grab a notebook

OK, next, think of *one* upcoming idea, negotiation, or decision that you're pitching, persuading, investing in.

- **WHAT'S THE NUMBER ONE REASON THIS MATTERS RIGHT NOW?** What do you stand to gain?
- **WHAT ARE THE STAKES?** What do you risk if it doesn't happen?
- **WHAT DO YOU WANT TO HAPPEN,** and what will you be happy with? What would you say your top motivation is?
- **WHAT DOES THE OTHER PERSON (OR PEOPLE) WANT MOST?** Could be anything from "Look good to her superiors" to "Look good to her kids"; could also be to earn money, to expand her own influence, or, in some cases, to cover his ass. Maybe they just want to make you happy, or keep the peace.
- **HOW WILL YOU POSITION THIS** in the best way possible to ensure your success here in getting buy-in, influence, or otherwise nailing it?
- **HOW WILL YOU KNOW YOU'VE SUCCEEDED?**

grab a notebook

Being flexible and open is as important as being prepared, but so is knowing what you stand to gain, why you're doing it, and how you'll know when you've succeeded—or how you'll compromise, which makes it a win-win.

CHAPTER 13

Never Rely on Anyone Again

What we want, what we need, what we must have are indispensable human beings.

—Seth Godin, *Linchpin*

There's this unicorn of an idea that when you work for yourself, you have no one to answer to *but* yourself. The only time that's true is when you have no work. That's not ideal.

What happens if or when you leave full-time employment (or it leaves you) and you decide to pursue self-employment is that you have many *more* people to answer to, in fact. And unless you're independently wealthy and don't need a dime, we're all dependent on *someone* to pay us for something. In short, you want people to come to rely on you in some way. The degree to which we can find success in that regard, full-time, part-time, or otherwise, is to be someone that someone else chooses not to do without. Seth Godin refers to this person as the *linchpin* (in his book of the same name). "What we want, what we need, what we must have," he writes, "are indispensable human beings."[1]

His point is that if we think we can be compliant and safe and do what everyone's always done and *also* be indispensable, we're mistaken. What being indispensable requires is risk, creativity, innovation, and the courage to deliver something only you can. Can I tell you how to do that? Yes and no—for the same reason Godin says you can find lots of cookbooks, but no *chef* books. There is no singular, fail-proof recipe for being a chef.

In their 2019 piece, "The Feedback Fallacy," in *Harvard Business Review*, Marcus Buckingham and Ashley Goodall point out that we spend so much of our lives pursuing excellence, thinking it's "hard" to achieve, when quite the opposite is true. "We've got it backward," they write. "Excellence in any endeavor is almost impossible to define, and yet getting there, for each of us, is relatively easy."[2] Excellence, by their definition, is idiosyncratic, in that it is "inextricably and wonderfully intertwined with whoever demonstrates it."[3]

And just as you come to appreciate someone's excellence and count on their ability, they can come to rely on yours. But there's a fine line between having appreciation and dependence. There's a liability in relying too much on one person or source to be everything to you, and vice versa.

"Talk to me about what's going on with your hair," Kelly said, tossing her glossy black bangs and looking at my reflection. I had just moved to New York City from the burbs outside Boston, where I'd spent a little too long in Dansko clogs and a serviceable medium-length bob. My bangs stood around my head like introverts at a party, unsure of where to put their hands.

I shrugged. "I think this is all it does."

If my hair could have spoken up then, it would have said I was demanding and lacked vision. It would have bristled at how I'm always checking out other people's hair and making it feel bad.

This wasn't a makeover; this was couple's therapy. Me and my hair, slumped in a chair, aware that the spark had gone out. Kelly wasn't there to cut; she was there to mediate.

"OK," she said. "How do you *want* to look?"

What did I want? I wanted to look like I lived in New York, that I belonged there. I wanted to look strong and sovereign, free and fuckable. To strut down the street with hair that simultaneously turned your head and flipped you the bird.

I have managed expectations when it comes to my hair. But we all hold out hope that we can be more than we think—a dream bolstered by an $85 billion hair industry, which tells us we have limitless potential growing out of the top of our heads when really a houseplant has more potential. Hair is nothing but keratin. It's lifeless tissue, a zombie thing—it's not alive, yet just keeps coming. No wonder I haven't been able to get my hair to *do* anything; it's been dead for years.

We certainly don't think of our hair that way. We think of it as a kind of chrysalis from which we're constantly emerging, as a version of ourselves that can be coaxed into a better version of itself. And so you don't just pay a top stylist to cut your hair; you pay her to have an opinion about it. That is what has made Kelly indispensable to me. She didn't just change my hair; she changed the way I saw it.

"Here's what we're going to do," Kelly said, waving a comb around my head in the sign for "do-over." "We're going to grow all of this out." Grow it out? Like long hair? "Yep," she said. OK. Does that mean I'm paying a stylist to not cut my hair? "I'm going to cut it *long*," she said. And because she's a goddamned artist and master of hair geometry, I swear to God when I left, it looked longer than when I'd arrived.

Fast-forward a few years. My hair has grown into its New York iteration, which is the longest I've had it since 1995. I'm on retainer for a small talent agency to media train their clients. Soon I wasn't just media training; I was helping with content strategy and platform development. I was going on sales calls. Meeting with prospects. I was bringing clients into the fold. I was thrilled that there was more work to be done, and it was fun to apply my existing skill set to new opportunities while adding others. It seemed I was quickly becoming indispensable to them: The more I did, the more they gave me to do. They paid for some of my time—and took pretty much all of it. Being indispensable can be a great thing, because it means our work is valued. The problem, however, is when you begin to believe that the job is indispensable to you, instead of the other way around.

Soon I was doing the one thing that, as a business owner, I would swear never to do again: become dependent on a single client. Because when you do, you're essentially a full-time employee with none of the benefits or security. And you're left with no time to build other streams of income. You are a shoemaker with no shoes.

My friend Ilise Benun is the creator of Marketing Mentor and helps creative professionals find better clients with bigger budgets. She's also a content *machine*; she's written dozens of books, including *The Creative Professional's Guide to Money.* But Ilise isn't so sure about the word "indispensable." "It sounds like a lot of pressure," she said to me. "I don't like pressure." She's cool with being indispensable only if it means "providing the utmost quality in a way that only I can provide"—and it doesn't come with an infinite time commitment.

It was right around this time that I started to get to know Ilise, whose grounded and sovereign nature appealed to me as it started to feel as if the waters were rising up around my neck. She has reminded me over the years that every project, every relationship, every *everything*, has a beginning, a middle, and an end. The idea is not to make things last forever, but to do your best and most valuable work for the right people at the right time. And to know when that time has passed. I'd lived that myself: My combination of skills as an editor, media contributor, and radio host might have made me indispensable when the magazine moved to New York, but once the leadership and the budget changed, I wasn't so indispensable anymore.

Ilise told an audience of entrepreneurs in a recent talk that it took her a while to realize that she doesn't need any *one*—not any one project, not any one client, not any one opportunity. She needs *all* of them. Because when she has access to options, she gets to choose—to begin a relationship or end one, to pursue an opportunity or quit while she's ahead.

That discovery, that realization, was incredibly freeing for her. And for me too. We all need more than one good option, one good client, one good idea. We need lots. Because if being indispensable by *her* definition is doing our best work for the people we choose to do it for, then *by* definition there should be no one we *can't* live without.

But I didn't know that back then. I was in too deep at the time, seduced by the inherent promise of what "more work" meant (and what it meant was just that: *more work*). I was starting to feel threadbare. This client had dangled all kinds of carrots, about how big they were going to be, how big I was going to be (because of them, of course), that I would maybe even own part of the business one day, and make millions besides. I believe they believed this, but I also realize it didn't matter if any of that happened; what mattered was that they had my full and unwavering commitment to them, right now.

The agency owners got by on their brilliance and charm, but the more I got to know them, the better view I had at how the sausage was made, and I was losing my appetite. Some of the promises they made to clients and others failed to materialize. Contacts I had introduced to them weren't returning my calls. Being around them made me seasick. One minute you were up—"Seriously, Terri, this is genius!"—and the next you were down: "Why are you so literal about everything?" You could feel full of momentum on a Monday but by Tuesday get sucked under by a strong undertow that drew your last bits of confidence out to sea.

"Terri, you know what your problem is? You think you're so independent. But you're not really all that tough. You're so sensitive! What do you think that's about?" And my favorite: "You know you're crazy, right?"

I rationalized: They were teasing. This is fine. I'm learning things. I'm good at this. They appreciate me. And in truth, I liked them for a long time. But something didn't feel right. *I* didn't feel right. The unhappiness started its distant simmer and in a few short years had reached a rolling boil. I was a frog in the pot, thinking, *Is it me or is this unbearable?*

One night, they were meeting a high-profile client—a best-selling author and psychiatrist who'd been on all the major networks—and invited me to come along. I was excited about being included. They seemed to be making good on the "We'll introduce you to all the best people" promise they'd made so many times.

We sat down at a hotel bar, and after they exchanged hellos they introduced me as their head of content and brand positioning and someone he'd be working with. Then they said, "And oh man, does she need you. Listen to how fucked up she was over her last relationship." Then, turning to me, "Tell the doc about you and what's-his-face. It's so crazy, I swear." They proceeded to pick apart my romantic life right then and there, over martinis. On one hand, they wanted to see this doctor do his thing. On the other, they enjoyed the spectacle. Except I was the spectacle.

When I told them later how stupid they made me look, they said, "Are you kidding? He thinks you're great!" and then, "It wouldn't be the worst thing for you to talk to a psychiatrist."

That was just one instance. There were others. More than I can count.

So why didn't you just leave? Ultimately, I did. But for a long time it was as if my life, my work, my identity, had been swallowed whole. It was like trying to get perspective from inside the belly of a whale.

Looking back, I cannot believe I stood for a fraction of what I did—I certainly wouldn't let *you* take that sitting down. Yes, they were my main source of income, but even I knew this wasn't just an economic decision. I fell under the trance of indispensability, of believing they needed me, and that I needed them, which set the stage for certain patterns of psychological abuse that even I, with my big opinions and my big mouth, endured. And if I could and did, I understand why others have, and do.

Finally, after a series of unspeakable insults and unforgivable fouls, the whole mess culminated in a holiday-party-turned-tea with the Mad Hatter, where a lot of drinking ratcheted up a raucous mood and tipped into a series of bad decisions that today would be considered an HR nightmare. Except, of course, there was no HR department; there weren't *any* departments. Just the owners, a few contractors, and several unpaid interns. I found myself in the bathroom crying (again), and said to myself, this was the last time. And it was.

Soon after, I issued my formal notice, ending our agreement. They told me I was overreacting, that I was rude and inconsiderate to leave them hanging, and that they'd move me to an hourly model. I said, "Pretend I've moved to the moon."

The whole thing felt incredibly dramatic—villains and heroes, climactic fights, escape plans, me at sea in a splintered skiff.

"I think you might be making a bigger deal out of this than you need to," Ilise said. "How is that possible?" I said. They were paying me more than anyone else! "What you need to do now," she said, "is replace them. And you will."

I surprised everyone *but* Ilise that year when I not only replaced that income but more than *doubled* it within the year. And grew it even more the following. How? Because once I freed up my time, energy, and attention, I could actively engage with my network and discover new opportunities that I had been too busy to see. It was as if I'd been holding my breath and clinging to an anchor for security. Only when I let go of it did I realize how much room there was to rise.

How to Think like an Indispensable Person

We can't control other people's tastes or preferences, budgets, the economy, or the weather, and you don't become indispensable by trying to do any of those things. But I've identified a few ways that have helped me deliver my best work to the people I most enjoy working with. Of course, providing excellent work or service is the floor. All things being equal, indispensability starts with not what you are expected to do but how far and above that you can go.

Here's what else I believe contributes to being indispensable:

- **QUESTION WHAT'S BEEN DONE.** When I first sat down in Kelly's chair, I believed a) that I was too old for long hair (wha?) and b) that a midlength bob was the best I could do. My assumptions, as well as my previous hairstyles, had zero to do with what she envisioned for me. She didn't just question what I'd done before; she disregarded it. Years later, she thought I should try bangs again, and well, we both should have questioned that decision a bit more. It's fine. I grew them out.

  What I love about being a consultant is that I get paid to do precisely the thing that I was discouraged to do as an employee: question what's always been done. I'm paid to kick tires, to explore, to try. And I'm able to do it not because I like to question things, but because I can back up my big opinions with well-executed solutions, and that's key.

  While I'm not a big fan of compliance in general, I've also done a lot of work in the financial services industry—an industry built on compliance! What has made me an indispensable brand advisor to some of the nation's top financial advisors is not that I'm "good" at being compliant; it's that I'm great at pushing compliance as far as it'll go.
- **HAVE AN OPINION.** Once, Kelly was away during a critical haircut window and so I saw another stylist whom I'll call Stacy. I sat down and she said, "So what would you like me to do?" She was trying to be a good service provider—accommodating, friendly—but that's when I knew I wouldn't be back. She had a skill set and a pair of scissors, but no ideas or opinions. She was the opposite of indispensable. Which is why I don't remember her real name.

Most people just want to get along and go along; they are hesitant to make waves (and then they wonder why the water is stagnant). Facts are important, but they're not the opposite of opinion; you need both to make a case for anything. The indispensable person doesn't just have information; she has insight into why it matters. She's not afraid to take a stance, or make a recommendation.

- **EXPLORE YOUR OFF-LABEL USES.** I get that people want to have their "thing," their niche, because they think that makes them marketable. A niche doesn't make you worth knowing about, though; you do. I also refuse to believe there's only one valuable outcome from your skill set (or mine). Niches can be an attempt to be indispensable, as in, if I do this one thing and one thing only, I'll be in high demand. That only works if . . . you're in high demand.

  I attribute my own success to being flexible about the ways in which I apply what I'm good at. I mean, if you can do "x" with this skill, what if you did "y" with it? What would it look like if you did this thing over there for those people too? I don't see the point of limiting what I do or how I can use what I know to solve a problem. You're not going to hear me saying, "I don't do windows." I mean, let's talk about your windows and what they really need.

  An obsession with finding your one thing is no different from believing you need to have one passion. While one is framed as practical and the other aspirational, the belief is that once you've figured out that one thing, you're all set. It's another symptom of the Industrial Age hangover, where we think the way to be successful is to make widgets of ourselves. You want specialized? I give you the garlic press. A big, bulky thing that takes up space and only does one thing. A knife took your job. Bye.

- **DON'T APOLOGIZE FOR NOT BEING A STANDARD POODLE.** OK, maybe you *are* a highly pedigreed professional. Or perhaps, like me, you're a mutt, who's worked in a few different industries.

Never apologize for having a varied, surprising, nonlinear career. You didn't do something "wrong." It's what makes your life yours and not someone else's—and it's what has given you the perspective you have. Your range of skills, unique experience, the unreplicable blend of your education, opportunities, and work, are in fact what will make you indispensable to someone. Why? Because you're the only one with it.

- **DON'T BE GRABBY.** Just because you have off-label uses doesn't mean you need to take every job or snatch up every opportunity. If it fits, great! But ask yourself, Am I grabbing this out of fear of not-enoughness? Do I think I have to take on more and more, or else someone else will eat my lunch? This will backfire, as things do when you grab for them for the wrong reasons and you know it.

  Once I took a PR gig for a supplements company. I didn't want it but was talked into it by someone whose entire argument was "take the money." I paid someone else to do the work and played miserable middleman all summer, and every time the phone rang I got a cramp. That's when I learned a valuable lesson: Getting someone to pay you for anything is not in and of itself the goal, and I would be well served to pass on jobs that didn't feel like a fit.
- **KEEP YOUR OPTIONS OPEN.** The only thing worse than grabbing for things you don't want is *clinging* to things you don't want. The biggest mistake I made back then was letting my own options narrow—not just by being too busy to accommodate other options but also by believing I had no others. You *always* have options. What makes you indispensable is knowing, really believing, that you do not need *any* one job, any one client, any one opportunity, as Ilise says. Needy and dependent is not a good look. And you don't have to exercise all options all the time. That's why they're . . . options. Because as soon as you fail to see any at all, you're cooked.

- **CHANGE HOW SOMEONE SEES THEMSELVES OR THEIR WORK.** Everyone feels good after a trip to the salon. The blowout may look fab, the color rich and vibrant. But that's not the only reason. It's because what you've done in that hour (or three; thanks, highlights!) is reconnect with the part of you that just won't quit, the part of you that's still there when everything else grows in or washes out. Of course you don't do it on your own. Kelly has a specific skill set that I don't have, and is able to do for me what I cannot do for myself. But it's not just that I like how I look when I walk out but that I like who I am as a result too.

  It's not enough to flatter, support, and complement (or compliment!) someone else. The power comes in helping someone see *themselves* in a new and better way. And you can do that by pointing out to them what they're doing right, by calling attention to the idiosyncratic ways in which they're achieving excellence. This is what it takes to be indispensable to anyone—a friend, a client, a colleague, a boss: That because of you, they get a glimpse of what's possible, are reminded of what's good, what's working, and what's worth doing.

Bottom line is that being indispensable isn't about dependency or deprivation, or pointing out just how much someone needs you (or vice versa). It means acknowledging where your skills end and another's begin, and appreciating what we each bring to the work or situation at hand. Also, it goes without saying that you don't endure less-than-stellar treatment in exchange for being deemed "indispensable." Nope! Not how that works. If you allow for that, simply because you so desperately want to be indispensable, well, that's like being psyched that a bunch of jagaloons who "aren't looking for anything serious right now" swiped right on you. Or worse, thinking you're winning this game when one dude, who asked you not a single question about yourself in ninety minutes, announces he'd like to see you again . . . as he leaves a 10 percent tip. You win, I guess?

There's power in being deemed valuable, even desirable, but the power is *always* about the choice you make. Because if you prey on need, then you're just as needy. The most valuable people on any team are those who support the team's ability to thrive, even independently of them. And the real power in an indispensable relationship is not that you depend on them or they on you, but that you keep choosing each other, each and every time.

write your next chapter

Indispensable is not an on/off switch or the indisputable truth. In fact, the fun of exploring what makes you indispensable is discovering the many ways in which you are. Don't overthink these prompts. Simply start writing and see what surfaces.

Write about a time you . . .

. . . Questioned what had been done before.

grab a notebook

. . . Voiced a strong opinion.

grab a notebook

. . . Took something (a skill, an insight) that you knew well and tried applying it in a totally different situation.

grab a notebook

. . . Let go of something (a project, a client, a relationship, a job) that just wasn't working anymore.

grab a notebook

. . . Helped someone feel better about who they were or what they'd done or achieved.

grab a notebook

Now go back and read through all the things that came up. What patterns do you see? What resonates? Where do you see similar ideas or moments or experiences floating to the top?

grab a notebook

Gather Some Indispensable Insights

Make a list of at least five (if not more) people you trust and admire. Be sure to include a cross section from different areas and periods of your life—a former teacher, a friend from school, your boss, a coworker, a colleague from another industry, a friend you volunteer with. Someone you talk to every day, and someone you talk to far less frequently. Tell them you're looking to gather some insights about yourself, and ask if they'd be willing to share some.

Invite them to answer a few questions for you via email. You can of course have a conversation about it, but I think there's tremendous value in seeing things written down in black and white.

- What are five words you might use to describe me? (Tip: Don't guide them too much here because you want to see what patterns emerge in their responses.)
- What's something you turn to me for first?
- If there's one thing you trust me to be able to do for you, what is it?

- What's one of your favorite stories about or memories of me (it can be something we experienced together or just one you know about)?
- What's one quality I possess that, if it came in a bottle, you'd stock up on?
- How would you describe me to someone I've never met?
- What's one thing about me that you don't find in most people, or that would be hard to replicate?

Spend some time with the responses. Print them out. Highlight the parts that surprise or please you the most. What patterns or similarities do you see? How do the things they say resonate with what you wrote in the first exercise above? What does it tell you about what people value most in you, and how does that change your approach to what you do?

grab a notebook

part three

---

unleash

CHAPTER 14

Abandon Your Plans

Good planning alone won't make your efforts successful; it's only after you let go of your plans that you can breathe life into your efforts.

—Twyla Tharp, *The Creative Habit*

One summer Saturday in 1985, we piled into the family van to go to Sesame Place and my mom asked my little sister Kim to quick make sure the back door was locked. She popped out of the car in her apple-red bathing suit, darted inside, caught her flip-flopped foot on the dog fence, and fell on her arm, breaking it—along with all the plans she had for that day. Sesame Place was not in the cards for Kim. I shuddered as I watched how quickly plans could be dashed: One minute you're sure of what lies ahead—you can practically taste the soft serve—and the next you're not. A dark shadow passed over the ball pit that day.

Up to this point, we've questioned what we've been taught, explored our own rules and values, and recognized the role that skill and practice play in creating a meaningful life. What we're about to dive into in this chapter—and this entire last leg of the book—is what to do when, despite all your best efforts, shit goes sideways. Because it will. There is no single guaranteed method or recipe for avoiding the human condition—with its pain, loneliness, and long stretches of tedium. But we don't have to assume that if and when that happens everything is wrong or ruined.

We start with plans because we love them so much—and they're often the first thing to go.

Why You (and I) Are Obsessed with Plans

In the moment we devise them, plans make us gods. I will do *this* and then *that* will happen. It makes us feel like the showrunners of this bingeable series called *Our Lives*, and yet what we're actually running is a puppet show, acted out on the miniature stage of our minds. And we're not necessarily pulling the strings of the universe when we do.

We all know the old Yiddish adage "Man plans, God laughs." Hard. A wheezing, coughing, I-just-choked-on-a-Cheeto hard. But we do love us some plans. Plans give us focus, hope, something to do next, something to gun for. Most important, they give us a sense of control, which is vital.

Planning is part of what allows us to face the unknown. Just ask a financial advisor whose whole life is helping other people plan—for the future, for worst-case scenarios. But they'll also tell you that the plan is not the point; the point is to know what you want to do and take measures to get yourself there, not because we know what will happen, but because we don't.

We plan to create some semblance of pecking order and priority—and something to pivot from. Without planning, you don't have options.

Our ability (read: obsession) with planning is fairly new in terms of human evolution, making it an exciting new app, but a buggy one. In his book *Stumbling on Happiness*, psychologist Dan Gilbert explains that it took about five hundred million years for the first protohuman brains to emerge.[1] Then the almost-human brain experienced a major growth spurt that more than doubled its mass in a mere two million years (two million! I've been on hold with Verizon for longer). The part of the brain that grew the most? The frontal lobe, seat of what is often referred to as our executive function, the part that solves problems and makes critical decisions, like who to hire or what restaurant to order takeout from.

The frontal lobe *plans*; that's what it does. You can no more stop it from leaping to the future than you can talk your heart out of beating, Gilbert says. As much as 12 percent of our daily thoughts center on the future, or one out of every eight hours, making each of us as Gilbert says "a part-time resident of tomorrow."[2] And you know what sucks? Paying rent on a place you never live in.

So while we may be obsessed with what we're doing tomorrow or next week or next year, imagine what it would be like if you had no ability to understand what "later" meant. This is not just a thought experiment. For some people, it's a reality. Gilbert references a famous case in the psych literature: A patient known as "N. N." suffered a head injury in a car accident in 1981, sustaining damage to his frontal lobe—and with that lost his ability to plan or even conceive of the concept of "later." When asked by a psychologist what he'd be doing tomorrow, N. N. draws a blank. When he's asked to conceive of tomorrow, he says it's "like being in a room with nothing there and having a guy tell you to go find a chair."[3] This man is not a part-time resident of tomorrow; he's not even a tourist. This man, like others with frontal lobe damage, Gilbert says, lives in a "permanent present" from which there is no escape.

You know who else lives in the permanent present? Your dog. My cat. Cardinals. Hippos. Centipedes. Elm trees. As Gilbert points out, living now is not the exception; *we* are. "Two or three million years ago our ancestors began a great escape from the here and now, and their getaway vehicle was a highly specialized mass of gray tissue,"[4] he writes. This nifty new app is what allows us to visit the past or tour the future, and, as with all time travel, has consequences; namely, the potential to get trapped in nostalgia or regret, or ensnared in the anxieties of what might happen.

Planning vs. Plans

There's a critical difference between "planning" and "plans." Planning is something we must do here in the matrix to avoid a nonstop logistical nightmare. But *plans*? Plans are different. Plans are flimsy. They change. They collapse under the weight of nearly anything, from a twisted ankle to a global pandemic. Think you're meeting Savannah for brunch on Sunday? You are, in theory. Until Savannah wakes up with a hangover that scores a seven on the Richter scale and brunch is not happening.

The problem isn't planning per se—it's an *attachment* to the outcome of said plans, to the idea that plans must align precisely with reality in order for you to be happy. And the more attached you are to your plans, well, the more disappointed you will undoubtedly be. If you plan to go to the beach and it rains, of course you'll be bummed. But your mood (annoyed, upset, down) isn't "caused" by the rain. It's caused by the mismatch of what you thought/hoped/planned would happen and what is *actually* happening. Enter, suffering.

The problem, says Eckhart Tolle, is that we're burdened not just by outcomes but also by the burden of psychological time, in which we're held hostage by the past or the future. The entire thesis of his monster best seller, *The Power of Now*, is simply that: The life you want, free of suffering and rich with meaning, vitality, and life, happens in one place: Now. The farther you get from Now, the more miserable you are.

"Unease, anxiety, tension, stress, worry—all forms of fear—are caused by too much future," Tolle says. "Guilt, regret, resentment, grievances, sadness, bitterness . . . are caused by too much past."[5]

I'm sure you have plans. Plans for next Tuesday, plans for next year. For your career. Plans buoy us, give us something to aim for. The point here is to understand our relationship to plans and allow the functionality and usefulness of plans to keep us moving, but not keep us bound. And to do that, we have to get real honest about what those plans do, and don't, mean.

"There's an emotional lie to overplanning," Twyla Tharp writes in *The Creative Habit*. "It creates a security blanket that lets you assume you have things under control, that you are further along than you really are, that you're home free when you haven't even walked out the door yet."[6]

Show me someone who lives and dies by plans, who clings white knuckled to How Things Are Supposed to Go, and I'll show you someone who does not trust—situations, or other people, or, more important, themselves. And if you cannot trust, it's hard to move forward with the confidence and ease we most want to feel and broadcast to the world.

Plan the Beginning, Not the End

Some people relish the planning process; I often get overwhelmed by it. But rather than let fear of plans get in the way, I have a simple strategy: I plan the first part.

I'd spent a single day in Florence with my uncle twenty years ago, and had always wanted to spend more time there. So in 2019, I booked my flight and reserved an Airbnb for a week and said, OK, looks like I'm going. I'll figure out the rest later. God bless you with your Excel spreadsheets with train times and museum hours and links to blogs. I see its value (which is why I travel with people like you), but I can't really get my head around any of it until I'm there. I woke up in Florence the morning after I arrived, made an espresso, and sat down with a guidebook and a Google search, booked a bunch of things for the week, and ended up doing half of them. Why? Because it was June and hot as an iron and touring all day was physically impossible. Also, planning every inch of a trip felt so, well, American—and the goal was to be Italian for a week.

The best parts of that trip were things I couldn't have planned for: Stumbling across a boutique where I discovered I *could* in fact pull off harem pants ("Bellissima, signorina!"). Falling in love with a perfume shop and spending a good hour sniffing every last bottle. I was proud that I'd booked the cocktail tour ahead of time. And guess what? *They* canceled on *me* because no one else signed up. So much for plans! Also, I don't need a group tour to drink cocktails. I can do that on my own.

Plan the Actions, Not the Ending

A goal is where you're headed; the plan is how you get there. That means a plan is not the same as an intention, an idea, or a wish. You can dream of visiting Iceland, but a plan involves dates and flights.

So what can you do? Plan your *actions*, not your outcomes. Because you can't plan an outcome anyway; you can only hope for one. So rather than make dangerous assumptions about what will happen, bank instead on the steps you will take. I plan to submit a short story to a writing contest this weekend; I do not, however, plan to win. Since I'm not one of the judges, what they think is out of my control, so it's not part of the plan. What I write is.

I'd be lying if I said I had some Grand Plan for my life, or that one got me here now. I created my plans as I approached goals I wanted, and sometimes they took shape rather quickly because that's when I realized I needed one. While a plan requires decisions, it does not require a vintage—which means a plan you come up with now can be just as viable as one you came up with ten years ago. You can plan for years to launch a business and not do it, but someone with a similar idea could plan it tomorrow and have a website up next week. The plan is only as good as its execution, and if the plan needs to change it can. I don't tend to stick to things just for the sake of sticking to them. I also don't see any reason why you can't come up with a perfectly good and actionable plan right now.

After ten years of living in that studio apartment, I decided to move to a bigger place. But that hadn't been the plan six months prior. Then, suddenly, it was. The plan began as a tiny idea a colleague planted in my head about hosting dinners. I'd never before given a hoot about hosting dinners. But the timing was such that the idea took root. After all, in my studio, I could only have one person over at a time to sit in the one other chair I had. Soon I became enamored with the vision of hosting not just a person but people. And I sure as shit wasn't going to do it here.

That's precisely where the plan began: because if I was going to host guests I needed to have a bigger place, and that meant I needed to download the StreetEasy app and go see a few places. Then I had to decide when I would move and how I would move. I created the plan based on the needs I had for the thing I wanted, and the resources I had, and that's how it went from a sprout to a fruit-bearing reality.

I found a place just down the street (same zip code, new dry cleaner) that had everything I wanted. I moved in, bought furniture, and by the holidays was ready to have people over. I strung up lights and sent out invitations to ring in the New Year at my place. I had snacks, paper hats, a bartender, and a smashing red jumpsuit. Boom! I was hosting a party!

Happy New Year . . . 2020!

Yup. And that was it for parties that year. I had the plan, executed on it, and then all the other plans were derailed. Was it worth doing? Absolutely. I might have moved because I was ready, could afford it, and liked the idea of stepping up my living situation, but what I was most grateful for later was being able to ride out the pandemic in an apartment with a full-sized refrigerator, and plenty of room to breathe in. I don't know what I would have done trapped in three hundred square feet for a year. Sometimes plans work out in ways you might not expect.

The pandemic took to our plans like an angry god, and in a single blow swept every chess piece to the floor. The tragedy was huge and incomprehensible on a global scale: Unemployment and mental illness skyrocketed; so did hunger and homelessness. No one planned for this. (Not even the people we paid to plan for it with our tax dollars. But that's a different topic!)

For those of us lucky enough not to get sick, our schedules (where our plans lived) vanished into the ether like when Angela Lansbury and those British kids tried to take a magic totem from one world into another in *Bedknobs and Broomsticks*. Poof! Gone like so much fairy dust. And as we emerged, we started planning again.

Consciously Uncouple Yourself from Your Plans

Does that mean we don't or shouldn't plan anything, or that we just consistently plan as if the end of the world is a week away? No. We still plan! We must! "Plan" is more verb than noun. And the relationship between ourselves and our plans is a long-running, long-distance romance by design. It would be wise to make like Gwyneth and Chris and consciously uncouple ourselves from our plans, not because we are mad at them or hate them or can't live with them anymore, but because we realize we are *not* them. And, while we're at it, unhook our plans from our future (just because you don't have a plan at the moment doesn't mean you don't have a future, and having a plan doesn't guarantee one either).

Let's keep going: What if we *also* unhooked planning from success, from happiness or the promise of happiness, from passion, from any of the things we're seeking—including protection? Yes, having a plan can give you options and allocate and secure resources. But it cannot protect you from the *fact* of what happens, from the unknown, or from the future, where we're all headed.

I was heavily discouraged from using inflatable swimmies as a kid, even though I wanted nothing more than a surefire way of staying glued to the surface of the pool. But anything you cling to can break, and in the moment that swimmie loses air it won't matter that it had a warranty or that you can maybe get a refund. At that very moment, what you want and need most to be able to do is swim.

Plans don't give our life meaning; they give it *structure*. We're the ones who inject and infuse plans with meaning, with what it means to be or become a certain thing, and it's not so much the plan but the loss of the meaning that hurts when one fails to transpire.

Think Preparation over Plans

Whereas an attachment to plans can keep you from being fully present, being prepared helps you dial in. Yes, planning is a way of thinking about what comes next. But if you're hamstrung by how you think things are "supposed" to go, you might be less able to adapt to a situation you do find yourself in. And it takes one kind of skill to articulate a plan: there's another equally brilliant, inventive, creative part of you that thrives when you're fully present.

"We often substitute planning, ruminating or list-making for actually doing something about our dreams," Madson writes in *Improv Wisdom*. "The habit of excessive planning impedes our ability to see what is actually in front of us. The mind that is occupied is missing the present."[7]

Rather than spend all your time planning, she says, direct your attention to what's happening right now, in front of you. "Focusing attention on the present puts you in touch with a kind of natural wisdom. When you enter the moment with heightened awareness, what you need to do becomes obvious. You discover that you already have the answers."[8]

What wasn't in the plan before but might be now? How can your existing plans expand to accommodate what's changing? Given all you now know about your skills, your practice, and your uniquely honed perspective, how can you prepare for the thing you want most?

In 2013, voice teacher Sarah Horn was called up out of an audience of several thousand at the Hollywood Bowl to sing

"For Good" from the show *Wicked*, with the woman who originated the role of Glinda on Broadway, the one and only Kristin Chenoweth. Horn did not plan for this to happen, which would have been impossible. When Chenoweth asked who knew the song, Horn simply raised her hand. She got up onstage and proceeded to sing the *fuck* out of that song, blowing away not just her friends and thousands of people but Chenoweth herself, who was visibly taken aback by Horn's performance. Her friend caught it all on his phone in the last few seconds of memory he had, and that video went viral overnight, racking up more than a million views in twenty-four hours.

Not only was that an incredibly exciting and lucky moment, but it opened doors for Horn, who was invited back by the Hollywood Bowl two weeks later to emcee an event, and it continues to draw all kinds of new opportunities to her. Horn says it's as if she had saved up all the luck in her whole life for that one moment.

She didn't plan it, no—but she was *prepared*. When you watch that performance (which has more than three million views to date), you see a woman crushing onstage with a major star—but what you don't see, says Horn, is what allowed her to turn a lucky moment into a life-changing one. What you don't see, she says in her TEDx talk, are the weekly voice lessons she'd had since she was eight; the times she sang when she was sick, so that she could make sure she could sing without sounding sick; the hours spent singing "For Good" on repeat in her bedroom, memorizing the harmonies on both parts.

What happened was a chance thing, for which she had no warning, no plan. But when the planets lined up for one miraculous moment, she was ready. And all that discipline, that preparedness, she said, led to what she calls her "moment of freedom."[9] Because that is what you're seeing there: a woman who committed to her craft and had planned on nosebleed seats that day—not on being "discovered." Planning for any of that would have been crazy, but if she hadn't been prepared it wouldn't have happened. It makes me cry a little every time, to watch this woman sing, her spirit rising through her skill like light through a filament.

Hold Your Plans like a Butterfly

Years ago, I had the opportunity to learn the ChiRunning technique from its creator, Danny Dreyer, who based his approach on thirty years of Tai Chi practice and forty-five years of competitive running and coaching. The goal is energy efficiency, injury prevention, and "intelligent movement," which allowed Dreyer to regularly run one hundred miles without hurting himself, and me to run two miles without dying. The key is in the posture, the foot strike, a strong core, and loose, relaxed body. I found that running became lighter, easier; less like gripping and huffing, more like leaning into the wind. I remember Dreyer's directive, to keep the chin up, the arms loose, and to "imagine you're holding a butterfly in each hand."

This is how I like to think of plans, and how I encourage you to think about yours: as delicate, beautiful, living things that must be held lightly so that you can keep moving forward. We want our plans to protect us, ideally, to keep us on track. But if we grip them too tightly, we keep them from doing the one thing we most want them to do: Take flight.

write your next chapter

Write about a plan you made. Any plan—could have been ten years ago or yesterday, and the scale of the plan doesn't matter either. What did the plan entail? What was the ultimate goal? Was the plan a necessary evil, or part of the fun, or even more fun than actually doing it?

grab a notebook

Now write about a time when plans changed. Maybe it was out of your hands, or maybe you called it off. Maybe you were disappointed (or relieved). It may have meant something better came along, or that you came up short.

grab a notebook

What's on the docket? What are you in the midst of or about to plan that you're really excited about? List a few, whether they're for six weeks, six months, or even a year from now.

grab a notebook

Plan of Action

Choose one of your plans to focus on and explore the actions for each:

- What's the first must-do part that will get it moving?
- What actions can you take, regardless of the outcome of the plan itself?
- What is the ideal outcome of the plan?
- What actions can you take if the plan falls through?
- What actions can you take now to make the plan a reality? Write them down, whether that means blocking time on the calendar, calling a friend, or researching options.

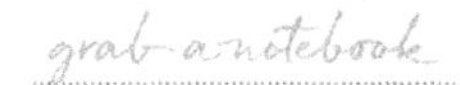

CHAPTER 15

Boredom Is a Detox for Your Soul

Boredom is the fear of self.

—Marie Josephine de Suin de Beausacq

I spent every Sunday of my childhood in church, where we were told that if we believed in God and didn't screw things up we would be granted eternal life. And it was during that interminable hour that we got a taste of just what eternity might feel like.

What was the point of doing this? I wondered. Church was a weekly do-over where you read the same things, did the same things. Catholic mass is the bootcamp of boredom, complete with calisthenics (stand up, sit down, kneel). While church taught some of us not to think, for others, like me, it's where we learned to entertain ourselves, wading through the tide of mumbled prayers, sharpening our thoughts like someone with a stick and nothing but time.

When we were kids, we thought boredom was something we'd grow out of. Yet here we are, all grown-up, and boredom didn't go anywhere; it just changed. And the ways we hide from it have also changed. How we respond to it, even how we think about it, can teach us something, especially if we're willing to look at it; but we're often not. And therein lies the risk.

It's Normal That You're Bored

Being bored is not a sign that something is deeply, critically wrong. It means you're alive. It means your brain is functioning correctly. Feeling ecstatic, heightened, pinched with anticipation, is metabolically expensive—so costly, in fact, that your ancient brain will allow it only sparingly, and shut off that valve as soon as it can. It's nothing personal. It's trying to run a business here and thrill is pricey. We were given very little budget for this.

Anything can become boring. Some things are innately boring: a pile of clean, unsorted laundry; a series of strip malls; red lights. But sex or steak can also be boring. Excitement can arise spontaneously some of the time, but we need to trick ourselves into it the rest of the time. Surfboards. Rollerblades. Costumes. Hot-dog-eating contests. We'll make do with whatever we have. Being bored isn't a disease; it's part of the human condition. What once opened you like a flower of attention and benevolence will later grind like a dull blade.

Why You Don't Have a Get-out-of-Bored-Free Card

In *The Power of Boredom,* teacher and philosopher Mark Hawkins says it's the fear of boredom, rather than boredom itself, that keeps us stuck. We avoid and fear it, he says, because we're taught that it's negative—not the other way around—thanks to a strong prejudice against "doing nothing" (which is where boredom is most likely to surface). "We live in a cultural climate where boredom is associated with laziness, lack of direction, and even criminality,"[1] he writes—which is why we're all driven to cram our schedules to capacity (and make plans to keep them full).

Think a demanding schedule or a host of obligations can give you a get-out-of-bored-free card? Guess again. It's not that demands on your time aren't real or pressing, but that the need to be busy at all times is a different issue altogether. Because more often than not, we stay busy to avoid boredom and the chasm of fear beneath, like the Road Runner, who bolts off the edge of a cliff and can only keep running as long as he doesn't look down.

Here in the twenty-first century, we believe we've bred boredom out of us like a weak gene or an impractical tail. We've got a stockpile against it. If entertainment were dry goods, we'd be set well into the zombie apocalypse: In 2019 TV programming reached an all-time high of more than five hundred scripted shows[2]—that's not counting, well, everything else on demand. According to recent statistics, there are currently more than two million podcasts with over forty-eight million episodes ready to fill your ears.[3] You can beam bookshelves' worth of titles right into your Kindle, the clown car of books, and it won't be any heavier in your purse. Every screen within reach is a black hole, ready to swallow our attention. Sure, we have the means to be endlessly entertained, says Hawkins, but that isn't the best way to cope with boredom, and may make things worse.

"The funny thing about life today is that we are all actually profoundly bored, but because there are so many distractions, we don't even know it," Hawkins writes. "In fact, the busier we are, the more bored we are likely to be."[4] That's because what being busy does, he says, is create "the illusion of a satisfying and meaningful life"[5]—not the reality.

Find Your Passion and Never Be Bored Again! (Kidding)

One of the off-label uses—and implicit promises—of the search for passion is this: that when and if you do find it, you'll be eternally stimulated and engaged, and free from the unblinking eye of the void. Sounds good, doesn't it? Except it isn't true. In fact, the search for passion is really just a great way to stay . . . busy (or, as we like to think of it, "productive").

As we learned from the Stanford study earlier, people with

a fixed mindset about passions are more likely to assume that once they find said passion they'll be endlessly motivated. If you believe that finding your passion will somehow safeguard you against a) the human condition and b) boredom, I've got *so* many things to sell you (and I do accept Apple Pay).

The Cost of Distraction

The reason we don't think we're bored is in large part due to distraction, which runs the gamut from fun to annoying. It also has a known productivity cost. The *Washington Post* reported on a University of California, Irvine, study that found that the average office worker is interrupted or switches tasks about every three minutes, costing them up to six hours a day.[6] Distraction eats up time, wastes resources, and can put us in harm's way, especially when heavy machinery is involved.

But it exacts a kind of spirit-level cost too.

Here's why: The opposite of boredom isn't pleasure. Or productivity. Or fun. The opposite of boredom is *meaning*, Hawkins says, which we need like food or air. The cruel irony is that in our attempt to fill our time with wonderful, worthwhile things we may be crowding out the very meaning we seek. Since we have so much to do and watch and read, we've all but barred the door to our own boredom like a room no one goes into anymore. And, in so doing, removed access to the very thing that would alleviate its threat.

"What we don't realize is that distraction is the death of meaning,"[7] Hawkins writes. It's why we tread water at a breathless pace—to avoid the abyss, the deep, dark tide that runs beneath everything.

Ever get that weird dead feeling when you turn off the TV or put away your laptop, like you've cut off blood supply from a vital, external organ? Even when I want nothing more than sleep, it takes everything in me to stop playing Boggle and put the phone *down* and go to *bed*.

Why? Because when faced with the void, we are faced with

what things mean—and what they don't. Being distracted not only keeps you from getting work done; it also keeps you from connecting to the work, or acknowledging just how disconnected from it you are.

That quiet, unpopulated space may be exactly what we need. "It is by embracing boredom and using it to learn about the truths in our lives that we can finally create a meaningful existence,"[8] says Hawkins. The real risk may be that to lose our capacity and tolerance for boredom is to lose the divining rod that points to where the water is.

Boredom Isn't a Problem; It's Potential

Hawkins suggests looking at that void of activity and attention as simply . . . space. Space is neutral, not menacing; it's pure potential. You could turn a space into anything: a family room, an office, a sex dungeon. If you're afraid of what it is and allow it to be a stage for your worst fears rather than your greatest potential, then you'll likely cram it so full of junk there isn't any space left. But if you don't have that space or an awareness of it, you are blind to potential too.

Deep down, we know that everyone and everything we know does come to an end, no matter how much splashing around we do. We're all fairly terrified that whatever lies beyond busy will suck the marrow of meaning right from our very bones.

Consider the final pose of yoga class—*savasana*, or corpse pose. A lot of people skip it. They show up, sweat hard, then peel up off their mat and skedaddle. The resistance to lying there is no surprise—surely we have better things to do. But any yoga teacher will tell you it's the most important pose of the entire practice because it "seals in the benefits of your practice" (must be in the script because literally *every* teacher says it). It calms, quiets, rebalances your body after your yogic exertions. But it's not called corpse pose by accident; there is a moment of dangling there in the void, especially when the lights are out, that can be relaxing . . . or unsettling.

Let's step back from the existential edge for a moment, though. Because while there is that deep river of death that runs through everything, there are also lots of smaller deaths that we suffer when we lose things or they leave us, and when the things we used to be so totally absorbed in don't hold water anymore: The relationship that once seemed so sparkling and alive that dulls or warps with time. The job we were psyched about that has turned lackluster and loathsome. The vibrance of the One Thing You Always Wanted—no matter what it is—that fades like a magazine cover in a sunny, south-facing window.

It's why I end up buying new perfumes; I just can't smell the old ones after a while. Nothing escapes the bleaching and leaching of meaning over time. Nothing.

And yet! Hawkins says *this* is the opportunity. Because this is how we reignite meaning. Rather than cling to the notion that we must feel scintillating and alive every second to make life worthwhile, we can loosen our grip long enough to see that the loss of meaning is not the end of the world; it's a shift of the light, the lengthening of a shadow. But what *we* tend to do the moment that shadow appears or the light flattens under a patch of cloud cover is to immediately flip on every light in the goddamn house, thinking that will help. (It doesn't.) This is not something to be fixed; it's a weather pattern of the human soul.

And it's not only something we will survive but also where our next great ideas come from.

How Boredom Can Make You Creative

Boredom researcher Sandi Mann, author of *The Science of Boredom: Why Boredom Is Good*, found that boredom may actually boost creativity. In a study published in the *Creativity Research Journal*, she and her colleagues had one group of participants copy numbers out of a phone book, another read the phone book, and a third, the control group, do neither of these things.[9]

Then they were asked to complete a creative task (such as: think of all the ways to use a pair of plastic cups). Guess who was most creative? The people who had to *read the fucking phone book*. In other words, their supreme boredom primed them for being creative.

You know who was really bored? Walt Disney. The story goes that he was sitting on a crappy park bench watching his daughter play on some anemic excuse for a playground when the idea occurred to him: Wouldn't it be great if there was a place where kids and their parents could have fun together? Out of that boredom grew an entire universe of stories and characters and cultural archetypes that are as American as apple pie. Disney didn't just buy up real estate to make that happen (though he did, scads of it); Disney as an entity resides rent-free in the landscape of our collective imagination. Would that have happened if he'd never experienced boredom that day? How many ideas aren't happening as we scroll through Twitter?

That gives us another great reason to let our mental real estate go fallow from time to time (and perhaps why, when we need to do creative work, we feel most drawn to cleaning out desk drawers). I'd say this is a good reason to go read something boring, but then I just realized what you're doing right now and so I'm having mixed feelings about that. I guess I'd feel great if I contributed to your daydreaming? But also, not.

Boredom Asks, "WTF Is the Point?"

We now know that while boredom can also inspire unnecessary risk taking and troublemaking ("Idle hands are the devil's workshop," Proverbs 16:27), it can give us the space for new ideas and insights to emerge. But there's another risk to crowding out boredom, and one I hadn't considered: that the less you tolerate boredom, the less you are *able* to tolerate it. "The fast pace of the world means that in an environment characterised by change, speed and novelty, we are losing the ability to tolerate the routine and repetition of everyday life,"[10] Mann writes.

We actually *need* that wide open space, that big, bland tide to wash everything out for a bit, because only then can we really call into question what we've been told matters versus what we *think* matters—and why. "Boredom provides the clarity to see that the meanings we buy into are completely arbitrary and assigned by someone else,"[11] says Hawkins.

Wait, don't glaze over that. Read it again. Boredom provides clarity—without which *you can't tell whether something actually matters or not.*

Think about that. Because if boredom strips things of meaning, then it gives us the chance to recalibrate what we have assigned meaning to and why. I'd say that's pretty important when we're talking about sovereignty and living a life of meaning, wouldn't you?

In other words, if we don't figure out WTF things mean to us we won't know why they matter, and we could very well end up staying very, very busy up until the hard stop of our lives doing shit we don't like for people we don't love.

Boredom and our ability to explore it may be the system-wide hard reset we need, so that we can flip switches to see which things still light up. "It is boredom that makes us realize that the world and all of existence demands that you attach meaning to it,"[12] says Hawkins. The world demands meaning—but you don't have to assign it, and you don't have to do what it says.

This—*this*—is the beginning of freedom. Because as long as you believe what everyone else tells you, as long as you take on meanings as assigned to you, whether they fit or not, you will not define your own terms and you will not choose your own life.

Now. Don't you have something to *not* go do right now?

write your next chapter

Think about a time you were bored. Where were you? What was happening? Maybe it's a montage of boring scenes or one particular moment stands out. Maybe you're bored right now. Writing about the boredom is in some ways the antidote, because what you're doing is laying it bare, saying what it was, looking at it without illusion. Don't try to force meaning or a big aha moment, or anything like that.

Set the timer for ten minutes. Start writing.

grab a notebook

Go back and read what you wrote. What surprises you about it? What came up that you may not have remembered or recalled, and why does that detail stand out to you now? What did you notice about being bored in that moment that may look different to you from this vantage point?

grab a notebook

Now zoom out and channel your thoughts about boredom.

- What does it mean to be bored?
- What will happen if you get bored, or what are you afraid will happen?
- What do you tend to do when you get bored—and why?

grab a notebook

Ho-hum, Do It Anyway

Where can you invite boredom? Yes, invite. We spend so much time snuffing it out that it's worth giving that space, that potential, a moment to exist, unfiltered, untouched. Can you go for a walk without headphones? Sit on a bench without a book? Lie on your couch—sans music, sans food, sans wine—and hang out for twenty minutes, forty minutes, an hour, and do nothing at all? I dare you. Do it and then report back.

grab a notebook

OK, so. What happened? Nothing, I know. But what was it like? Where did your mind go or attempt to do for and to you? What ideas, monsters, or dancing girls emerged and what did you do about it? What happens when you allow there to be space, with no obligation to do a thing, think a thing, make something with it? What is it like to just be?

grab a notebook

CHAPTER 16

Questioning Commitments Doesn't Make You Noncommittal

Obligation . . . is not the same as commitment, and it's certainly not an acceptable reason to stick with something that isn't working.
—Twyla Tharp, *The Creative Habit*

The best way to describe what we were wearing was Janet Jackson meets Victoria's Secret. It was 1995, so it worked: sheer black lace half top, black bra, black biker shorts, black knee pads. It went Lycra-flesh-Lycra-flesh. We looked like a line of women whose private parts had been redacted.

The problem wasn't the outfit exactly, but the fact that I had two numbers back to back: There was no time to go back to the dressing room in between, which meant you had to change in the wings. Another dancer assigned to you would help you step into the next costume and tie your shoes. I was the queen of the quick change. I stepped into the shorts while another dancer pulled the lace top over my head. Then I dashed out to center stage with the other dancers to get into position. That was always the most exciting moment, right before the lights went up, that long, taut pause when your lungs were heaving and the room went quiet, except for the occasional call out from someone's roommates ("Go, Shelly!"), followed by a ripple of laughter. Then that beat of silence before it all began.

Lights, go! Music, go! The song was something I'm sure was popular at the time; the dance started slinky and tight before bursting into percussion with a stiletto edge. We weren't so much dancing to a song as drawing it along on a silken string. Then I heard some whispering in the front row.

"Her shirt!"

Without moving my head, I could see that my lace top had retracted like a cheap window blind that someone had jerked down and then let go of. I had put it on upside down. There was nothing to be done. You never, *ever* touch your costume on stage. Every time I met another dancer's eye, our eyebrows shot up in surprise and stifled laughter. Josh the stage manager put his hands over his eyes.

To train as a performer, of any kind, is to be committed to performance. And the measure of professionalism is the degree to which you keep going. The show must go on, as they say, with good reason—because it's bigger than you or your problems or your wardrobe malfunction. Doesn't matter what goes wrong. Doesn't matter that you're dancing around the stage with your shirt up around your armpits as if you're being dangled by your ankles off the side of a building.

When people talk about commitment, they tend to think long term. Commitment to a partner, an industry, a cause. We tend to measure commitment in terms of duration, years, decades of resilience. But commitment can be measured in moments. That song lasted four and a half minutes. We were never going to dance it again. We were never going to wear this again. It was my last show, my last year of college. Every minute of it counted. So I committed to the very last beat.

We're told that if we want successful lives, fulfilling careers, we need to commit. It's not that you and I don't know what it means to commit or that we're incapable of doing it. It's that it's not always clear what to commit to, or, perhaps more important, *why*. We just know we "should" be committed—to something, someone. Searching for something to be committed to isn't unlike searching for your passion or trying to fall in love; it assumes that you can aim straight for it and find it, which isn't how that usually works. Leading with commitment makes no sense if you're not sure what it's for; it would be like leading with advocacy without knowing whose side you're on.

Commitment isn't "easy," but that's not the point; it's that once you've made it, it makes other decisions easier. That's why the biggest choices we have to make aren't whether to commit, but what to commit *to*. We tend to rush to the "what"—when it's worth thinking about how we choose what commitments we make to begin with. Don't let anyone tell you that you're incapable of commitment; the expansiveness and depth of your own ability to do so can surprise you. What's limited is time, energy, and attention. So you must choose. Which means you're defined as much by what you *don't* commit to as what you do.

It never occurred to me to walk offstage in the middle of a number—not because I'm an unflappable exhibitionist, but because my concern was no match, in that moment, for the commitment itself. My stakes didn't come *close* to the collective stakes. Anything I did at that moment would be an act of self-consciousness, fear—and would disrupt the delicate symmetry that we'd spent months getting our bodies to learn. One single scared look or tug would break the spell that we'd worked so hard to create and to maintain, just to draw attention to the thing that mattered the *least*. Another thing I knew in my bones was true then and has been 99 out of 100 times since: Most people don't notice most things, and the ones who do usually don't care.

Your Commitment Tells the Story

I knew that this onstage situation was going to make a funny story, and in that moment I got to decide which story I'd tell.

I didn't want it to be The Time Terri Ruined the Show. And while most audience members didn't notice and probably zero remember even being there, that memory for me and a few of my friends serves as a bookmark of that time. After all, it's the one I'm telling you right now.

And honestly? I wanted to dance. That's why I was there. If I took myself out of the moment, not only would it disrupt the other dancers and distract the audience; it also would mean that I, too, would lose that moment I had waited and worked for.

We might think of capital *C* commitment as square jawed and stalwart, with all the joy and levity of a fundamentalist preacher; however, the point in committing or giving yourself wholly over to something, no matter what it is—a dance, a job, a career, a person—is because there's something in it for you, too, because there's rigor and worthiness but also a sensual, even animal pleasure to it, a deep, instinctual wanting for it that disregards any minor obstacle or deterrent.

None of this means I'm better at commitment; it just means that I knew why I was there. And if we know why we're in a place or doing a thing, it makes it easier to keep doing it—which is the one thing that commitment requires.

Dropping a Commitment Doesn't Make You "Noncommittal"

I let things go all the time. I drop the threads of more conversations than I can count; start projects I don't finish, abandoning them like old woodsheds or stalled-out cars. I've slept with people I didn't feel committed to, and slept with people who weren't committed to *other* people. Does that make me noncommittal? Not a chance. And it doesn't make you noncommittal either.

Because the term "noncommittal" assumes that either you can't do it or you're afraid of doing it. For a long time I used to joke that I was noncommittal—because I liked to date and wasn't interested in settling down in the way a lot of people do. I wasn't noncommittal; I was quite committed—to freedom. I'm also committed to doing my best work, and that means I do it the way it works for me.

Commitment Is Not a Thing; It's an Act

Commitment doesn't exist in a vacuum. If you don't apply it to something, it's just an idea, a floating notion of all-in-ness without something to be all into. It's like any core value (trust, excellence, et cetera); if you have nothing to tether it to, it just hangs on a wall as an idea of something you like.

What's critical is getting clear on *why* we make the commitments we do, and it won't always be obvious to anyone else (not that it matters).

In *Essentialism: The Disciplined Pursuit of Less,* Greg McKeown says the instinct to overcommit, to say yes, to think, *I can do both,* is where focus and productivity break down. You can do anything, in other words—you just can't do *everything.* True productivity is not about getting the most things done, he says. It's about getting the *right* things done. "Only once you give yourself permission to stop trying to do it all, to stop saying yes to everyone," he writes, "can you make your highest contribution towards the things that really matter."[1]

Take my life, for example. I have a group of friends I'd lie down in traffic for. Some I talk to every day; some I see once or twice a year. I have a cat but no kids. A bike but no car. I rent my apartment; I own my business. I do work I love for people I respect. I spend my disposable income on excellent skin care, good food, and soft clothing. And maybe a pair of badass boots. I keep occasional company, but I cherish my alone time above all.

You might look at my life and say, "Wow. I want that life! How can I get that life?" But for every person who thinks that, there are ten others who say, "Poor thing, never had a family, and she's compensating with face cream and sushi."

Or you could conclude, based on my relationship status,

lifestyle, and choices, that I have a "commitment issue." There are men I've been involved with who probably think I have a commitment issue (which I did—because I didn't want to commit to *them*). But in fact there's nothing in my life that actually suggests a lack of commitment. It's not even a matter of whether I "believe" I'm committed; I show it. There really isn't any other way.

You might also be totally OK with how things are and your life as is, and wonder why you're questioned on it, and then think maybe there really is something wrong with you (there isn't). Maybe you're doing what you always wanted to do, or never expected to, and both are equally wonderful. Your life might look starkly different from others', perhaps strikingly different. You might have resisted the clarion call to "settle down" (oy). You may be committed to a cause but not a role, a career path but not an industry, a feeling but not one person. There are as many things to commit to as there are people to commit to them. The point is, every choice to commit should be a choice, not a default.

Commitment is not a binary—it's not that you are or aren't committed, which is why the word "noncommittal" is tough to apply across the board. Commitment itself is defined as the state or quality of being dedicated to something. But its secondary definition is "an engagement or obligation that restricts freedom of action." That means being overcommitted is the same as not being committed at all.

Commitment, like love, is an action, a decision. Not a free-floating thing or trait we all lay occasional claim to. "We often think of choice as a thing," McKeown writes. "But a choice is not a thing. Our options may be things, but a choice—a choice is an action."[2] The risk is that if you feel you must prove how committed you are, you may end up clinging to wrongheaded, ill-serving commitments that capsize your life and sanity. I believe in worthy effort; I do not believe in going down with the ship.

When to Bail

After college, I joined a semipro dance company in the Boston area. I was working full-time as an office admin and this group became the vibrant, pulsing oasis of my life. I loved the people, the music, the two hours every Tuesday and Thursday when I could get out of my head and back into my body.

But after many happy years of rehearsals and shows, things changed; with new leadership, the tone of the group felt different. I sensed distrust, suspicion, and jealousy rising like roots in a crowded planter. The group had evolved, as groups do. But I didn't recognize it anymore. Something fundamental had shifted and I found myself bumping up against new edges a lot. They suggested a leave of absence and I took it; I never went back.

We should be clear here that commitment isn't the same as compliance, or dependence, or need. No one else can commit for you or "make" you do it, especially if you don't want to; if they do, you can call it many things, but you can't call it commitment. And just as choosing what to commit to is critical, so is choosing when that commitment has run its course.

When Your Healthy Commitment Costs You More Than You Thought

My friend Alex Jamieson became vegan in 2000 in an attempt to reboot her body from years of unhealthy eating. And it worked; she felt great. As she learned more about the effect of food, not just on her health but also on the health of the planet, her commitment deepened. This, she said, was the answer to obesity! World hunger! Climate change!

Her partner at the time, filmmaker Morgan Spurlock, decided to eat McDonald's every day for a month and see what happened, resulting in the award-winning documentary *Super Size Me*, and Alex was heretofore introduced to the world as the vegan girlfriend. She started to gain a following and was enjoying success as a noted name in the vegan movement, which allowed her to reach and help even more people.

It was all great! Until, years later, something changed. She started feeling . . . off. She became anemic, and was diagnosed with hypothyroidism. And for a full year, she tried everything within the vegan framework to address the issue, essentially mainlining sea veggies and green juice, thinking that recommitting, more intensely, would save her. Nothing worked. The body has wisdom beyond diet or agenda. And her body was no longer whispering; it was shouting. It didn't matter that what she had believed in was virtuous or, to her mind, "better." The body does not make such commitments. One day she sat across from a friend who ordered a burger and instead of being disgusted . . . her mouth watered. One day she put an egg in her mouth for the first time in many, many years. And rather than revolt, her body screamed, *Yesssss!*

What followed was a torrid and unspeakable months-long affair . . . with animal products. She was sneaking around with meat. And as she fed her body what it wanted, her cravings quieted. She felt different. She felt . . . better.

What did she do about all this?

Well, for a while, she went ahead and shut the fuck up about it. After all, she was the poster child of vegan virtue, a model for thousands of followers, clients who came to her, often weeping, feeling like failures, because they couldn't do what *she* was doing. Talk about pressure. She thought about coming out sooner, but she says she was afraid—of what not just her vegan friends would think but also her family, her clients, her friends.

You can only live in a state of cognitive dissonance like that for so long. What's more, she realized that by keeping this secret, she was contributing to the hostile food culture that caused perfectly rational people to sneak food home and eat in the dark while hating themselves.

Finally, she came clean. In her viral blog post, "I'm Not Vegan Anymore," Alex shared what had happened and was happening, which was that "after working for twelve years as a health and wellness professional," she said, "I'd developed an eating disorder."[3] She realized she had become part of the problem. Just because she wasn't vegan anymore didn't mean she gave up and ate glazed doughnuts all day. "I began to see my cravings for animal foods from a different angle," she wrote. "It wasn't immoral or wrong. It just was. I came to believe that trusting your body, living your truth, whether it be vegan, part-time vegan, flexitarian, or carnivore, is all inherently good."[4]

She may have broken a commitment to a strict vegan diet, but it's not like she was turning on vegetables; rather, her health and her perspective had evolved, and she had something new to offer. By helping people accept, rather than resist, cravings, she writes, she could help them "create lives of meaning, freedom and radical self-acceptance."[5] What changed was the tool she'd been using to do that, and it allowed her to offer something that people obsessed with weight and crippled by shame need even more: compassion.

Her post, as you can imagine, sparked outrage and debate and she got more than her fair share of vitriol. (She even got death threats! From vegans!) She lost plenty of die-hard vegan fans and followers, and gained new ones. It also led to a pivotal discussion, a best-selling book, a new podcast. In short, Alex Jamieson's story isn't about a "broken" commitment; it's about one that *evolved*. And for every vegan who unsubscribed in a huff, think of how many more she can reach and help in ways she might not have before. I recently met up with her for dinner (we split a rib-eye steak!), and she told me about how her coaching practice has changed. It's not even just about food or diet; she's helping women in high-stress careers gain clarity and creative agency in their work and lives. Her website reads: "You can't be defined by one box." And she should know.

The choices we make and commitments we made are not prehistoric spiders locked in amber. They're actions we take over and over again because we believe in what we're doing, want and need to do them, and feed them because we are in critical ways fed by them as well.

Commitment Has a Cost

I told you about how I left a consulting role that I'd been in some ways overly committed to, and how it taught me a hard lesson about being too dependent. Commitment is an action, not an attribute. I say this because we can get it twisted and end up staying in things (jobs, relationships, you name it) way beyond the expiration date simply because we fear that to end that commitment says something bad about us. Commitments are not "owed"; they're given and given freely, for as long as you choose to commit. Full. Stop.

The moment I got laid off from my full-time job in 2011, the company ended its commitment to me, which meant I was relieved of my commitment too. I walked away from a desk full of work. Commitments are conditional; when the agreement changes, you reconsider the deal. Of course, since your commitment is yours, you can choose to stay in the game even if the money runs out. You can hang in there with a scrappy start-up as long as you like, but no one would blame you for leaving if you can't afford your life. You can play lame gigs with a band for years and quit the day before they get signed. It's a risk you take.

If you're not allowed to end a commitment, you're being kept against your own will and someone needs to call the authorities. The idea that commitment is sacred in and of itself, regardless of what it's attached to, and thus should supersede money (equitable pay, cough cough), quality of life, health, or anything else is not only nuts; it's not true.

What Are You Committed to (and How Do You Know)?

You might be committed to a job, a cause, a mission. Or you might be committed to improving your health, working out, writing a book. Here's the rub: You can't just be committed to an idea; you have to actually do something. And if you don't make time to do it, don't find ways to make it happen, are you really committed? If a tree falls in the forest . . . OK, fine. You get it. You can tell me you're committed to the idea of meeting me for a drink, but if you can't pick a date I can assume you're not all that committed.

Your life is richer *and* more limited by the commitments you make, and there are zillions of ways and things to commit to. They don't have to look like anyone else's, and they require no defense. Commitment, like passion, is the energy and attention you give to one thing at the expense of the others. And it stops when you stop.

You are not the promise you made two, ten, twenty years ago, whatever that promise was. You are the one you keep making, every day, every moment. What that means is that you're capable of commitment and can plug it into whatever you do—but more important, you can change it, because your commitment begins and ends with you.

write your next chapter

Let's Look at the Commitments

First, make a list of the things you're committed to, right now. Things that require time, attention, deliverables, and actual space on your calendar (regular and healthy family dinners versus solving world hunger).

grab a notebook

Next, rate each commitment on a scale of 0 to 5. Go back over the list and do a gut check, rating each item on a scale of 0 to 5, with 0 = I feel no or low energy when I think about this and 5 = I feel energized and aligned when I do it.

- How are the items that you scored a 3 or lower detracting from what you rated a 4 or a 5?
- What decisions can you make that will allow you to give more of your time and attention to the 4s and 5s (ideally, even, just the 5s)?
- What scored the highest on your list? If there's only one crown, which one are you giving it to?
- What would it look like to make that the priority? What can you cancel, delegate, or gracefully bow out of?
- What would the next step be?

Think of a time when your own commitment surprised you. Maybe you didn't realize you could *do* that or have that kind of courage, resolve, or even fun. Set the timer for fifteen minutes. Start writing.

grab a notebook

CHAPTER 17

Tell Your Critic to STFU So You Can Get Some Work Done

Do what is natural, what is easy, what is apparent to you. Your unique view will be a revelation to someone else.
—Patricia Madson, *Improv Wisdom*

Years ago, at the invitation (and benevolent urging) of a friend, I attended a writing workshop in Tiverton, Rhode Island. We huddled around the living room with blankets and pillows as the first autumn chill settled across New England. We were told that this was going to be different from any other writing workshops we'd likely been in before (and I'd been in *plenty*). The retreat leader, Suzanne Kingsbury, gave us a prompt and told us we would write silently for about twenty minutes. Then we would read aloud what we had just now written, and give one another feedback. Only not the kind of feedback we (or at least I) expected, where people tell you what they were confused by or what you should fix. Or worse, what they didn't like.

No. This would be a dramatic departure from all that. There would be no questions. No suggestions. No criticism of any kind. Instead, we would share what we loved about it, what was working, what really sang on the page. The reason, she said, was that when we mute the incessant mental chatter that tries to talk us out of doing anything risky, our writing becomes rich, powerful, and fascinating. Whereas criticism, even just the *anticipation* of it, is like throwing cold water on a flame when what we need is to feed that fire.

This threw me. I'd always loved to write but had spent my life doubting whether I was a "real" writer—regardless of the As, the contest awards, the master's degree in creative writing, the fact that I was employed by and writing for a national magazine. *Didn't matter.* It was impostor syndrome of the highest order. All those external forms of validation? Pshaw. Didn't do shit to move my work, or me, forward. A real writer, in my mind, would . . . work as an intrepid reporter or write screenplays or novels and have Big Ideas about the World. A *real* writer was fearless and bold and knew things that I didn't. I figured I was just good with words, the way some people are good at organizing closets.

But like many writers, I wanted to write a book, and was afraid I never could or would, that if I did no one would buy it or read it. I had a million reasons why, and I believed them all, including that I could be good at a thing and yet never good enough.

As you can imagine, this warm, welcoming room where all you heard was what was good, powerful, and strong in your work was . . . disorienting. Too good to be true. The more closely I listened to the work being read, the more I trained my brain on what *was* working, the more the synapses in my brain started firing. When it was my turn to read aloud, the feedback felt like lightning shot straight into my veins. I was told what I wrote was funny and relatable and real. The other participants told me not just that they liked it but also *what* they liked about it. This blew me away. As Suzanne will tell you, it's quite unusual to receive validation for any work, but creative work specifically—which is why it feels so foreign to us.

But my inner critic, the unbearable Karen of my brain (and

likely yours), piped up: *That's all very nice, but we'd like to speak to the manager, please.*

I approached Suzanne at the break. "How will I get better if I'm only hearing good things? How will I know what people really think?" Suzanne smiled, the way she smiles at someone on the verge of a breakthrough who doesn't know it yet (I've seen it many times since)—beaming me in like a lighthouse through a smog of self-doubt.

"Sweetheart, this *is* how you improve. I know you think hearing what's 'wrong' will help. That's how we're conditioned to think, but not how it works. Trust me, you'll see."

Turns out, almost every writer she had worked with had the same knee-jerk response that I had—suspicion, doubt, disbelief. If it doesn't hurt, we think, how will we grow? If I gonked you over the head with a firm but flexible object every day and told you it made you stronger and then one day started handing you chocolates instead, you'd be suspicious too.

We think something should hurt to be good for us, but it really doesn't have to. In fact, it can feel like the opposite of hurt to take a risk, to make something, and to share it with someone else. Remember what Marcus Buckingham said about comfort zones? Take us out of them and "our brains stop paying attention to anything other than surviving the experience." Where we're comfiest, we're also the most creative and insightful.

And as for improvement? "Learning is less a function of adding something that isn't there," Buckingham and Goodall write, "than it is of recognizing, reinforcing, and refining what already is."[1] For two reasons, they say. One: because we tend to become better at things we're already good at. And two: because attention to what's working helps us learn more quickly. "Learning rests on our grasp of what we're doing well, not on what we're doing poorly, and certainly not on someone else's sense of what we're doing poorly,"[2] they write.

Suzanne has spent years studying how our (traditional) approach to feedback can block and discourage the creative process. After finding early success as a best-selling novelist only to find herself creatively blocked while earning her MFA, she became fascinated at this disconnect, this way in which the conditioned mind and the cult of criticism work against us. As a Fulbright scholar, she studied the research exploring the intersection between neurology, Zen Buddhism, and literature—all of which informed her approach as a workshop leader and developmental editor-slash-"book shaman" who helps writers and makers of all kinds access their creative genius. The result is what she named the Gateless Method, a specific approach to creative work, originally developed for writers, to help get past the blocks put there by the internalized critic and reinforced by cultural conditioning.

"What the studies out of the University of Pennsylvania, Harvard, Johns Hopkins, and the National Institutes of Health have shown us," she says, "is that when criticism, competition, and judgment are present, the amygdala goes into fight or flight—which makes it very hard to access imagination and memory, which are critical to writing." But when those subjects were nurtured and taught what worked, the amygdala relaxed. What this means, she says, is that to reach our highest creative potential, the part of our brain associated with criticism and resistance needs to be quieted.

That means that hearing criticism, which we think will hurt so good it'll make us better, doesn't. In fact, it may hinder growth. "The research is clear," say Buckingham and Goodall. "Telling people what we think of their performance doesn't help them thrive and excel, and telling people how we think they should improve actually hinders learning."[3]

You'll get (and grow) more from leaning into what you're good at. Criticism causes a contraction, or "squeeze," causing you to tighten up and shut down—and so if we want to create or learn or actually improve in anything we care about we need to do the opposite and seek expansion—and ease.

Are there times when behavior must be corrected and instructions taught? Of course. Does a writer need an editor? Yup. This isn't about glazing over flaws and deciding everything is wonderful exactly as is. It's about feeling ownership and sovereignty in your work, rather than someone who needs to be "fixed." It's about replacing criticism with craft, and antagonism with agency. Because how can you lean into what's working if you're only told what's wrong? How can you find a confident stride if you're worried about where to step? And chances are, if I ask you to recall the last time someone specifically pointed out to you something you did that was fantastic, genius, impressive, or great, you're going to need a minute. Whereas the last time someone gave you "feedback" or advice for improvement? You can recall it like *that.*

The whole experience reinforced for me just how critical comfort is—especially when you're feeling blocked. A sense of safety and camaraderie, trust and security, emerges when you work within a space defined by a simple set of rules that seal out criticism, judgment, and doubt.

I'll tell you what happened that weekend: A dam broke. Not just inside me but inside every person in that room. I saw it. I felt it. Freed from the worry of whether we were doing this or that right, from the fear of being judged or criticized or picked apart by our peers, we could just . . . write. Writing went from trudging upstream to floating down a river. The effect of having spent four days hearing what was working in my own writing, and training my ear on what was working in others', completely shifted my focus, attention, and mood.

By Sunday afternoon when we left our little comfort zone in Rhode Island and one another, I had all the symptoms of falling in love: I felt expanded and weightless, filled with fresh air and fairy lights, flying down Route 84, all five bars blinking on my internal battery. Things felt easier, frictionless, as if until that point I'd been driving around with the emergency brake on and finally let it go. I also got a glimpse of myself at my very best, a version I had not seen in ages, which alone was worth the price of admission.

Two of the women on retreat, who've since become close friends, started writing scenes for fun that weekend—and today are in the final edits of their novels. Some of the people there have since left their spouses; others became better spouses. Better parents. Better friends. Why? Because when you decide to see what's working, Suzanne says, you can let the rest fall away. And: You become less tolerant of not only what isn't working but also the people who love to keep reminding you of that.

Not long after, I left a go-nowhere relationship and a toxic client (which you now know all about), upleveled my business, and started to take my writing seriously again. I had no idea what it would be, any more than you can see New York from Boston—but I knew what direction to head in. I attended all the retreats I possibly could, and went on to certify as a Gateless Writing instructor, creating and holding that space for other people, and using it to great effect in my work as a creative professional and brand advisor. It was and is the rising tide that lifts all of my boats.

Maybe this is really speaking to you because you want to write. Or maybe you don't want to write, but you want to make, or bake, or take pictures. Something in you is screaming for self-expression. One of the most powerful, transformative things you will ever do is make something. The second most powerful thing you can do? Share it.

Why should you—because you're a secret genius? Because it will make you money? Maybe. But that's not the point. Making isn't just for people who identify as artists; the inclination to make something—draw or construct or write or invent or find a solution—is inherently human. We can't help it. It's hardwired. But some of us might have stopped doing it years ago and instead just did what other people wanted, for any number of reasons, not the least of which is that it felt like the safest route to take. And safe comes at a cost too.

When People Tell You It's "Hard"

When I went to shop this book around, years later, I expected a blend of rejection and radio silence. I knew this would be a steep climb that guaranteed all the heartbreak and none of the results. The "no thank yous" aren't part of the problem, of course; they're part of the game. You only need one yes.

There are many ways up that mountain. Traditionally (though certainly not always), you send your proposal to an agent who decides whether it's something she a) likes and b) can sell to a publisher. That's not always how it goes, but that's the path I took. What I heard from some of the brightest, most successful, and most responsive agents (since most didn't say boo about it) surprised me. It wasn't just "no thanks," which would have been easy enough. I expected that. What I heard, instead, more than once, was this:

"What you are trying to do is hard."

They told me that writing is hard. Publishing is hard. That particular genre I want to write in? Hard.

Of course, I knew this already. I didn't decide to be a writer the week I started contacting agents, nor did I pitch them on a whim of an idea I'd come up with the night before. I'd been in the muck of it for a while. I knew what felt hard, and what was, statistically speaking, hard to accomplish (landing an agent and getting a book deal). Yes. What they said wasn't a lie. I didn't expect a glitter bomb.

But what they said was not only profoundly unhelpful and mildly patronizing; it was a way to act as if they weren't making a decision when really they were. Throwing your hands up that "publishing" is hard is a great way to deflect blame. Because rather than just own a decision and say, "I don't think I can sell this book," they made it about how I'd chosen a thing that was too hard for me *and* for them. Or that the genre was hard (show me one that isn't).

I'm sure they were just trying to be nice. But I respected the people who simply passed on it more than the ones who tried to teach me about the world. Because then it was less about owning a decision and more about "why I know more than you." To my mind this friendly fire is lethal, because while a gatekeeper is well within her rights to make a decision, the "life is hard" approach attempts to tell you why you can't get where you want and that it's out of all of our hands. I call bullshit. And now I'll wait while you go read every biography of every writer, musician, actor, teacher, inventor, philosopher, or business owner who was told they couldn't do what they wanted to do, and who proved them wrong.

Done? Moving on.

We all have to say no to most things to get even *one* thing done, to pass on opportunities, sometimes even good ones. But telling someone that xyz is "hard" is insidious: It disempowers the other person by passing the buck and blaming the world/market/industry. ("It's not me! It's just . . . the world is hard.")

There's also no good response to it. What was I supposed to say when they said the book I wanted to write was hard? "Oh! OK. Then I'll now pitch you my other book on the mating habits of the helmeted water toad. Want that one?"

Fact is, *everything* worth doing is hard. Building a business is hard. Ending a relationship is hard. Raising kids is hard. Getting out of bed is pretty damn hard. Even the holidays, which at this point swallow a sixth of our entire calendar year and are singularly dedicated to lights and music and gifts? That's one of the hardest times of the year for too many people.

If you listened every time someone told you things were hard, you wouldn't be anywhere. And neither would I. This is how blocks, even the things other people think are "helpful," get in our way. And if we let them tell us what to do, we wouldn't do a thing. No one would try anything new, and we'd all be in our homes without electricity or internet or machine-washable fabrics.

When you look back over your life, the things that were hard to do were also worth it. And you did them for a reason. What we have to be careful of, myself included, is falling into the trap of telling ourselves that things are hard, even too hard, and use that as a reason not to do them.

And here's my point: Calling something hard is actually really easy. It's the easiest thing in the fucking world, which is why you hear so many people do it.

What if, instead of talking about how hard things are, we talked about why they're worth it?

Why Quieting the Critic Works

The Gateless Method, originally developed by Suzanne Kingsbury to help writers push through blocks, creates the conditions and container for generating and creating great work, regardless of what you make or do. I found this so profound in my own work that I went on to certify as an instructor and I use this tool in just about every kind of work I do.

Here's how it works: The workshop leader brings you into a relaxed state with a brief meditation, and then gives you a writing prompt and short window (anywhere from five minutes to a half hour) to write freely. Then members of the group take turns reading their unedited drafts aloud to one another, and the group shares feedback that focuses specifically on what's working and why. It sounds simple, and it is in theory, but the experience of it can be profound.

Here's a bit more insight into why (and how) this approach works:

- **YOU ARE GIVEN A SET OF GUIDELINES.** At the outset of every workshop, or salon, as they're called, we establish the rules of engagement: No questions, criticisms, or suggestions; we talk about the work, not the writer/creator; we stay on the page rather than refer to our own personal experiences or work. These rules pacify the part of the brain that craves order and control, while freeing up the creative mind to explore freely.
- **YOU STIMULATE THE CORPUS CALLOSUM.** Joseph Bogen, a neurophysiologist and clinical professor of neurosurgery, found that the corpus callosum—a bundle of nerve tissue that connects the two lobes of the brain—is thicker in people who score high on creativity tests.[4] When you're engaged with the prompted writing exercise and not worried about critique or judgment, you can support more activity between the two lobes.
- **YOU DECREASE NOREPINEPHRINE.** Dr. Kenneth M. Heilman, professor of neurology at the University of Florida, found in brain studies that during heightened creative thought the neurotransmitter norepinephrine—responsible for anxiety, low energy, and decreased focus—is greatly reduced.[5] Heilman also found that

students working with lowered norepinephrine made novel connections, and were more likely to come up with new ideas.

- **YOU FREE UP YOUR LIMBIC CENTERS.** When neuro-researchers Charles Limb and Allen Braun performed brain imagery scans on jazz musicians, they found that when the musicians were spontaneously composing—without risk of critical analysis—the brain functioning in the prefrontal cortex associated with conscious control and self-monitoring was suppressed.[6] In other words, the limbic centers of the brain were set free, which allowed for intense, highly emotive work.
- **YOU BEGIN TO RETRAIN YOUR BRAIN.** A negative bias is great for avoiding danger, not great for generating creative work. Dr. Rick Hanson, neuropsychologist and author of *Hardwiring Happiness: The New Brain Science of Contentment, Calm, and Confidence*, says that the practice of "taking in the good" can shift the brain from negative to positive. A focus on what's working can actually help retrain our brains to do that, rather than only get snagged on the negative.
- **YOU LEAVE ON A HIGH NOTE.** Suzanne says it's not uncommon for Gateless students to feel something akin to postcoital after an experience like this. I can attest to that. It's wild. It's so rare to hear what's working in your own work that it can stimulate a kind of expansiveness, arousal—the sense that you can do just about anything.
- **YOU TAKE IT WITH YOU.** What happens in a Gateless session doesn't tend to stay there—meaning: Once you start to find ease in your own work and look for what's working, you might find that this has a lovely spillover effect in your job, your relationships, your family. You start to see evidence of what's working everywhere; you spot new potential and possibilities where none existed before. And while the world doesn't adhere to the rules of this methodology, being in that environment strengthens your perspective and sense of self so that you're less tolerant of people who cling to the negative, and less interested in doing it yourself.

write your next chapter

Try the Gateless approach on for size. You can put the principles of this method to work for you, even outside of a salon, just to see how quickly and profoundly it can shift your mood and the way people respond to you too.

Point out what's working. For one full day (I'd recommend longer), make it a point to call out, write out, point out, precisely why someone's work is brilliant. This is not flattery, mind you. This isn't "great shoes" or "I love your jacket" (though that's nice too). This is about listening and paying close attention to what they're doing that's working, and specifically why. *Why* was that presentation strong? Why was that an excellent point to make? *What* did you notice about what someone said or did that was effective? Make a practice of it and you'll find people opening up to you in new ways. Jot down a few specific instances or observations that you've noticed, admired, or appreciated recently. Then, tell them.

grab a notebook

Look at what's working in your own work. You don't have to believe your work is flawless or perfect—that's not helpful. Rather, look for, highlight, write down what you're doing that you like, enjoy, and are finding a connection to in your work. If you can't see what's working, how do you expect to do more of it? List at least three things that are working in what you're doing right now.

grab a notebook

Hear out the critic. That critic isn't going anywhere. She (or he, or they—whichever pronouns apply) will find ways to stop you from taking risks. When the fears arise from the critic chatter ("What if I look dumb?" "What if I ruin everything?"), it's worth taking five minutes to sit down with the critic and let her voice all her concerns at once.

- LET IT OUT. Write "What are you going on about?" or "What is your problem right now?"; set a timer for five minutes (ten if you need), and then dump it out on the page. Write it out of your system and let her tantrum wind down. You might write it in first person or second person. Whatever works. Don't react—just let her get it out.

grab a notebook

- REREAD—AND QUESTION. What you will find is that the critic generalizes, contradicts herself, makes outlandish, unsubstantiated claims, and flat out lies. Now it's your turn to do the critique. Underline, circle, write question marks in the margins. Is that true? (Probably not.) Is it always true? (Nope.) Is this a foregone conclusion? Note the contradictions; i.e., one moment she's telling you you'll never accomplish X but that when you do it'll be an embarrassment. Really? Which is it? Neither, that's what.
- ASSESS RESOURCES. The critic may be calling attention to holes in your knowledge or toolbox ("You don't know anything about X and you're gonna look stupid!"). What you can say is, "What I'm hearing is I could use more training around X or help with this thing." Who can you ask? What help can you get? Meet the critic's fears with resources, ideas, and actions. She doesn't get the last word; you do.
- CLOSE THE NOTEBOOK. Now that she's had her tantrum, the critic can return to her restless sleep while you get back to work.

CHAPTER 18

Stop Fixing What Isn't Broken

Everything can be taken from a man but one thing: the last of the human freedoms—to choose one's attitude in any given set of circumstances, to choose one's own way.
—Viktor E. Frankl, *Man's Search for Meaning*

I throw my back out once in a while. It happens. One particularly difficult spasm comes to mind. I was leaning forward to move a box on a high shelf. The dumbest, most boring injury in the world. But you feel it so hard you can literally almost hear it, echoing through every nerve like a silent scream.

Muscles overreact; it's what they do. You may not break your spine moving a box, but your muscles *think* you're about to, so they step in to save you from yourself by biting down hard—that's it; no one's moving, not today, not for days. Muscles aim to protect, but they also hold grudges, and they can hang on a long time.

I went to see my chiropractor, a lovely woman about my age with a quiet sense of humor and a handsome jawline, a woman who goes rafting and does yoga in Costa Rica, and who I imagine can pitch a tent in the dark. She explained "subluxation," or a misalignment of the vertebra. She didn't say I had that—because what I had were spasming muscles. But chiropractic theory holds that misalignment in the spine creates pain and tension and can ultimately lead to illness and disease. Different experts describe subluxation in so many ways it's become a catchall theory for everything related to the spine, and for the most part conventional medicine thinks it's a lot of bunk.

Here's what I found interesting: You could have a spinal misalignment and experience no pain or symptoms whatsoever. Or you could have pain and discomfort without appearing to have what might be deemed a subluxation. The theory that misalignment equals pain can be inaccurate but diagnostically convenient: It's easy to pathologize pain when you have evidence of a problem. You might get an X-ray and be told by a health professional, "Oh, see that subluxation? That's the cause of your pain," when that may not actually be true.

We'd all love to draw a clear line from problem to symptom to solution. A plus B is causing C. And while you'd think having a picture of your actual spine would be a foolproof way to get at the cause, that's not always true. It seems like a good idea—that is, if we believe pain is a crime and an X-ray is a lie detector test. But in fact you can have a subluxation and no symptoms, or you could have pain while nothing seems obviously wrong. Pain is complex in that way. Though you see the danger: You could have pain, find a subluxation, and assume they're causally linked, go through treatments, even surgery, only to find that your back pain is not better; it's worse.

That's a thing, by the way. It's literally called Failed Back Surgery—and it occurs in anywhere from 10 to 40 percent of lumbar laminectomy surgeries.[1] Would you take those odds on restaurant reservations? ("We can hold a table for you, but there's up to a 40 percent chance it won't be available when you show up.") What's more, as much as 36 percent of people who undergo surgery for a herniated disc see their leg and back pain return *two years later.*

Not only do we sometimes end up trying to fix the wrong things—the fixes don't even *work*. And if we make the big leap from back pain to your actual, literal life, then it's worth considering that whatever pain we feel, whether it's shockingly sharp or a deep, roaming ache, the cause may not be what we think it is. And even if you find the root cause, it may not be as helpful as you hoped.

So it stands to reason that if you believe there's a hole in your life because you haven't found X (a man, a woman, a hypoallergenic dog, your dream job, your ultimate purpose), how sure are you that that's the answer? You're not, of course. I'm not trying to tell you not to want what you want. But to pin everything onto one goal, to believe that *one* thing would "fix" your life? Do you believe that's true? What are the odds? Ten to 40 percent, would you say?

If It Ain't Broke . . .

We think to fix a thing is to troubleshoot it, to remove a flaw. That's not actually the definition of "fix." "To fix" means to fasten securely in a particular place or position; to make permanent or secure.

When things are "fixed," it makes it *harder* for us to grow, change, evolve, any of it. A fixed mindset, as we discussed earlier, is one that sees everything as a zero-sum game, on or off, black or white. Good or bad. The problem is that we're always bumping up against "fixed" (and conflicting) ideas about how things *should* be—at work, home, in relationships or just the general #patriarchy. Things that we believed were permanent or right or the way to be often aren't quite so simple or set.

Believing things are fixed or need to be fixed *is the problem*.

Everything is in flux and in flow. Your career, which may look "fixed" on your résumé or LinkedIn profile, a stack of experiences linked by date, is actually a living, changing, arcing thing. You're always ahead of it, living into the next phase. A résumé is always past tense; it could change ten minutes from now.

Your relationships, too, must move forward or they wither. Your address, your job, your taste in footwear, your feelings about a strong lip versus a smoky eye—all in flux!

It's not that it's all out of our control or that we can't change things on purpose. Of course we can. In fact, the less "fixed" we are in our mindset, the more we can change and evolve the way we want to. The problem is when we might assume parts of us are flawed or permanently damaged, when they're anything but.

A Life-and-Death Situation

When I was thirty-two, I got sick. It wasn't flu sick, and it wasn't cancer sick; it was the kind of sick that strikes like lightning and nearly kills you on the spot.

I was on a business trip to a conference in Baltimore, and had a deep ache in my abdomen that continued to worsen. When I woke up, the pain was no longer a tiny, aching seed, but full-grown. It had stood up inside me and assumed full height; it had taken over. I called my doctor, who ordered me to get to the ER, stat. I called a cab. "Where would you take your daughter if she was sick?" The driver dropped me off at the entrance to University of Maryland Medical Center.

The doctors didn't know what it was. They crossed out one diagnosis after another: pelvic inflammatory disorder, appendicitis, syphilis. In the middle of the night, my blood pressure dropped to something like 60/40, an entire river slowing to a stop. I was rushed into surgery. The doctor unzipped me from stem to stern, took out each of my internal organs, turned them over in his hands like fruit, looking for the bruised spot. There was nothing to see. There was nothing to fix.

I had acute sepsis, which is when wayward bacteria get in and turn your whole body against you. For many, sepsis is the very last phase, and then it's over. However, I came to, fully intubated and disoriented in the shadowless light of the ICU, feeling as if I'd woken up inside someone else. The antibiotics saved my life. A week later, I left the hospital with a nine-inch scar that started above my navel and cut a rough path down through the center of me, laddered with staples like railroad ties. I couldn't sit up or move easily; I was pinned at the center like a butterfly.

The scar has gotten both tougher and softer with time, as have I. I often forget it's even there, except for when I put on a bathing suit or a lover runs a curious thumb along the edge. And sometimes, during yoga—the practice of expanding, of making room in the body—that's when I feel the hem of it, a single stitch pulling toward the earth. The surgery wasn't a mistake; they had to do it. The antibiotics are what saved my life; the surgery (which we often see as the ultimate fix) didn't change anything—all it really did was complicate and delay my recovery. In other words, I spent more time healing from the fix than from the sepsis itself.

It took nearly a month to recover. I couldn't work, or teach in the evenings. I had to postpone all those side-hustle jewelry parties. I watched as a schedule once teeming with activity slowly emptied of its chaos like a beach at sundown. How odd, to uncouple your purpose from your obligations, from your schedule, from the work that defines you. I had so identified with what I did that I almost didn't know who I was without it. When I gave away, canceled, and let go of all my obligations, I almost couldn't believe there was anything of me left. But there was. And what's even stranger was how full I felt, how cared for, how grateful I was to be that lucky and that loved. I lay on my mother's couch those first nights home, teary eyed, not because I felt bad for myself; rather, I felt so light I thought I might just float away. In the days and weeks to come, I started putting weight back on, felt my energy rising in my spine like mercury, ready to weather a new day.

If you've ever had an experience like that, a life-quake moment (and I'm guessing you either did or were close to someone who had), you realize pretty quickly who you are and what you aren't. And if you've ever mistaken yourself for your job, your commitments, your dreams, or even your relationships, you probably know (or will learn) that you *aren't* those things—that you survive them, in fact.

Our Collective Life-Quake Moment

We all did live through something like that—the year 2020. It will live in infamy as one of the most terrifying, disruptive, and, oddly, boring years of our lives. All of life as we knew it to be—what it looked like, felt like, moved like—came to a grinding halt. Things we used to care about and do were stripped of their meaning and value because we didn't even *do* them anymore, and the most popular tool of communication became . . . virtual business conference software (WTF?).

Of course, not everything could be solved by Zoom: People lost their lives, their businesses, their jobs, their minds. What we thought mattered fell away and what really mattered made itself clear. A year at home was enough to raise the very critical question of WTF am I doing here, exactly? The Prudential Pulse of the American Worker Survey, published in March 2021, found that one in four working adults were planning to leave their jobs and seek out new opportunities as the threat of the pandemic receded.[2] We reconsidered what we were doing but also with whom: Bloomberg News reported that March 2020 saw a spike in divorces in China, record-high requests that led to backlogs in government offices so long that workers barely had time for water breaks.[3] At the time of this writing, we don't yet have all the data on post-pandemic divorce rates. I imagine many of those spouses are still eyeing the door.

When You Forget Who You Are for a Sec

In the first TED talk ever to go viral, Harvard-trained neuroanatomist Jill Bolte Taylor details the workings of her mind during a severe brain hemorrhage in 1996.

What she describes is inexplicable: When her left hemisphere, which governs that sense of us being separate and self-contained, began to shut down, her right hemisphere took over, and she experienced a kind of euphoria. Her brain went silent, as if she'd hit the mute button. What remained was total peace. In the shower, she looked at her arm and couldn't tell where she ended and the wall began; instead of her body here and the rest of the world there, she saw a swirling mass of atoms and energy, indistinguishable one from the other.

She struggled to operate the phone while drifting in and out of a dreamy, ecstatic state. She described feeling large and uncontained, an expansive flow of energy, a whale bounding through infinite waves. She couldn't imagine she could fit all of that energy back into her tiny body, even if she tried. When she was rolled into the ambulance, she realized this might be it; she felt her spirit surrender. She was surprised to wake up hours later.

It's no wonder her TED talk went viral. It's not only a feat of incredible storytelling (I challenge you to watch it and not feel moved); it's also a powerful reminder that we do in fact have the capacity to change the way we experience the world and one another. That our loneliness, resentment, anxiety, may be a side effect of our overemphasis on left-hemisphere thinking, enforced by a culture that believes that for each of us to be worthy of love we must be different, separate, better. You don't need to have a stroke, she says, to experience the peace and oneness she felt. The more we cultivate that right hemisphere, the part that sees us as one rather than separate, the more we can feel that bliss, that sheer and utter atomic connection.

I was able to recover from my very-near-death experience, as was Taylor, as are lots of people, every day. It's unimaginable, really, the wreckage people can rise from. Sometimes we know what saves us; other times it's a mystery. As I write this, we're starting (*starting*) to put the pandemic in the rear view, and while the world is nowhere near back to normal, we're beginning to believe it could be.

"Everything can be taken from a man but one thing: the last of the human freedoms," writes Viktor Frankl in *Man's Search for Meaning*, "to choose one's attitude in any given set of circumstances, to choose one's own way."[4]

People don't typically walk around every day worrying

about whether they'll have a stroke or go septic. We worry about what that person said, or what that guy thinks, about what will happen at 2:00 p.m. or next Friday, or five years from now. We worry as we squint in the mirror, as we stare at the news, as we wonder about conversations we're part of, and those we're not. Worry is like hygiene in that way—a mindless, habitual, daily effort, our anxiety collecting empty glasses and dishes in the middle of a party, wiping surfaces, and checking the locks. It lets us exert control while also fearful that we'll lose it. But all of it is somewhat fruitless and wasted effort when we have no idea what's coming our way or when. And then sometimes you're blindsided by a realization that stuns you.

What If There Was Nothing to Fix?

In the introduction to *The Power of Now*, Eckhart Tolle recounts how he woke soon after his twenty-ninth birthday in a state of utter dread. The world suddenly felt alien, hostile, loathsome. "Why carry on with this continuous struggle?" he asked himself. "I cannot live with myself any longer."[5] And that thought struck him as peculiar—because if he couldn't live with himself, who was he referring to? Who else was there? That stunning realization changed him forever, because he realized that the suffering he felt was in fact optional. That there was, inside him, an observer, something separate from the mind, with its churning, teeming thoughts, and the less he identified with that mind, the more at peace he was.

When people ask him, "How can I get what you have?" his response is: "You have it already. You just can't feel it because your mind is making too much noise."[6]

Everything in our lives makes too much noise, messages that start in our heads and that barge in from outside it. There's that voice that says you are lost *unless*—unless you find this, do this, buy this, accomplish this. The encultured, and then internalized, belief is that your life has a yawning blank inside you and you'll fail the test if you don't fill it.

But what if it wasn't that? What if there was nothing to fill, or to fix? What kind of self-help book would this be if I didn't offer a fix? Except you don't need fixing. There isn't anything *to* fix really. There's just what happens, how we respond, how we heal, evolve, and change as a result of whatever comes to pass. And lest you think I'm just like Eckhart Tolle, wandering around in a state of indescribable bliss—I assure you, I am not. I find it hard to live with myself, too, sometimes. (Though I'll admit it is easier now that I moved into a bigger apartment.)

Just because things fall apart does not mean we are beyond repair, or that we are not whole. No one knows this like my friend Sarah Montana (you might have seen her TEDx, "The Real Risk of Forgiveness and Why It's Worth It"). In a subsequent talk, "What Shapes You Can't Break You," delivered at the Aha Women's Speaker Series in Saint Louis in 2018, she recounts how as a Catholic girl she was taught that what made her whole was her purity (aka her virginity). So when she was seventeen and her boyfriend took her virginity without her consent, she believed—and feared—that part of her was beyond repair. Years later, when her mother and brother Jim were shot and killed in a botched burglary in her home, people flat out told her she'd never be right again. But none of these things broke her. What happens to us can wound, she says, without robbing us of our wholeness.

"Give yourself permission to heal your wounds. That's where you discover who you really are," she says. "And once you've seen everything you are, it becomes impossible not to show up fully in every aspect of our lives."[7]

Unfix Yourself

You can tweak and tinker, worry and wonder, or you can stop fussing with the itty-bitty parts in an attempt to fix, and embrace that you are, in fact, a whole, sovereign, and unbreakable person, and act accordingly—out of intention and purpose, not out of fear or defensiveness.

The opposite of fixing, which for lack of a better term I'll call "un"fixing, is in fact what helps you get closer to what you want—to experience a life of meaning, value, and connection. When you're not fixed, or fixated, on one part or one idea of yourself, you're free to shift and change, and to discover new things about the world and yourself, which is one of the most exciting things about being alive. Recognize that nothing is a foregone conclusion—not your job, your genetics, not your address, not even whatever it is you're doing right now.

Omega Institute cofounder Elizabeth Lesser says that the key to getting through any and all of this—our own lives, the world—isn't to shut down or to numb ourselves in order to get through, but to do the opposite. "If we can stay awake when our lives are changing, secrets will be revealed to us," she writes in *Broken Open*, "secrets about ourselves, about the nature of life, and about the eternal source of happiness and peace that is always available, always renewable, already within us."[8]

This is the source of freedom and sovereignty: To realize that the idea of fixing things forever *is* the illusion. That the only way to keep going—through sickness or storms, through boredom or struggle—is to know that staying in a still or locked position doesn't help. Your cycling or yoga or any other fitness instructor will remind you that the only way to keep going without running out of gas is to relax your grip, unlock your knees, keep breathing.

What Your Future Holds (and Why It's Not Worth Guessing)

Worrying about the future, that we're missing something, that we don't have all we need to meet it, or that it won't be what we expected? It is a waste of time—because, as Dan Gilbert says in *Stumbling on Happiness*, the future is never what we expect, because we don't have the tools to imagine it with. He describes a comic strip that never fails to delight him, in which a fish asks a sponge, "If you could be anything in the world what would you choose?" And the sponge says, "Anything?" "That's right," says the fish. The sponge thinks for a moment and then responds, "I guess I'd have to go with a barnacle!"[9]

The joke is that we can't conceive of more than where we are right now. We can't see beyond "barnacle." "We think we are thinking outside the box only because we can't see how big the box really is,"[10] he writes. This is good news. Because what it means is we have every reason to be optimistic. We're not only *not* supposed to know or plan everything; we also literally *can't* imagine what's possible. Why else do we so often say, "If you had told me back then that I would be . . ." and finish that sentence with literally what we're doing right now? Because most of us are walking around incredulous that *anything* has happened in the way it has.

The urge (pressure, inclination) to define ourselves by anything—our passions, our fears, our pasts, our accomplishments—will always be limited and limiting. We live in a world where we're expected to spit out a self-summary in thirty seconds flat, and of course nothing we say will feel right or enough. I was doing some brand work with a women's empowerment coach who was frustrated by that title—even though that is who she is and what she does. "But I'm so much *more* than that," she said. And it's true. She's more than her title. And so are you: You're not only *not* the sum of your parts; you are more than anything could contain or describe. If you know that, believe it, and lead with it, pouring yourself into the opportunities that present themselves to you and the ones you seek out, and contribute to people and projects in ways that only you can, that's the most any of us can ask for or dream of.

write your next chapter

Think about a time when you felt whole. What memory or moment comes to mind? Where were you, what were you doing, thinking, and feeling the moment you felt whole, and loose, and decidedly unfixed? Set the timer for ten minutes and start writing.

grab a notebook

What can you unfix? Next, think about something, maybe a few things, in your life that you've tried to fix or fasten, and which seemed to resist that effort. Maybe it's something you're struggling with now. What would happen if you did the opposite of fix it? What would that look like, sound like, feel like?

grab a notebook

CHAPTER 19

Why It's Not Worth Obsessing Over Forever

It is always important to know when
something has reached its end.
—Paulo Coelho, *The Zahir*

The video of my sister Lori's wedding is five minutes of the most perfect wedding you've ever seen. It's set to "Somewhere Only We Know" by Keane and shot in slow motion, like a montage in a movie that reminds you who the characters were at their best. You'll see a (posed) shot of me painting lip gloss onto my sister's mouth, my other sister zipping up her dress. A shoe being buckled. Every moment is weighted with purpose and ceremony.

It was a crisp New England day, cool around the edges but still warm in the middle; our bridesmaid dresses were gray frost. Instead of floral centerpieces, I remember bowls of Siamese fighting fish at each table, although in retrospect they might have been at the tables at my other sister's wedding (they both went through a Siamese fighting fish phase; don't we all). I can still see that fish, one per table because they do not get along. That might have been a sign. The bowls seemed lit from within, the brilliant plumes twitching and fierce.

Weddings are exciting, optimistic, centered on everyone's favorite part: the beginning—the promise of something eternal, something that will not end. We are dangerously, frighteningly, head over heels in love with the idea that something is worthwhile only if it never, ever ends. As a rule, we cast beginnings as great and endings as bad. Beginnings are thrilling and optimistic. Yet, we are infatuated with forever and what we envision is the thrill of a beginning without end.

Obsessed with Forever

Forever is in everything we talk about, dream about, pray for, pay for. From happily ever after to everlasting gobstoppers, eternal life to lifetime guarantees. My friends love a bottomless brunch: For $24.95, you can drink as many mimosas or Bloody Marys as you can handle for two straight hours. I have a Quip toothbrush and if you subscribe, as I do, you will get new toothbrush heads every three months *forever.* When I die, they'll just pile up in the mail until someone tells them to stop.

Most of us rail against the endings, even other people's endings. You could have a shitty boyfriend, whose last name *no one* bothered to learn, but when you roll in solo to the holiday dinner someone will ask, "Where's what's-his-name?" And if you say, simply, it didn't work out (which is the truth), you'll be met with, "Oh, why *notttttt*?" as if being with anyone is better than being with no one. And when you go to make your case to your Aunt Rhonda about why things went the way they did, Aunt Rhonda may press you on it: "It's a shame you couldn't work that out." It is? And was that the only option? To just work it out . . . *forever*?

I Want It Bad, Your Bad Romance

In the wedding video, you'll get highlights from the ceremony: a sweeping shot of the string quartet, the singers, the vows, my sister Kim wiping a tear from her eye, careful not to smudge anything. Then it shifts to the reception, from emo soundtrack to Jamiroquai, slow-motion embraces, high fives, knowing smiles, the room swaying and pulsing in one uncut congenial flow. And then a glimpse of the moment when 150 guests leapt from their seats, rushed the dance floor, and started moving in unison to "Land of a Thousand Dances." (This was the last gasp of the flash mob trend.)

What you won't see on the video is the moment during the cocktail hour when I slipped away to an empty coatroom to whisper hotly into the phone to a man on the verge of ending his own marriage. I craved his attention the way some people crave nicotine, knowing you need it and that it's bad for you. He was tipping over the edge of his life like a shelf teeming with quarters in those vending machine games. If you dropped a coin in at just the right moment, the robotic arm would send all those quarters into your waiting hands. But I've never actually seen that happen. All that money, in a perennial state of not falling.

We were entering the middle of the affair just as heat, having found an outlet, starts to escape. It wasn't lost on me that just as my sister was locking in for the long haul, I was in the midst of a flameout. I had been manic and lingering, making out with him in elevators, going blocks out of my way to walk with him, which runs against the basic creed of New Yorkers. One night, I was talking about him to my level-headed friend Carina, who's known me for twenty-five years and doesn't give a shit who I sleep with. She shook her head slowly. "This will not end well," she said.

Most things in our lives have a beginning that leads, inevitably, to a middle and finally an end: Songs. Books. Orgasms. Any good story (even "The NeverEnding Story," which is one hour and 42 minutes long). Childhood. Our life, in fact. For some, the end doesn't come soon enough; for others, it's swift and stunning.

Things That Don't End Are Terrifying

The things that never close—casinos, all-night diners, twenty-four-hour convenience stores, the New York City subway—aren't marked by joy and thriving. And the longer you stay, typically the less thrilled you are. Head to a casino or convenience store between 2:00 and 5:00 a.m. and you'll find most people staring into the middle distance, dancing on the very edge of despair. When and if you find yourself in such a place, get in, get what you need, and get the fuck out.

Every end is a reminder of the ultimate end, and we push hard against it. Some people think we live multiple lives; some think this is it. My grandmother used to wonder if "we just go out like a light." We are immortal souls, animating a meat puppet for a short time, and it's very hard to reconcile that divide between the part that will keep going and the part that will end. We're continually confounded by our limits, by the dread that an end must, ultimately, come.

Endings Aren't Always a Choice (but They Can Be)

I don't think we end *enough* things, actually, and certainly not soon enough. The idea of living forever, for me at least, is unappealing; the prospect of a Black Mirror–enabled immortality, where my soul is extracted and placed inside an endless simulation or a doll's head? Sheer horror. I can't even stand a meeting that goes over, a party that won't wind down. When things don't end on their own, I will find an ending. Big fan of the French Exit. There's nothing wrong with slipping out the back.

In the weeks after Lori's wedding, the married man I'd been seeing became slow to respond, vanishing behind a wall of his own complication. I say "complication" and not "complexity" because they are different; this man was not complex; he was simple and Catholic and confused. He texted me that he needed to take a break; he would come back later, when things cooled down. But things had already begun the process of cooling. I knew it was over.

It was right around Christmas when I got the text. I was underground at 42nd Street, waiting for the subway. I read and reread it, and my heart became the apple I watched on a time-lapse video once, weeks of decay collapsing into seconds, the spots and spores rising, the skin caving, folding in on itself like a fist. It was both devastating and unsurprising. I looked up and saw that the 2 train had come and gone. Usually, I see it coming. Even in the fullest, most fragrant bloom of a relationship, my mind will tiptoe to the window and peer out to see if an ending is making its way up the road—in a black SUV with tinted windows, on a sporty green Vespa. I asked my mother through high school, college, and beyond, not how to find everlasting love, but how did she propose I get out of this thing with this boyfriend or that one? "You'll know," she said. "The end will become obvious." She was right, as the endings, when they came, usually were.

It's Not Just Romance That Flames Out

The end of a friendship is perhaps even more heartbreaking, because the only reason to really end it is that you simply don't want that person in your life anymore. We don't have an infinite capacity for friendships, but you have room for more than one. So when you end it, it's not sexual or circumstantial; it's, *No, really, I'm done.*

I had a close friend for years; we talked every day. She was the only person whose travel schedule I had on my calendar. I listed her as my emergency contact when I went in for an endometrial ablation. I still don't know what happened. This was a woman who was capable of articulating precisely how she'd been wronged (that I knew). But she never said anything definitive. We never even fought. One by one, my invitations were declined, my texts fell down a well. The silence was deafening. I'd been ghosted by dudes, too many times to count. But ghosted by a good friend? I wouldn't have thought it possible. Until it happened.

I didn't tell her We Need to Talk. I didn't send pleading emails or voicemails. I didn't attempt a come-to-Jesus moment (and who would Jesus be, in this scenario? Not me). You kind of get the hint. And, given the chill and finality with which she'd so completely departed my life, I didn't think anything I said would matter. It actually doesn't matter anymore why. For reasons I may never know, she decided that a life without me suited her better than one with me. She doesn't actually need another reason than that. No one does.

We expect the best things will not, should not, end, that to even think it is a sacrilege. We expect this from our lives (things should always be like this), our bodies (I should always look like this), our relationships (I should always be loved like this). And so we've gotten attached to the idea that a life of meaning and value will also spring from a singular, eternal love affair with one person, one industry, one job—and somehow that you're supposed to pick these things and commit to them when you're in your twenties, when no one knows anything yet. And that you'll do that and be that, *forever.*

We spend most of our time, most of our *lives*, in the middle. But if we don't and can't learn to love and really appreciate an ending when it comes, we risk being stuck there, in suspended animation. While we don't have to obsess over or focus on endings, we can anticipate and expect that they will come. We could let go of the belief that denying or preventing them will make things matter more, make us matter more.

The ending isn't the failing of an effort, great or small. It is the punctuation on a sentence you care about, and the punctuation matters. It doesn't just *need* a place to end; it deserves it.

My sister is no longer married. But if you ask her, she knows exactly why she got married: They wanted the same things, at the same time, and there was enough synergy and chemistry to keep the wheels turning toward those goals. And it worked, until it didn't. The end of it was fraught and wrenching, as these things usually are. It's not that one couldn't live without the other, because they both knew their lives would be more peaceful apart. The hardest part of ending it wasn't the loss of a difficult marriage, but a loss of the imagined future, which looked a lot different at the start.

The same goes for you, and for me—whether you've been married or not, whether you've lost friends or not. Chances are something turned out differently than you expected and it ended in a way you either couldn't have predicted or had known, achingly, all along. This doesn't mean we should hasten endings, nor that we drag them out, but that we treat them, well, not unlike we did our firsts: as pivotal, meaningful, yes, but also as something we move through in order to get to what's next.

The moment on the wedding video I love most comes at the 1:12 mark, before the ceremony, the reception, dancing. It's during the "first look," which gives the bride and groom a private moment together before the ceremony (and also lets you take advantage of the light while you've got it).

Lori moves down the hallway through the last few bars of golden light, her hair a dark wing against her back, to where he is waiting, as the song plays ("I'm getting tired, and I need somewhere to begin"). There's so much ahead of them that will broaden and deepen their lives, the two children they will have and love so much it shocks them, even when they no longer love each other. There will be pain too. Somewhere, years away, a car is slowly making its way up the road. But for now, she is dressed and ready and beaming. She stands behind him, just slightly out of focus, as he turns to see her, as if for the very first time.

write your next chapter

Think about something that ended. It may be a catastrophic, larger-than-life loss; maybe it was small, forgettable. It may have been sad, bittersweet, or a flat-out relief. You can revisit a major event in your life—but you really don't have to, especially if you've gone through it many times. Rather than pick something broad like "the end of my youth" or "the end of my career," focus on a moment you can actually get inside, and write out the sensory details you remember, the things you recall (and what you recall may surprise you).

The point of this exercise is to exist inside an ending for a few moments, even if it wasn't The Big End, even if it wasn't life changing in and of itself. So that you are able to not just recognize an ending but also remind yourself that you can experience it and survive it. The goal isn't to change your mind about endings, or make it all OK, because it may not be OK. But if we cannot at least acknowledge and understand them, we risk getting stuck there.

Pick a time that rises to the surface for you, even if it's small and subtle, or funny or sad, such as:

- The end of a first date when you knew there would not be a second
- The end of a book you read that wrecked you
- The end of a long, boring summer
- The end of a lousy relationship
- The end of a crazy night
- The end of an awkward drive
- The end of a long weekend with people you liked, or didn't like

Don't worry about wrapping it up with a bow or finding a moral to the story. Just write and see what floats to the surface. Set your timer for fifteen minutes. Start writing.

grab a notebook

CHAPTER 20

Set Yourself Free

> *When you reach the end of your life and are wondering whether it's all been worthwhile, you'll be measuring whether you did everything you possibly could with the gifts you've been given.*
>
> —Gay Hendricks, *The Big Leap*

My uncle Bob drove me to Calvary Cemetery in Drums, Pennsylvania, where his parents are buried, and where he would be too. It was mid-August and the summer hadn't left yet, but you could tell it was thinking about it. He parked and got out, walked over, and lay down on the empty plot beside his parents. "This is it," he said, looking up at the sky. "This is where I'll be. Not a bad spot."

Bob had taken me on a tour of Hazleton that day, an old mining town, less than an hour from Scranton, where he lived and taught at the university. The last time I'd come here it was to bury my grandmother, when I was thirteen. I couldn't believe we were going to simply lower her into the ground and leave her there.

While Bob's cancer was in remission, he'd traveled as he always had, and I joined him for trips abroad each summer, which I told you about, traipsing through tunnels in Jerusalem, walking the white-hot streets of Rome. The cancer had started in the prostate, but, like him, it had traveled. He'd never had a single symptom. At one of his doctor's appointments, he pointed to his urologist and said, "My only symptom of cancer is you."

I'd love to tell you that choices are the same as control, and that as long as you do xyz you can have whatever you want. But I don't think that's fair to say. What I can tell you is that your choices matter, not because they control the outcome, but because you'll find more success in flexibility than in trying to bend life to your will. There's a kind of freedom that comes with allowing life to unfold, knowing you can't singularly dictate it.

As we round the last bend here together, you and I, it's worth looking at what we've covered. And it's a lot. We've not just taken stock of our skills and contributions but also thought about what "indispensable" really means (and doesn't mean); how to uncouple ourselves from plans and question our commitments; make peace with boredom, and with endings. We've come to terms with the fact that life can be tedious one day and disappointing the next, no matter how good or talented or focused you are. And most important, that there is nothing to fix about yourself or your life—only ways to rise into whatever comes next.

The goal, at the end of all of this, is not just to rack up more successes, or more money, or more likes. I think you know that, but it bears repeating. Because what I want for you is the thing I want for myself, and what every human on the planet wants: *Freedom.* The freedom to decide for yourself, to choose your path, your partners, your work. To have a say in what happens. For most of human history, people did not have that freedom, and they still don't. Pick a problem, any problem: from power and greed to fear and corruption, autocracy to abject poverty, a lack of education and awareness to a deep, perennial distrust.

There are a million reasons why most of the world is not as lucky as you and I are right now and doesn't have a fraction of the choices. I don't say that to shame you, but to wake you up to that fact. Maybe you think, *But I'm not free! I have to take care of my parents and my kids and do a job I hate and pay for things I don't even want!* I hear you. But freedom doesn't have to mean we gallop off into the sunset with total abandon. I don't know too many people who can or would do that. But you do have choices, and that means it's worth looking at which ones you're making and which you aren't.

What does it mean to you, to be truly free? Does it mean having all the answers, or being free to ask the questions? Is it having all the info or just enough to keep going? Maybe you're like my friend Sarah Montana, whom I told you about earlier, who loves spoilers—you can tell her the end of anything and she'll enjoy the movie just the same. (I do not understand this.) I find freedom in a bit of mystery, only because if I think I know what can't happen I might not be as open to what can.

My uncle Bob believed more information did not always equal more freedom. He trained his doctors not to give him bad news unless there was something he should do about it. He told them he had nowhere to store that information, so better they just keep it to themselves.

"Beautiful view, isn't it?" Bob said. The sun was setting over Hazleton, the far-off sound of cars on Route 80 like a distant tide. It was time to eat.

"Would you mind rising from the dead, please, Bob? I'm starving."

Bob sat up and brushed the grass out of his hair. "Sure," he said. "Let's go grab a slice."

Later, when his cancer came back, Bob wouldn't change his life one iota, and would stick to his regular teaching schedule until the very end. No one even knew he was sick. One day he said to the class, "I won't see you again." When they asked why, he said, "I just won't."

Bob showed me a world I wouldn't have seen without him;

he's the one who showed me what freedom could be. As a Catholic priest with a deadly diagnosis, he was still the freest person I ever knew. And, ironically, it was while we were traveling through ancient cities ruled by centuries-old patriarchal traditions where he taught me what it meant to be truly sovereign.

Govern by Your Own Rules

We were walking through the Piazza San Pietro in Rome, eating gelato as the sun left a maraschino glaze along the edge of the city, when Bob told me I might just have a gift: the gift of celibacy.

I must have made a face.

"I don't mean like *that*," he'd said. "I mean, you would be fine on your own." We passed a violinist in a fedora serenading an American couple. Bob explained that to be celibate was simply to be unattached—which wasn't a problem to be solved; it was a gift, something you had a talent for.

I was at the age where my friends had begun to pair up, settle down, invest in kitchen appliances. The wedding invites had started to wash up in my mailbox like a pretty, cream-colored tide. Everyone else wanted to reassure me that the next move would be obvious and plain, that the great rom-com director in the sky would cue the Perfect Person to enter the scene. I imagined hopping from one thing to the next like a series of lily pads: *boyfriend, fiancé, wedding, baby, house*.

"Or you could teach, write, take summers off, travel the world," Bob said. "You don't need to do what anyone else does."

I hadn't considered life quite this way before—as something you made up as you went along. I didn't know you could just dive right in and swim anywhere you wanted.

A female boss in her fifties had once whispered to me, "If you don't want kids, don't get married." I tucked that deep in my pocket to think about later. Most other people would say that if I couldn't have both, then definitely consider one or the other, as if marriage and parenting were the only two things to consider. Most people told me to have *hope* that I might get to do them. I'm not sure women need hope for a single outcome. What we need are more outcomes to choose from.

Of course, for most of my young life, I'd assumed I'd want those things. In high school, I'd asked Bob if he wished priests could get married. While he believed priests should be allowed to, he said that, if given the chance, he probably wouldn't. That was hard for me to believe when I was sixteen, harder still when I saw his yearbook pictures—Bob was the star of his high school basketball team, with lean, winking good looks, plenty of girlfriends, all of whom wept bitterly when he entered the priesthood. Back then I thought it was nuts to turn down the freedom to marry, to commit to such a restrictive institution. If you ask me, he opted for the less restrictive of the two.

On March 11, 2004, my mother got an early call—the one she dreaded—from a friend of Bob's: *Come quick; come now.* Bob was in his bed when we arrived the next day, but he wasn't *actually* there, not anymore. My mother and I were sitting with him when he died. When the air left his body and the room, I braced myself for the world to crack in half, which it did, my mother's cry rending it in two. She had buried her mother and father and now her only brother—her family of origin, gone. There would be no fixing this, no putting it back together.

We buried Bob right on that spot where he had lain on the grass and looked up at the sky four years earlier. It might have been odd for a young woman to aspire to be just like her priest uncle. But I did. And in many ways, I am.

I didn't stay close to the Catholic religion, but he did teach me about faith—the white-hot fire of it—and the power it has to light up whatever it touches. I also knew he had tremendous faith in me, probably more than I had in myself. Then again, the only way you know you have any kind of faith is if you have an occasional crisis of it.

Bob was sixty-two when he died in 2004; I was thirty-one. Like him, I am unmarried, with no children, and live quite contentedly on my own. I love to read and travel and teach, to enjoy people's company for a while and then go the hell home. I don't for a moment think everyone should live the way I do (or want to). For the balance of human history, women have not always been free to do as they damn well please, and so if you have the chance, do it. Start to see yourself like the Vatican City and function as your own sovereign nation, independent of other countries, even while you live in harmony with them. Govern by your own rules.

When You Return from Paradise

In May of 2008, my parents, sisters, brother-in-law, and the kids took the first full-tilt family vacation we'd taken in years. We spent a week in a resort inspired by and named for the lost city of Atlantis, that mythic place first described in Plato's dialogues as a highly evolved civilization destroyed by an earthquake around 9500 BC and swallowed whole by the sea without a trace. Many argue that Atlantis was never an actual place, but a metaphor for utopia. Though the Atlantis resort is a very real place, located on Paradise Island in the Bahamas—complete with swim-up bars, water slides, a different pool for every day of the week.

It was a respite for all of us, but in particular for my sister Kim, whose two small children were barely a year apart. She hadn't had a break in a long time, and what became clear to me is that for parents there was no break, ever. There isn't really a vacation, even; just doing what you do in a place far less convenient, albeit with a few more hands on deck. Kim had always been the sunniest of the three of us, and is. But I saw how parenting brought out a dimension in her that I hadn't previously seen: She had acquired a heightened awareness and worry that had risen to the surface, the way your triceps, with enough lifting, become strikingly defined. There was a new edge to her strength that I marveled at but did not envy. When you had children, every place was a potential disaster—even paradise.

Every morning on our way to the pool we walked through The Dig, a mock archaeological excavation site where you can wander dimly lit caverns, admire ancient cave drawings (circa

1998), and peer through floor-to-ceiling glass walls at all manner of aquatic life—shimmering schools of fish, pacing sharks, stingrays that shuddered along the bottom, lifting off like flying saucers. Behind them, a scene worthy of a Hollywood set: tumbled stones, rusted artifacts, crumbling staircases that lead nowhere, a forged memory. It called to mind the classic poem by Marianne Moore, about "imaginary gardens with real toads in them."[1]

That was where we encountered one of the largest and most stunning sea creatures I'd ever seen up close. He emerged from a dim corner of the lagoon, as if from the very depths of our subconscious. With a wingspan of twelve feet, weighing in at about one thousand pounds (think Smart car with wings), Zeus was a giant manta ray, the king of this underwater lair, undulating with incredible grace and ease. We all stared up agog as he cast a shadow, and a kind of spell, over everyone and everything in his path.

While Bob used to say a good trip will ruin your life, a good family vacation will make you grateful to be home. Soon after, I got a call from my friend Bridget Slotemaker whom I'd known since college, who was pregnant with her second child. She'd been having odd symptoms, blood clots. She called from the hospital where they'd finally done a round of exploratory surgery and tests.

"OK, so what you're saying is we wait and see what they—"

"They know." I went silent. "It's not good, T," she said.

That's when she told me she'd been diagnosed with stage 4 terminal cancer, that when they went in to take a look they'd closed her right back up again as there was nothing to remove unless they were going to remove everything. Trying to find where it began was like trying to find a match when the house is ablaze.

I'd known Bridget since we were sophomores on the Golden Eagle Dance Team at Boston College. She was a skinny, vibrant thing with a big personality, a booming laugh, a Julia Roberts smile. When we graduated and I was feeling lost and lonely, Bridget invited me to her New Year's party, to the Cheesecake

Factory for my birthday. When our leases were up, she suggested we find a place together.

We spent nearly four years with a rotating roster of roommates in a big empty house on Route 9 in Newton, Massachusetts, which none of us had enough furniture to fill. We had a series of memorable house parties and boyfriends, both of which required considerable cleanup when they were over.

But when her parents divorced, things changed. A light went out in Bridget, as she tried to hold her mother and brother together through the tumult. I would say Bridget had a crisis of faith—not because she lost faith, but because that's when she found it. She came to religion when most people our age were sloughing it off like old skin. She reached for it like a sturdy bough and hung on hard, the only thing she could find.

There's a reason they call themselves born-again Christians; it was a total do-over. Gone was the Bridget who gossiped, who talked about, or even had, sex (to the chagrin of her boyfriend; they soon parted). She went from the person I'd always known to someone who didn't drink anymore, who went to Saturday morning Bible study and mass on Sunday nights. She had new friends. She started bowing her head for grace at every meal, even when it was microwave pizza and we were in the middle of a conversation.

Her new piety irked me. I told myself this was what she needed, something bigger and sturdier than herself. Still, I quietly resented it, and told my friends that Jesus stole my best friend.

When our lease was up that year, Bridget announced she was moving out. She wanted some time alone now; she was about to be engaged to a man she'd met at church, a very sweet, very tall guy named Steve, and, given her newfound faith, couldn't move in with him before they were married. Bridget and I remained friends, of course—I was in her wedding, proud of her as always, thrilled when she had her first child. Though I felt more slack let out when she announced she was moving again—this time to the West Coast, near Steve's family in Portland.

The day she called me from the hospital with news of her

diagnosis, I tumbled through denial, anger, tears, acceptance. And when we hung up—Bridget to make her next difficult call, and then another—I was changed, too, the sinews of pending loss tightening. I became acutely aware of a silent metronome in my head, counting down. And while I wasn't one for traditional prayer, I prayed. Or rather, *assumed* a posture of prayer, because everything I did, I did inside that one prayer, in hopes that it would help, somehow. I went from banging around my days as usual to stepping very carefully, afraid I might break something.

I saw Bridget once after she was diagnosed, the day she started chemo. I flew out with my mother, and we watched *American Idol* in her hospital room. She was in high spirits that day, the MVP of the maternity ward. I stayed as long and late as I could. Then I said, "See you soon," when what I really meant was goodbye.

The doctors delivered her miraculously healthy, tiny daughter, Chloe Faith, by C-section at twenty-six weeks. Bridget never got to hold her; they were both in a fragile state. There's a photo of Bridget smiling, pointing through the glass at her the way you might at an exotic fish.

One thing Bridget said from the beginning was that she wasn't brave and didn't aspire to be. She had no interest in suffering. So when things took a turn for the worse, while she was under anesthesia, the family made the hardest decision of all—to let Bridget go. She died August 12, 2008, just three short months after her diagnosis. Her mother told me that, in the end, Bridget's faith kept her strong and unafraid in the face of the unthinkable. While I'd rolled my eyes at her newfound religious rigmarole and all its rules and regs, Bridget had been building the boat that would hold her aloft when the waters rose. I like to think it's what kept her free.

The Last Act

The Pacific octopus lives a short, brilliant, solitary life, which ends, rather than begins, with motherhood. In *The Soul of an*

Octopus, naturalist Sy Montgomery writes about one octopus she developed a relationship with, Octavia, who was captured young and spent most of her life in the New England Aquarium. Montgomery also had the privilege of witnessing Octavia's final act: the laying of her eggs. A typical octopus will lay as many as one hundred thousand of them in a few weeks—each with a tiny cord that she'll weave into beaded strings, sheets of jeweled curtains.

In the wild, an octopus does this once, and will not leave the eggs until they hatch—not to hunt or to eat, often starving to death. Octavia's love and care for those eggs was instinctual and purposeful, if futile, because Octavia was young when she was captured and the eggs were not fertilized. Still, the drive was strong, her care unceasing; Octavia spent her time fluffing and maintaining her treasures, Montgomery says, looking as if she were vacuuming the curtains.

There's a point when those thousands of fertilized eggs in the wild will break open like tiny pearls, freed like milkweed to the watery wind, where they become part of the ecological landscape, like so much plankton and other teeny, life-giving things, most of them gobbled up by other life-forms, so many cellular sacrifices that keep the ocean teeming and alive. Maybe five—*five!*—will survive to become full-grown octopuses. If the mother doesn't starve to death, she may develop a form of dementia, where she'll forget where she is, what she knows, and ultimately surrender to the sea.

We are not octopuses, certainly, and not all of us are parents or will be. But this, too, is our work. This is the work we must do—regardless of the timing, conditions, or how we feel about it: We tend to what we are given and what we create; we pour ourselves into the care of that which feels instinctual and urgent and real. It doesn't matter why we're doing it; it doesn't matter what someone thinks of it. It doesn't matter, even, the outcome. Of all the things you will ever do or care about, the many thousands upon thousands of things, the goal is to set as many of them free as we can—not because any singular effort is meaningful or perfect, or because it's *meant* to be or do a certain thing. But because it's what we can do.

No one can know a wild animal's mind—we can barely know our own. But Octavia didn't peer into each egg and wonder if *this* was the one her legacy would be built on, or maybe that one—or if she should spend time caring for it, or call in a consultant to find out before she "wasted" any time on it. In the end, none of her eggs grew into anything at all, but that didn't affect how she cared for them, not one iota.

What else is the point, really—what's the point of *anything* we might do—if we cannot and will not wring ourselves out for the few things we *can* do, make, contribute, no matter what they are? We can control where we put our attention and effort, even if we cannot control where those efforts take us, or how they will succeed. You live it out, give it what you have, *all* of what you have, knowing that there's always a chance that one egg could beat the odds, sure, maybe five if you're lucky, but that that was never the point. Most of what the octopus sets free into the underwater landscape doesn't end up full-grown like her, and the ones that do certainly bear no memory of her. Most of them go on to enrich the landscape itself, contributing to the great cycle of it all, in very real ways, most of which are impossible to know.

A week after Bridget called from the hospital, I was getting ready for work while the *Today* show chattered away when I heard something that caught my attention. Meredith Viera cut to Kerry Sanders on location in Atlantis. The big news was that the largest manta ray in captivity was being set free. The people who care for the wildlife there had noticed that he had been scraping the leading edges of his wings against the walls of the aquarium—a clear sign that he'd simply grown too large for the space. Even paradise could get cramped after a while. I watched in utter disbelief as Zeus was airlifted from the lagoon in what looked like a giant diaphragm, and gently lowered into the open water.

We're all living in some kind of constructed space, some

habitat, some situation, job, or relationship that we may very well outgrow. We may expand so much that what was comfortable isn't anymore, and we'll continue to expand, beyond who or what we loved, our mothers and our homes, this job or that career. And that *is*, in fact, the goal—not to fit into this place or that one, nor to waste time trying to find a fit, but to feel yourself forever in the midst of an upward arc. At some point we'll each outgrow *all* the things that used to fit—including this body, this planet, this life.

As Zeus fluttered free of his net, I thought about what that might be like, to stop swimming in circles, to feel yourself expand instead to your widest possible wingspan, a whole world opening up ahead; a deep familiar pull drawing you farther, and farther still.

write your next chapter

What can you do, right now, to set yourself free?

grab a notebook

ACKNOWLEDGMENTS

When you choose to write, you are choosing a life of homework, most of which you'll do alone. Which is why, when you get the chance to sit with other people, especially kind, creative, open-minded people, you do it.

There are lots of people who kept me company as I wrote this book—on throw pillows in Connecticut, crowded coffee shops in the city, a sun-drenched tent in someone's backyard, Zoom. They listened and read, and told me to keep going.

Thank you to my agent, Johanna Castillo, for your advocacy and insight, for talking me up (and, when necessary, talking me down), and believing that this wasn't the one book I would write, but the first one—and for finding a home for it in the middle of a global pandemic. To my editor, Michelle Herrera Mulligan, whose direction, support, and above all, trust, helped me make this book better by a mile. To Emma Van Duen for ensuring the book was dressed, clean, and ready for the world. Also big thanks to Libby McGuire, Lisa Sciambra, Falon Kirby, Karlyn Hixon, and the entire marketing, publicity, and sales team at Simon & Schuster—because writing a book is a tree falling in the forest; it takes many other people to ensure that work is heard.

Thank you to Mike Lundgren at TEDxKC, who changed the scope and scale of my career—and my life—by granting me access to his prestigious event in 2015. If we hadn't met, I might have written a book, but it wouldn't have been this one! And to Chuck Brandt, whose invitation to throw my hat in the ring changed everything.

Of course there would be no book to speak of without the love, vision, and guidance of Suzanne Kingsbury and the entire Gateless community. While I've been writing my whole life, it wasn't until my first Gateless retreat in Rhode Island that I woke up to the writer I could be. Thank you, Suzanne, for not only believing in me and my work but for making it a reality—and helping me give to others what you have so graciously given me.

To Becky Karush, for being both dear friend and willing reader, for introducing me to Gateless and Suzanne, and inviting me into a community of writers. To Daisy Florin and Sheena Cook, for years of friendship, colleagueship, and late-night editing eyes. To Sarah Montana, for being fearless and fierce, a force for good in my life. To Nicole Watson for reading and listening and never doubting that I could do it. And to Laura Belgray, for your beloved snark and unflagging feedback on the book (and everything else).

And a very big thank you to Kate Vanden Bos, for being the guiding force behind my exponential growth, and making it possible for me to do more than I imagined. Your sage counsel and friendship are invaluable to me.

Thank you to Daria Gregory and the whole gang at Pinnacle and Parabl for your indispensable support, energy, and ideas, and for creating a gorgeous digital runway for the book. To Ilise Benun, for changing the way I see my work and myself. And to Cass McCrory, for seeing me for who I am.

Big shout-out to all my friends and colleagues from Emerson College and the Alumni Board, with a special thanks to Rebecca Glucklich. To the Women's Media Group for keeping me connected to the inspiring women committed to the art and the business of words. And to Paula for making this and many other introductions that opened doors.

A deep bow to Seth Godin for being a source of endless inspiration and encouragement along the way.

To Kim Vandrilla, for being my own personal influencer and brand advisor, and for touching your magic wand to every element of the book—from what's on the outside to what's on the inside, to the title of the book itself. And to Cameran Hebb, Lyndsay Romano, Rachel Zeolla, and Tegan Harcourt, for being a big part of the experiences that found their way into this book (and the ones that didn't). To Jenn Lederer for laughing through all of this with me. To my dear friend Carina Wong, who for decades has offered a level-headed perspective and listening ear. And Janice O'Leary, for your enduring friendship, humor, and support.

Thank you to Elisabeth Egan for more than thirty years of friendship, and for not only telling me it was time to do this, but knowing that I could.

To Bridget Slotemaker, for being a bright beam of light to everyone who knew you. And for staying as long as you could.

To Dan, for being both unflappable and attentive, and the loving, grounding force I need—and am grateful for.

To my sisters, Kim and Lori, for always being in my corner, for reading early and often, for making me laugh in ways no one else ever has or can. To Joe, for decades of friendship and family. Dad, for being generous to the core, and making sure I had what I needed, even if you weren't totally clear on what I needed it for. And my mother, who knows me better than I know myself, and who has had the biggest influence on how I see the world and respond to it. I love you so, so much.

And finally to my Uncle Bob, who inspired this book and my life in so many ways, and whom I believe has given this book his blessing.

NOTES

CHAPTER 2

1 Martin Scorsese and Fran Lebowitz, "Pretend It's a City," Episode 5, Netflix, January 2021.
2 Marcus Buckingham and Ashley Goodall, "The Feedback Fallacy," March-April 2019, https://hbr.org/2019/03/the-feedback-fallacy.

CHAPTER 3

1 Cal Newport, *So Good They Can't Ignore You: Why Skills Trump Passion in the Quest for Work You Love* (New York: Grand Central Publishing, 2012), 22.
2 Scott Adams, *How to Fail at Almost Everything and Still Win Big* (New York: Portfolio/Penguin, 2013), 14–15.
3 Viktor Frankl, *Man's Search for Meaning* (Boston: Beacon Press 2006), Loc 80.
4 Pete Docter, "Soul," Pixar Animation Studios (2020).
5 Ibid.

CHAPTER 4

1 Twyla Tharp, *The Creative Habit* (New York: Simon & Schuster, 2006), 124.
2 Paul A. O'Keefe et al., "Implicit Theories of Interest: Finding Your Passion or Developing It?" *Psychological Science* (October 2018): 1653–1664, doi: 10.1177/0956797618780643.

CHAPTER 6

1 Jack Holland, *A Brief History of Misogyny: The World's Oldest Prejudice* (Robinson, 2019).
2 Elizabeth Lesser, *Cassandra Speaks: When Women Are the Storytellers, the Human Story Changes* (New York: Harper Wave, 2020), 30.
3 Ibid.

CHAPTER 7

1 Seth Godin, *The Practice: Shipping Creative Work* (New York: Portfolio, 2020), 103.
2 Twyla Tharp, *The Creative Habit* (New York: Simon & Schuster, 2003), 173.

CHAPTER 8

1 Mel Robbins, *The 5 Second Rule: The Fastest Way to Change Your Life* (New York: Simon & Schuster, 2017), 43.
2 Ibid, 50.
3 Marie Forleo, "How to find the motivation to keep going when you're feeling stuck," MarieForleo.com (blog), https://www.marieforleo.com/2021/05/3-steps-to-getting-unstuck/.
4 Jeff Haden, *The Motivation Myth: How High Achievers Really Set Themselves Up to Win* (New York: Portfolio/Penguin, 2018), 35.
5 Ibid, 16.
6 Seth Godin, *The Practice*, 38.

CHAPTER 9

1 Patricia Ryan Madson in *Improv Wisdom: Don't Prepare, Just Show Up* (New York: Bell Tower, 2005), Loc 229.
2 Ibid, Loc 233.
3 Tharp, *The Creative Habit*, 120.
4 Ibid.
5 Seth Godin, *Linchpin: Are You Indispensable?* (New York: Portfolio/Penguin, 2010), 19.
6 Ibid, 14.
7 Ibid.
8 Madson, prologue.
9 Ibid, Loc 706.

CHAPTER 10

1 Amy Wrzesniewski et al., "Jobs, Careers, and Callings: People's Relations to Their Work," *Journal of Research in Personality*, Volume 31, Issue 1 (March 1997): 21–33, https://www.sciencedirect.com/science/article/abs/pii/S0092656697921620.

CHAPTER 11

1 Irving Stone, *The Agony and the Ecstasy: A Biographical Novel of Michelangelo* (New York: Berkley/Penguin, 1987), 83.
2 Ibid.
3 Ibid.
4 Austin Kleon, *Keep Going: 10 Ways to Stay Creative in Good Times and Bad* (New York: Workman Publishing Company, 2019), 80.
5 Kleon, *Keep Going*, 82–83.

6 Ibid, 84.
7 Godin, *Linchpin*, 8.

CHAPTER 12

1 Mark Vicente, "The Vow," HBO Documentary Films, 2020, https://www.hbo.com/the-vow.
2 Darko, "19 Amazing MLM Statistics You Should Read in 2020," jobsinmarketing.com (blog), https://jobsinmarketing.io/blog/mlm-statistics/.
3 Kerri Ann Renzulli, "The highest-paying sales job in the US pays as much as $185,000 a year—here are the other 6," CNBC Make It, April 2019, https://www.cnbc.com/2019/04/23/glassdoor-the-7-highest-paying-sales-jobs-in-the-us.html.
4 Grant Cardone, *Sell or Be Sold: How to Get Your Way in Business and in Life* (Austin: Greenleaf Book Group Press, 2012), 1.
5 Ibid, 3.
6 Ibid, 66.
7 Haden, *The Motivation Myth*, 34.

CHAPTER 13

1 Godin, *Linchpin*, 8.
2 Buckingham and Goodall, *The Feedback Fallacy*.
3 Ibid.

CHAPTER 14

1 Daniel Gilbert, *Stumbling on Happiness* (New York: Alfred A. Knopf, 2006), 10.
2 Ibid, 16.
3 Ibid, 14.
4 Ibid, 15.
5 Eckhart Tolle, *The Power of Now: A Guide to Spiritual Enlightenment* (Novato, California: New World Library, 1999), 50.
6 Tharp, *The Creative Habit*, 122–123.
7 Madson, *Improv Wisdom*, Loc 317.
8 Ibid, Loc 336.
9 Sarah Horn, "Be Ready—Lessons from the Hollywood Bowl," TEDx-Riverside, 2014, https://www.youtube.com/watch?v=-cmjNfU2rIs.

CHAPTER 15

1 Mark A. Hawkins, *The Power of Boredom* (Mark A. Hawkins, 2016), 21.
2 Julia Stoll, "Number of original scripted TV series in the United States from 2009 to 2019," Statista, July 14, 2021, https://www.statista.com/statistics/444870/scripted-primetime-tv-series-number-usa/.
3 PodcastHosting.org. "2021 Global Podcast Statistics, Demograph-

ics & Habits," April 10, 2021, https://podcasthosting.org/podcast-statistics/.

4 Hawkins, *The Power of Boredom*, 7.
5 Ibid.
6 Brigid Schulte, "Work interruptions can cost you 6 hours a day. An efficiency expert explains how to avoid them," *Wall Street Journal*, June 1, 2015, https://www.washingtonpost.com/news/inspired-life/wp/2015/06/01/interruptions-at-work-can-cost-you-up-to-6-hours-a-day-heres-how-to-avoid-them/.
7 Hawkins, *The Power of Boredom*, 9.
8 Ibid, 10.
9 Sandi Mann, "Does Being Bored Make Us More Creative?" *Creativity Research Journal* 26, no. 2 (May 2014): 165–173, https://www.tandfonline.com/doi/abs/10.1080/10400419.2014.901073#preview.
10 Sandi Mann, *The Science of Boredom: Why Boredom Is Good* (London: Robinson/Hachette, 2016), Loc 57.
11 Hawkins, *The Power of Boredom*, 43.
12 Ibid, 42–43.

CHAPTER 16

1 Greg McKeown, *Essentialism: The Disciplined Pursuit of Less* (New York: Currency/Crown, 2014), 3–4.
2 Ibid, 35.
3 Alexandra Jamieson, "I'm Not Vegan Anymore," AlexandraJamieson.com (blog), https://www.alexandrajamieson.com/alex-jamieson/im-not-vegan-anymore.
4 Ibid.
5 Ibid.

CHAPTER 17

1 Buckingham and Goodall, "The Feedback Fallacy."
2 Ibid.
3 Ibid.
4 Joseph Bogan, "Creativity and the Corpus Callosum," *Psychiatric Clinics of North America*, 11, 3 (September 1988): 293–301, https://pubmed.ncbi.nlm.nih.gov/3067226/.
5 Kenneth M. Heilman, "Creative Innovation: Possible Brain Mechanisms," *Neurocase*, 9, no. 5 (November 2003): 369–79, https://www.tandfonline.com/doi/abs/10.1076/neur.9.5.369.16553.
6 Charles J. Limb and Allen R. Braun, "Neural Substrates of Spontaneous Musical Performance: An fMRI Study of Jazz Improvisation," *PLOS One* (February 2008), https://doi.org/10.1371/journal.pone.0001679.

CHAPTER 18

1 Harel Deutsch, "What You Need to Know About Failed Back Surgery Syndrome," SpineUniverse, December 24, 2019, https://www.spineuniverse.com/conditions/failed-back-surgery.

2 Pulse of the American Worker Survey Special Report, "Is This Working? A Year In, Workers Adapting to Tomorrow's Workplace," Prudential (March 2021), https://news.prudential.com/presskits/pulse-american-worker-survey-is-this-working.htm.

3 Sheridan Prasso, "China's Divorce Spike is a Warning to Rest of Locked-down World," Bloomberg Businessweek, March 31, 2020, https://www.bloomberg.com/news/articles/2020-03-31/divorces-spike-in-china-after-coronavirus-quarantines.

4 Frankl, *Man's Search for Meaning*, 66.

5 Tolle, *The Power of Now*, 1.

6 Ibid, 3.

7 Sarah Montana, "What Shapes You Can't Break You—The Power of Your Whole Story," Aha Women's Speaker Series, November 29, 2018. YouTube video, 17:38, https://www.youtube.com/watch?v=Or4hrTAwJts.

8 Elizabeth Lesser, *Broken Open: How Difficult Times Can Help Us Grow* (New York: Villard, 2005), xxiii.

9 Gilbert, *Stumbling on Happiness*, 125.

10 Ibid.

CHAPTER 20

1 Marianne Moore, "Poetry," *Poems* (London: The Egoist Press 1921).

INDEX

ABOUT THE AUTHOR

Terri Trespicio is an award-winning writer, speaker, and brand advisor whose TEDx talk, "Stop Searching for Your Passion," has been viewed more than seven million times. A former magazine editor at Martha Stewart Living Omnimedia, her writing has been featured in *Marie Claire*; *Jezebel*; *Business Insider*; *O, The Oprah Magazine*, and others. She earned her MFA in creative writing from Emerson College, and won first place for creative nonfiction in the Baltimore Review's 2016 literary contest. A certified Gateless instructor, she leads writing workshops and retreats, and consults with individuals and organizations to craft their brand messaging. She lives in Manhattan. Visit territrespicio.com for more information.